D1519991

THEISM AND EMPIRICISM

THEISM AND EMPIRICISM

A. BOYCE GIBSON

SCHOCKEN BOOKS · NEW YORK

Published in U.S.A. in 1970
by Schocken Books Inc.
67 Park Avenue, New York, N.Y. 10016

© SCM Press Ltd 1970

Library of Congress Catalog Card No. 70-111210

PRINTED IN GREAT BRITAIN

CONTENTS

Contents

'Ἀποβαίνει δ' ἐπιστήμη καὶ τέχνη διὰ τῆς ἐμπειρίας τοῖς ἀνθρωποῖς   *Aristotle*

'Philosophy may be described as the experiential or empirical study of the non-empirical or *a priori*.'   *S. Alexander*

INTRODUCTION

THERE is a long historical association between theism and rationalism on the one hand, and empiricism and atheism on the other. This work arises from the personal discomfort which such an alignment produces in me. On the one hand, I believe in God, not merely on authority, but because I think there are good reasons for believing in God: I am, that is to say, not merely a believer, but a theist. On the other hand, my belief in God is based not on inference but on experience: and my background is one which has not been much represented in recent controversy on the philosophy of religion: that of a Christian independency which rests on the assembled testimony of believers and not on the authority of church or academy. Both as a thinker and in my own religious experience, I find myself pulled in both directions. This is a schizophrenic condition from which I am impelled to extricate myself as best I may. And the first expedient which presents itself is to challenge the traditional alignment. If it could be shown that there is no contradiction between the theistic and the empirical outlook, my problem would be solved for me.

Both traditional theists and traditional empiricists will protest that it is impossible. The former will insist that the concept of God is bound up with that of necessity and that, without it, it is reduced to the status of one finite concept amongst others – not unique, but at best *primus inter pares*. What, it will be said, can be made of a God who merely *happens* to exist? In the same way, and arguing from the same premises, the latter will maintain that from presented data it is never possible to infer necessity, and that any being who is not necessarily might *not* be – the support on which everything stands might slip from under at any moment, and therefore cannot be called God. Both ways, God is defined so as to make the empirical approach to him self-contradictory.

To meet these objections, it will be necessary to re-examine

much of the traditional natural theology, and also much of the
recent philosophy of religion. It will be necessary, first of all,
to explore the foundations of empiricism, and to ask why it is
that it is held to be impossible to be empirically acquainted
with the non-empirical. In the second place, it will be necessary
to explore the foundations of philosophical theism, and to ask
how the concept of God has become associated in the minds
of all kinds of philosophers with the concept of logical necessity.
Thirdly, it will be necessary to explore the religious conception
of faith, for if God is not logically necessary but practically
necessary, faith must carry the weight which logical necessity
has been made to carry and cannot carry. And, fourthly, this
will entail a further exploration of a topic at the moment of
much interest to philosophers: the relation of theoretical and
practical reason. The programme is formidable, but the predicament demands no less.

The problem is discussed mainly in a Christian setting, not
thoughtlessly, which might have been arrogant, but with a
deliberateness which I hope will avert offence. The Christian
religion is the only religion which I can feel from the inside,
and it is the only religion which I know enough of to think
about from the outside. Moreover the issues with which I am
concerned, though certainly not restricted to Christianity, or
even to the Jewish-Christian-Moslem family of religions, present
themselves to modern Western philosophy with a Christian
accent, and in any other setting would have to be differently
stated.

Much has been written lately in the modern style on the
philosophy of religion: indeed, the deployment in this region of
British analytical philosophy is a welcome sign of its maturity.
If in these pages there is no attempt at a general review of
these contributions, and they are mentioned only when the
argument calls for it, it is not for lack of respect, but because
both the point of departure and the course of the journey are
radically different. What follows is an essay in metaphysics,
not an attempt to rescue religion from the wreck of metaphysics.
It is possible, however, that the 'empirical' metaphysics here
attempted may stick less obstructively in the modern gullet
than older models.

My obligations stretch over a period of years. Firstly, to the Carnegie Corporation of New York, which enabled me to visit centres in the USA, as far back as 1953, with the present set of problems in mind. I remember with particular gratitude the opportunity thus afforded me of meeting philosophers and theologians at Union Theological Seminary, New York, at Yale University, and at the University of Chicago. Indeed, the Woodward Lecture which I had the honour to deliver at Yale has turned out to be the germ of this whole work. I am further grateful for the opportunity, as Visiting Professor at the University of Texas in Austin ten years later, of presenting a compendium of the first chapter to a meeting of philosophers in that centre, from which I received most helpful suggestions. On both these occasions I owed much to the personal and philosophical friendship of Professor Charles Hartshorne. I have also been privileged, on several visits to the United Kingdom, to discuss issues in the philosophy of religion with Professors John Macmurray, J. N. Findlay, W. G. Maclagan, D. M. MacKinnon, and R. B. Braithwaite, and, most particularly, with the then Nolloth Professor at Oxford, I. T. Ramsey, now Bishop of Durham, for whose continuing encouragement and advice I am deeply grateful. Inside Australia, I owe more than he might have suspected to the challenge of that grand old militant atheist, the late Professor John Anderson of Sydney; I have been helped by constant discourse with my Catholic former colleagues at the University of Melbourne, Dr M. J. Charlesworth and the Rev. Dr Eric D'Arcy; by participation in the work of the Australian Student Christian Movement over a period of 30 years; by the friendship of the present editor of its journal, *Crux*, Mr J. R. Howes, and of Mr G. E. de Graaff, Director of International House in the University of Sydney; and by the stimulating interest in my work shown at all times by the Rev. Professor E. F. Osborn, of Queen's College, University of Melbourne, who has spared hours for discussion with me cheerfully and without complaint. Needless to say, I do not hold any of them responsible for the opinions here expressed, which in their various ways they have helped so materially to form.

I am grateful to the Australian Research Grants Committee

for a grant in aid during the year following my retirement, and also to the typists who have helped to prepare the work for publication: in particular Miss C. Donovan, who carried the main burden of the first draft direct from my handwriting, and Miss N. Cazas, who has made a clean job of chapters much mutilated by necessary revision.

Finally, I am grateful to the SCM Press Ltd, and to its Managing Director and Editor, the Rev. John Bowden, for their interest in the work, and for their unfailing consideration.

July 13, 1969   A. Boyce Gibson
Mont Albert
Victoria, Australia

I

THE MISADVENTURES OF EMPIRICISM

1. *The Initial Misunderstanding*

THE WORDS 'empirical' and 'empiricist' derive from the Greek word ἐμπειρία (*empeiria*), the ordinary translation of which is 'experience'. It is etymologically related to πειρᾶσθαι (*peirāsthai*), 'to try', and its persistent overtone in Greek is 'trial and error'. An 'empiric' is not one who knows the rule and applies it, but one who, not knowing the rule, plays about experimentally with the appearances, accepting them as his starting-point, organizing them on the basis of habit, never going behind them to challenge them, anticipating, if at all, only on the basis of past experience, and greatly resenting the claim of reason and calculation to overrule him. He may have a kind of practical skill or 'know-how' better, perhaps, than what is strictly the opposite of 'experience', i.e. ἀπειρία or inexperience,[1] but standing lower in the scale of excellence than τέχνη (*technē*, 'craft'), which works to a rule, even if it does not understand it, and still lower than ἐπιστήμη or understanding.

In the brilliant campaign of Plato on behalf of τὸ λογικόν, rational discourse and behaviour, ἐμπειρία, 'experience', was certain to be an early casualty. The decisive battle is to be found in the *Gorgias*, by common agreement an early dialogue, and the terms in which the issue was there stated have influenced discussion ever since.

It might have been expected that the downgrading of experience would be the result of excitement about Pythagorean mathematics and the theory of Forms. In the *Gorgias*, however, the contrast is between *empeiria* and *technē*, 'craft', though there

---

[1] Even Plato admits that much: ἀπείρου . . . ὧν ἔμπειρον χρεὼν εἶναι, *Timaeus* 55d.

are signs that craft is being dignified by embodying *epistēmē*,
knowledge. The difference is that craft 'is based on a rational
principle, and can thus explain the reasons for its procedure',[2]
and *empeiria*, experience with the controls of *technē* removed
from it, varying between sheer fumbling and successful guesswork,[3] is fundamentally uninstructed and unable to give an
account of itself.[4]

Right from the start, we should note what has happened.
Partly through a sharpening of concepts, and partly through
sheer verbal manipulation, 'experience' is represented as cut off
from its informing ideas. This may be good enough for the
lower-grade experience of lower-grade minds in their off
moments, but it is not true of empirical science, or even of
ordinary reflective behaviour. More or less, but always to some
degree, experience is not just routine[5] nor just an 'empirical
knack';[6] it has just enough intelligent anticipation to guide it
into fruitful paths. The point is important, because 'knack' and
'routine' are not the only alternatives to *a priori* argument, as
Plato would so brilliantly persuade us.

Part of the trouble is that the contrast between *technē* and
empeiria is introduced *à propos* of oratory. We can see what Plato
is about, and can applaud his intentions. The orator does not
produce anything determinate. He produces whatever may
happen to please the majority of the people. He does not know
what this is; he has to find out. Even if he has his own ideas
(and they may be sufficiently unprincipled anyway), they may
be twisted and inverted in the give and take of popular discussion. This is not the fulfilment of a craft according to rule:
and in the *Republic* we see the orator supplanted by the philosopher. But again (as reports of proceedings in the *ecclesia* in

[2] The summary is that of E. R. Dodds in his edition of the *Gorgias*, pp. 228f.
[3] στοχαστική, 463a7: cf. the prizes awarded in the Cave to successful
guessers, *Republic* 516c.
[4] 465a3: οὐκ ἔχει λόγον οὐδένα ᾧ προσφέρει (ἢ) ἃ προσφέρει ὁποῖ' ἄττα τὴν
φύσιν ἐστίν.
[5] *Empeiria* is thus translated by W. D. Woodhead in his version of the
Gorgias in the one-volume edition of Plato's works, ed. E. Hamilton and H.
Cairns, 1961, p. 245.
[6] Dodd's translation of ἐμπειρία καί τριβή, *op. cit.*, p. 225. The difference
between 'routine' and 'knack' is considerable, but it is secondary to the
main issue: both are lacking in clear and conscious insight.

Thycudides show), though decisions were not always wise, there was plenty of discussion, and even though oratory is an unfavourable specimen of activity not governed by its end, again we are confronted by a hard-and-fast distinction from which the gradations have been artfully erased.[7]

That the suppression was quite deliberate is clear from the sentences assigned to Polus at the beginning of the dialogue, 448b. He draws the distinction allowed by Plato himself in the *Timaeus*, between ἐμπειρία and ἀπειρία, experience and in-experience, but adds that it is experience which makes our life proceed in orderly fashion (κατὰ τέχνην), while inexperience exposes it to chance (κατὰ τυχήν). The contribution is put aside as irrelevant (as indeed it is, in the context), and buried under a derisive parody of Gorgias' prose style. But it is never resurrected; and the connexion between empiricism and disorder is firmly established in the reader's mind.

The conclusion is all the more curious in that *technē*, in a non-industrialized society, is very much a matter of use and wont, and that its order is built on precedent. When Plato writes of ἐμπειρία καὶ τριβή, this order seems to be what he is attacking. But in the *Gorgias*, as R. W. Hall has pointed out,[8] Plato is in the act of proceeding beyond *technē* to a 'transcendent ordering principle' and distinguishes the philosophic life from that of the vulgar, including the vulgar expert. During the transition, the conception of *technē* is upgraded by association, linking up with that of *epistēmē*, knowledge, and their combined testimony is brought to bear against *empeiria*. And when *epistēmē* finally takes charge of *technē*, the case against the empirical is stronger by the weight of the new unprecedented passion for science.

To show that Plato did not change his mind, we conclude by citing two vital passages from the *Laws*. In the first (938a), *empeiria* is specifically labelled ἄτεχνος (almost 'unscientific');

---

[7] In *Phaedrus* 269a, Pericles is described as a true rhetorician (because he learnt about the nature of things from Anaxagoras), and in 270b rhetoric is said to be for the soul what medicine is for the body, i.e. a *technē*. But that can happen only when the rhetorician is instructed by the philosopher and is no longer, as is normally the case, 'ignorant of dialectic' (269b). Mere oratory can never be more than 'knack' and 'routine', and any oratory that *is* more is no longer *empeiria*.

[8] *Plato and the Individual*, 1965, pp. 127f; *Gorgias* 507–13.

exactly the doctrine of the *Gorgias*. The second (720c) makes
an interesting distinction between slave doctors who are said
to prescribe τὰ δόξαντα ἐξ ἐμπειρίας, what seems good from
experience, and the doctors who have ἰατρικὴ τέχνη, medical
science, who prescribe from the skills of their craft. The skills,
then, are *not* learnt from experience; and the test, no doubt,
would be how to act in an unfamiliar situation. The slave doctors
are routineers; only the scientists, who can vary the treatment, are
practitioners. It sounds convincing, till one asks how the practitioners acquire their skill; not, it would seem, without experience.

In short, in this preliminary sparring Plato succeeded in
forcing on the discussion of reason and experience an 'either-or'
which it will be the main object of further discussion to remove.
In what follows there is a systematic attempt to blur the out-
lines. In the interests of a modern philosophy of religion, this
procedure is indispensable: 'either-or' places a barrier between
God and man.

Before we leave the classical scene, three unconnected comments are perhaps appropriate.

In the first place, Aristotle, who wisely preferred hierarchies
to alternatives, gathered together in one masterly sentence the
elements which the dialectic of the *Gorgias* has thrust apart.
'Knowledge and skill,' he wrote, 'descend to men through experience' [ἀποβαίνει δ' ἐπιστήμη καὶ τέχνη διὰ τῆς ἐμπειρίας τοῖς
ἀνθρώποις, *Met*. A.981a 2]. The passage is particularly to our
point, because Aristotle proceeds to quote with approval the
distinction made early in the *Gorgias* (448c) by Polus, between
the experience which produces *technē*, and the inexperience
which can at the best be the occasion of luck. Now Polus is one
of the main targets in the *Gorgias*, and to quote him approvingly
is indirectly to attack Plato. Aristotle makes it clear that
'experience' includes and is informed by intelligence, and not
merely the responsive intelligence of the craftsman (τέχνη), but
also the knowledge of the philosopher or scientist (ἐπιστήμη).
A priorism in modern philosophy comes not from Aristotle, but
from the Neo-Platonists, and from Aristotle's seventeenth-century critics.

In the second place, the attack on experience in the *Gorgias*
is part of a campaign against subjective testimony which runs

through the whole of Plato's politics. He never shows the
remotest inclination to put himself in another's place, and
unless the other is an established good man he condemns the
practice as immoral. That is why, in epic and drama (*Rep.*
396c), he will not allow the bad man the advantage of *oratio
recta*; that is why he writes (409b) that judges must know of
evil by understanding, and not by private experience.[9] Contrast the procedure of Father Brown,[10] who, with his creator,
moves in a Christian setting.

I don't try to get outside the man: I try to get inside – the murderer . . .
thinking his thoughts, wrestling with his passions; till I have bent myself
into the posture of his hunched and peering hatred; till I see the world with
his bloodshot and squinting eyes; looking between the blinkers of his half-
witted concentration; looking up the short and sharp perspective of a straight
road to a pool of blood.

Father Brown describes this imaginative substitution as a
'religious exercise'. For Plato, the moral adventure would be
too perilous, even for a judge. His attitude throws further light
on his constant theme, 'knowledge versus experience'. Knowledge keeps a man clear of risks and experience takes him into
them. There is, as so often, a moral edge to Plato's epistemology,
the knowledge which is everbody's knowledge is sanity and
soundness, experiential knowledge is suspect and precarious.
As we shall see, as an approach to religious knowledge, this
healthy-minded extroversion is far too simple.

In the third place, there is the cognomen of Sextus Empiricus.
How did he obtain it? His writings are those of a therapeutically
minded sceptic; like many of our contemporaries, who do not
acknowledge him, he hopes to ease mankind of the burden of
metaphysical contradictions by dissolving them. He attacks
'dogmatists' (including, most particularly, 'mathematicians'),
and commends the average man's *status quo ante intellectum*. He
is not an enthusiast for empirical science, and does not consider
the possibility of empirical philosophy. He is, in fact, the
prototype of those modern philosophers who find satisfaction,
and a living, in demolishing philosophy, without a thought

[9] ἐπιστήμη, οὐκ ἐμπειρίᾳ κεχρημένων: note again the contrast between
'knowledge' and 'experience'.
[10] G. K. Chesterton, *The Father Brown Stories*, 1929, pp. 817f.

about what might happen to them if they succeeded. Yet from
early times Sextus has been known as Empiricus. We are thus
presented with a view of the antithesis between experience and
rational discourse from the other end – a view which was
widespread enough to get a man a nickname. Reason having
disowned experience, experience disowns reason. Nothing could
better illustrate the operation of the 'either-or' introduced in
the *Gorgias* and despite the influence of Aristotle bequeathed
to the modern world.

2. *The Empirical Complex*

Empiricism as a modern phenomenon is part of a complex of
ideas which broke upon the world in the sixteenth and seventeenth centuries. Its philosophical expressions cannot be isolated
from its technical, economic, geographical, moral and literary
expressions, and least of all from its religious expressions. The
common error of historians of philosophy is to seal them off
from all contemporary developments except those of the
natural sciences, and to treat of them in themselves, with due
regard to other philosophies, but without a proper sense of the
mounting excitement which accompanies the growth of a way
of living. A philosopher can hardly hope to re-create the
historical context: he can only hope that historians will do so.
But as it is part of his business to discern unlikely resemblances,
he may fairly draw attention to a common factor in the following activities of the period: exploration, private industry, the
growth of inventions, experimental science, personal Bible-
reading (and indeed reading generally), the insistence on conscience and freedom of interpretation, the dominance of private
will in the home and in palaces, the priesthood of all believers,
introspective biography (Montaigne), dramatic soliloquy, and
finally the empirical method in philosophy, whether employed,
as by Descartes, merely to set the enterprise going, or, as by the
British empiricists, as a continuing inspiration of the enterprise
itself. What unites all these activities is that they are personal
rather than public, and are attempts, not so much to apply
what is known, as to find out. Discovery, and under one's own
steam, is the leitmotiv of the period; and it is woven in and out

of the solid relics of a feudal and objective world, permeating, sustaining, outflanking and displacing them, building out of them and in the teeth of them a new adventurous intersubjective world held together by free contract and a personal sense of responsibility. That world is the context for the examination of modern empiricism.

And, in that connexion, it should be noted that the factor of privacy and the factor of finding out, in this particular complex of ideas, go together. It is *because* enterprise, conscience and religious conviction have personal contexts that they are adventures and not certainties. The quest for certainty stems from the belief in authority and solidarity, buttressed, in the case of philosophers, by objective demonstration. The empirical approach to things is entailed by the personal; from his own resources, whether in meditation or in practice, no man can cover the whole ground; there is always more to know and there is always more to dare. On the other hand, the personal approach is entailed by the empirical; discoveries do not discover themselves. Traditions and even arguments are by comparison impersonal; they have to be appropriated or apprehended, but they do not have to be made or made again. The piecemeal advance of knowledge[11] depends on a continuing inquirer, or on a continuing team or succession of inquirers. The point is crucial, for the empiricist has frequently practised a reductive analysis leading back to the impersonal unit of sensation, or to the equally impersonal unit of point-event, in which his own activity is itself reduced to sensation or event, and his personal role in the act of reducing disappears, along with what he is reducing, into the depersonalized unit to which he reduces it. It may help to dissociate empiricism from this unempirical deviation if we replace it in its cultural context and reunite it with the zest of personal enterprise. For a philosophy of religion, no move could be more important.

Having thus noted the context in which empiricism as a philosophy came into being, we may proceed to a few explanatory comments:

1. The notion that it is the business of the thinker to find out is unquestionably a challenge to the acceptance of tradition or

[11] As Locke saw. See *Essay on the Human Understanding*, Book IV, ch. 9.

authority. It does not entail their rejection – the conviction
that it does is, in an empiricist, one of the disorders of childhood
– but it does entail calling them to account. Whereas *technē*,
industrial or moral, is based on routine, the man who wants to
find out must at least suspend judgement. He may, as Plato did,
succeed in supporting *technē* with *epistēmē* – he may become a
rational conservative instead of a conventional one. He may,
as revolutionaries do, use the moment of intellectual suspense
to launch a rival dogmatism of his own. In neither case will the
process of finding out be more than an interregnum or a means
to an end; and in the interests of common action this may well
be inevitable, though it should never be allowed to silence the
qualms from which the next progressive moment will be born.
But the philosopher, in his professional moments, not having
to act, may maintain the suspense indefinitely, reserving only
the right to tilt the balance according to the evidence or the
probabilities. Far more than the practical man, he is committed to finding out as a way of life.

Two asides at this point:

(i) When philosophers become dogmatists, it is always because of moral commitments which they cannot lay aside. In
their practical capacity they are not to be blamed, because
they are also human beings, and as such have to commit
themselves; but they are thus involved in a split-personality
situation which they do not always understand. They cannot
ignore their practical necessities, and they are part of what they
have to inquire into: and they cannot be dominated by them
because that would put an end to the inquiry. They can only
balance as best they may.

(ii) If they are also religious believers, they take a short cut,
and properly so, because their lives are at stake, and their lives
are more than their professions. Nevertheless, even as believers,
they are always finding out: 'the Lord hath yet more light and
truth to break forth from his word'. Moreover, there is a
difference between the situation of the believer and that of the
moral agent. Religion has an intellectual as well as a moral
component. It is not a way of life imposed on a state of affairs;
it is a way of life with a conviction about a state of affairs
built into it.

2. Like all cultural complexes, the many-sided movement we have called 'empirical' contains potential discrepancies. Thus the introversion of introspection and the individualism of the private conscience are poles apart from the publicity and objectivity of experimental science; the sense of equality engendered by the priesthood of all believers clashed early with the inequalities inherent in the private conduct of industry. The same attitude, poured into different moulds, solidifies into incompatible formations. What holds the complex together is its antipathies: when it removes the obstacles it divides against itself. As the process takes centuries and is rarely if ever completed, and as there are usually counter-currents to keep the unity of inspiration alive, it is difficult, even in the case of revolutions, to say when the split takes place and a new antithesis begins to dominate the stage. It is possible to discern lesser splits within any one aspect of the complex: both capitalism and communism hark back to Locke's definition of property as 'that which a man hath mixed his labour with'; an empirical definition invalidating the principle of heredity, and substituting for tradition and experience 'the industrious and the rational'. It is the next move which sets them against each other, within the order of modern industrialism: and it then appears that the communists are the conservatives. It is also possible to discern alliances between two disparate expressions of the complex, e.g. the support given to experimental science in the English dissenting academies of the eighteenth century. What held them together was the educational counter-current: both science and Dissent were spurned by Oxford and Cambridge.

3. The impression prevails in many quarters, both religious and anti-religious, that the attitude of finding out is incompatible with religious faith. The believer has assurance, it is said; how can he amalgamate with those who disclaim assurance? The question leads to a full discussion of 'faith', which will be developed in chapter VII, and can here only be briefly anticipated. But this much must be said, as a prolegomenon to everything that follows: that the believer's assurance does not rest on intellectual certainty, whereas it is such certainty which empiricism as a philosophy disclaims. In

the one case as in the other, there are probabilities: the philosopher can afford to go on keeping them open; the believer,
having to act, has also to commit himself.[12]

It is true that the believer is reinforced by certain constant
reminders and examples; that there is an area of conviction
beyond which his discourse may not wander. But it cannot be
said too often that the same is true of anyone else whatever.
Scepticism takes as much for granted as dogmatism. Liberals
are not free to wander into authoritarianism; unbelievers are
not free to wander into believing. There is no thinking which
does not follow in the wake of a commitment. Show me a man
with an 'open mind', and I will show you a simpleton or a
hypocrite.[13]

Thus the contrast between the believer and the inquirer
rests on the assumptions that the believer does not inquire
and the inquirer does not believe; and both assumptions are
false. The believer, equally with the inquirer, develops his
convictions; the inquirer, equally with the believer, has convictions to develop. Both have commitments and both can be
reasonable. The trouble arises when believers ask for a certainty
which belief cannot provide, and inquirers ask for a mental
vacuum in which one could never begin to inquire. To both
kinds of extremists the empirical approach may be recommended.

4. It may be said that the conception of belief adumbrated
in the preceding paragraph is not that which is usually accepted,

[12] Cf. the impressive and judicious reminder of Butler: 'In questions of
difficulty, when more satisfactory evidence is not to be had, or is not seen;
if the result of examination be that there appears upon the whole . . . a
greater presumption on one side, though in the lowest degree greater; this
determines the question, even in matters of speculation, and, in matters of
practice, will lay us under an absolute and formal obligation . . . to act on
the presumption or low probability, though it be so low as to leave the
mind in very great doubt which is the truth.' Butler is particularly instructive
because he sees that speculation, as well as actions, falls under the rubric of
practice – being itself a kind of practice. The reference is to the *Analogy of
Religion*, Introduction, Sect. 4, and I owe it, together with a re-introduction
to the best book on natural theology ever written, to Bishop I. T. Ramsey's
quotation, in *Religious Language*, 1956, p. 16.
[13] This applies particularly, as Michael Foster pointed out in his contribution to the collection *Faith and Logic*, to those modern philosophers
who say 'we', purporting to present uncorrupted human nature, when
they are merely elaborating the habits and prejudices of a secular society.

and that to depart from established usage is sinful. So it is, if one does not explain what one is doing, or if the departure covers a conceptual confusion between old and new. It must, therefore, be clearly explained that the conception of belief here adopted is one which has long been current among Christian Independents (and among other Christians who would not accept that designation); that it has a certain established usage in the circles in which I feel at home; that it is at variance with more authoritarian conceptions which are often taken as standard; and that the case illustrates with peculiar force how easily usage can be cited to promote, without argument, one or another of competing alternatives.

With these explanations, we may proceed to that element of the cultural complex which is known to historians as 'empiricist philosophy'. We ask that its cultural situation be borne in mind, as we explore its implications. For what we shall see, as so often in philosophy, is that as it develops the cultural context is discarded. This may be inevitable: any broad movement of ideas is bound to contain fissures which indeed it is a main business of the philosopher to explore. But he should not be stranded on one side of the fissure or to stand astride of it without realizing that it is one. That is what happened to the empiricist philosophy of the seventeenth and eighteenth centuries.

3. *The Epistemological Misadventure*

Any broad philosophical movement, as it forms to maturity, attempts to accommodate the main interests of the epoch it grows in. (A good example is the recent considerable concern of logical analysts with the philosophy of religion. It was the last thing they were concerned about in the first instance. They became interested when they saw in religious discourse a fruitful field for their theory of different logics.) But the initial drive comes from a single direction. The stimulus to seventeenth-century philosophy came from seventeenth-century science. The philosophers may have practised, e.g., a new kind of religion; but Locke, who notably did, a liberal Christian of the establishment strongly sympathetic to the confessionally under-privileged, saw no reason in his religion to question the rationalist formulae; on the contrary, he treated the existence of God as a matter of proof as emphatically as Descartes, who practised an older kind of religion. It was contemporary science which made him resort to the 'new way of ideas'.

He wanted to apply to our knowledge of nature the method of 'composition' or, as we should now say, 'analysis', which had proved itself successful in the study of nature itself; to show the elements from which it has grown, and of which it is constituted; to supply, as Kant percipiently put it, a 'physiology of the human understanding'. It was in that context that he set out to prove (with significant exceptions) that 'all knowledge begins with experience'. Empirical philosophy began by trying to account for our knowledge of things in the same way as the scientists had tried to account for the sequences of things. It was geared to science from the start.

This is not the place to consider the *actual* procedures of seventeenth-century science, or to estimate how far its procedures were empirical. Certainly in so far as it depended on the development of mathematics, it was more stringently *a priori* than ever before. But it also depended on experiment. The telescope was in the true tradition of the great navigators, whereas the natural philosophy of Aristotle, with its aura of stability, was built into the tradition of a self-contained feudal Europe. There was, then, something empirical about them, with the overtones attaching to the word in its full cultural context. But just how far the factor of experiment was controlled by the mathematician's questions is another matter. The answer, for the natural sciences at least, is that the control was complete and properly so. Observation became at the same time more ample in scope and far more subject to leading questions; and that was how knowledge was extended. The empiricism of the seventeenth century was only one side of it, and was actually held in place by its opposite, the *a priorism* of the mathematicians.

It would, then, be a mistake to underrate the *a priorism* of seventeenth-century science in actual practice, as the philosophers of the Continent, from Descartes down to the end of the eighteenth century, quite properly insisted. But the English reaction was to stress the element of inquiry. Reference may here be made to the florescence in England of other aspects of the empirical complex, in navigation, industry and, not least, religion, which supplied the undercurrent of operative analogy on which the shape of philosophical movements so unexpectedly depends. And in one respect the English reaction was the right one. The English philosophers saw far more clearly that, whatever else was happening, the working programme of the sciences was not merely organization, but discovery; in the language of the *Gorgias*, *epistēmē* was achieving itself in *empeiria*.

Unhappily, the attempt to empiricist philosophers to give an account of human knowledge in the new style was incomplete and self-contradictory. It was incomplete, because until Hume it exempted the conceptions of God and the soul.[14] It was self-contradictory, because the atomic model, having been a convenient device for exploring physical nature, was transferred *a priori* to the understanding of the human mind. By an analogical short cut, 'sensation' takes the place of 'atom'; an alien unit is planted upon the delicate complexity of mental life by the prestige of physical science. The *tabula rasa* is not *given*; how could it be? The separateness of impressions is not given; they have to be disentangled with care and ingenuity. The principle that separate 'sensations' impinging on a *tabula rasa* are the source of knowledge is not given, nor is it put to the test as a hypothesis: it is just taken for granted. Empiricism is thus installed *a priori*, from a base in a single field of experience over-simplified by logical manipulation.

It is clear from this cursory sketch that the empirical philosophy of the seventeenth and eighteenth centuries did not fairly represent the empirical complex and its contribution to human culture. Awareness is not only not atomic; it is its nature not to be. To be aware of things is to grasp them as a whole in their relations and their sequences; they are mutual signposts in the complex to which they belong. Nor is awareness only subjectively continuous in the face of an atomic world; it discerns continuity objectively in that world. It does not require the idealist hypothesis to assure continuity; that

---

[14] The exemption of mathematics is another affair altogether. Mathematics ought to be exempted, because numbers do not, in any relevant sense of the word, exist.

hypothesis is needed only when the given is represented as discontinuous. Still less is knowledge a secondary product from the discontinuous self – distilled through the association of ideas. If we follow our noses and try to find out, we shall be led far from these inapplicable constructions, and shall be set free to contemplate, later in the day, the first things in their duration. This, it must be insisted, is not an unempirical activity, unless experience is unempirically confined by definition to the discontinuous.

The importance of this discussion may be seen by reference to Hume. Hume thought that the exemption of God and the soul from the empirical scheme of reference left empiricism incomplete. Hence his use against 'spiritual substance' of Berkeley's weapons against 'material substance'. Because he accepted the atomic view about sensation he could not contemplate the empirical approach to the soul and to God. The soul he reduced to its constituent factors, without remainder and without overtones; God he was prepared ironically to allow, but only on faith, making it clear that the sceptic and the fideist stand together against rational theology, and launching the most powerful criticisms in history against the only contemporary argument with a definite empirical premiss, the argument from design.

The usual attempts to meet Hume are unsatisfactory, because they accept from him the equivalence of 'empirical' and 'atomic', and in trying (rightly) to challenge the latter find themselves (wrongly) at odds with the former. Given the equivalence, Hume was in fact justified in carrying the programme of his predecessors to its logical conclusion; and in the process (despite his dislike of 'enthusiasts'), he gave an airing to the mainly sectarian view that *believing* is a more appropriate category for the discourse of worshippers than knowing. (Moreover, as his treatment of the causal relation shows, it was part of his programme to insist that much of what passes as demonstration rests on belief: so that, in respect of what exists, there is only a difference of degree between them.) But it is the equivalence which should have been attacked. Experience does not give us snippets; it gives us, in and through what changes, successive glimpses of what endures.

This is not to say that the constructions of science are not of the first importance. It is merely to say that they *are* constructions. Sensation is a sophisticated scientific concept, achieved by paring away and disaggregating organic wholes. It may be convenient to isolate it for special scientific purposes, but in that case it is those purposes that effect the isolation: it is not simply found there. If we go simply by what we find, the complex structures which include sensation are prior to sensation. All this has been said so often that it should be needless to repeat it; but the conclusion usually drawn is that the early empiricists were wrong because they proceeded empirically, whereas the point of the present argument is that they were wrong because they did not. They operated not with data, but with abstractions, and, chief among them, 'sensation'.

This, indeed, was clear to the early empiricists themselves. To select at random: Locke (*Essay*, Book II, ch. XXIII, Sect. 1), describing the composition of 'complex ideas', writes: 'the mind, furnished with a great number of the simple ideas conveyed by the senses . . . takes notice, also, that a number of these simple ideas go constantly together'. Is the 'mind' which thus 'takes *notice*' a sensation? Again, Berkeley (*Principles* CXXXIX, and again CXLII) distinguishes between 'ideas' and the 'notions' that we have of spirits ('a spirit is an active being, whose existence consists not in being perceived, but in perceiving ideas and thinking'). There is little to choose between these 'empiricists' and the 'rationalist' Leibniz, commenting on the scholastic doctrine to which, after all, sensationalism is much indebted: '*Nihil est in intellectu quod non fuerit in sensu: excipe ipse intellectus*' (*Nouveaux essais*, Book II, ch. 1). Hume took the only way out, by resolving mind into constituent sensations, and thereby depriving his conclusions of any claim to truth.[15] It is notable, however, that he found them impossible to live with. What his dialectic achieves is to drive a wedge between philosophy and the ordinary course of life: backgammon, for example, or making merry with his friends. His philosophy is not a reponse to environment, but the pursuit of an unempirical thesis unempirically to its logical outcome. He does not listen

---

[15] Dogmatic and sceptical reasons 'both vanish away into nothing, by a gradual and just diminution' (*Treatise*, Part IV, Sect. 1).

for contexts or overtones. He is just a Scots dominie who has
got the better of the minister in argument.

If, instead of following atomic analogies drawn from the
natural sciences, we put our ears to the ground and observe
what happens, we shall find that sensation is an extract from
experience, and presupposes an experiencing of which sensing
is only a part. With this much admitted, factors excluded by the
sensationalist dogma – voluntary effort, other minds, and even
the structural features of the world enumerated, for example,
in Plato's *Sophist* – reassert their claim to consideration. Now it
is the linking of empiricism with sensationalism which, more
than anything else, has made it implausible to talk about the
empirical approach to God. If it is possible experientially to be
aware of one's self and other people and Platonic 'kinds', distinguished from sensation by activity on the one hand and
permanence on the other, one of the *a priori* objections to an
alliance between theism and empiricism is removed.

4. *The Misadventure of Subject-object Parallelism*

There is a long tradition, going back to Book V of Plato's
Republic, that that which is most real is most knowable. On the
face of it, it is most unlikely. The most real things are not the
most obvious. To apprehend things in their range and complexity, without bias or abstraction, is difficult to a degree. If
there is any incorrigible knowledge, it relates to abstractions
serving specific purposes. Of things as they are, knowledge can
be only piecemeal, and is highly corrigible. This point is
relevant to knowledge as a component of religion. So far from
being clear and distinct, one would expect knowledge of God
to be fragmentary and enigmatic. This, in fact, is part of the
Christian tradition – the tradition of *deus absconditus*. It is often
combined with the view that the *existence*, as opposed to the
nature, of God can be demonstrated: that we shall consider in a
later chapter. At present we are discussing the knowledge of
God, not the knowledge of his existence; and of this there is
every reason, both of philosophy and (if it matters) of orthodoxy
for supposing it to be imperfect and fallible. That is why the
standard view that ways of knowing stand in a defined one-one

relation to ways of being is, for a philosophy of religion, startling, and has to be considered before we proceed further. For our further instruction, if this standard view can be refuted, we may admit, at least as a possibility, an empirical knowledge of the non-empirical.

But in challenging it, we shall find ourselves at odds with all the main traditions, empiricist and rationalist alike, and also with Kant's notable attempt to arbitrate between them. We collide head-on with Plato's dictum that 'the fully existent is the fully knowable' (*Republic* 477a). But we collide also with the empiricist conviction that as knowledge is of particulars there is no whole or source of things to know. Moreover, though Kant broke down these barriers, though he understood that the science of his time was a *necessary* knowledge of *empirical* phenomena, he did not similarly admit that there might be an *empirical* knowledge of *things in themselves*. The programme of a necessitarian science matched with an empirical metaphysic, which his reversal of the Platonic parallelism might seem to have facilitated, was not worked out, because being, in Kemp Smith's words, 'a rationalist by training, temperament and conviction', he could not conceive of 'empirical metaphysics' except as a contradiction in terms.

It will be objected that a challenge to both the alternatives of the philosophical tradition will take a good deal of justifying. This is only too true. All that is claimed in this section is that a dogma which would invalidate it from the start is indefensible. As we have already suggested, it is just the most difficult and far-reaching problems the approach to which must be most sensitive, the answers to which most provisional, the convictions concerning which most cumbrously cumulative. Not to mention the concept of God, which introduces the complicating reference to being, consider the more abstract concept of 'unity' – one of the 'highest kinds' of the *Sophist* and a possible example of Strawson's 'massive core of human thinking which has no history' (*Individuals*, p. 10). But to think about 'unity' is not to think about a concept given from the beginning in all its clarity. It has a focus but a shifting and variable periphery. To encompass it, we have to think about mathematics, about art, about society, and about religion, edging in here and there,

noting analogies and sorting out differences, taking up stances
and abandoning them and gradually feeling our way into the
diversified complex of ideas for which the term is a general
description. Even if Plato and Strawson are right about the
hard core, the procedure is empirical, because we are required
to examine the different instances and arrange them in a
provisional order. It is much more like finding one's way in the
bush than like reading off destinations from a signpost. And it
is never completed, because we can never be sure what shapes
the concept may assume in the future. (In the field of political
philosophy, the concentration of discussions about unity, since
Bodin and Hobbes, on the nation-state, at best only one kind
of political unity, is a warning against particularizing standardization.) It is not something to be applied; it is something to be
understood. It has to be sought out with circuitous circum-
spection over a wide range of situations. In short, the inquiry
is an empirical inquiry into kindred but by no means uniform
structures[16] though, unlike empirical inquiry in the sciences, it
depends entirely on observation and comparison and cannot
fall back on planned experiment. This sample of metaphysics
as actually practised does not bear out the traditional conviction
that empirical metaphysics is impossible. On the contrary, that
conviction is imposed on the metaphysician by an unreasonable
expectation of finality. Why should the harder enterprise be
expected to be finalized when the more straightforward enterprises of science are subject to revision? What is, is hardly
likely to be more transparent than its more accessible offshoots
and appearances. That being so, the traditional alignment of
knowing with what is and 'opining' with what appears, in all its
direct, inverted and consequential manifestations, should not
go unchallenged and will in all likelihood prove to be indefensible.[17]

[16] Structures, not meanings: the meanings of words are directed to things.
If it is said that this is itself a question of words, I reply that I prefer mine.
[17] The reasons for extravagant metaphysical expectation will appear
later: cf. pp. 108f. They arise from religious authoritarianism on the one
hand and from the dogmatics of science on the other.

5. *Misadventure in a Crucial Instance:* '*Intuition*'

When empiricists protest against *a priori* methods, they are attacking two distinct and separable procedures. They are attacking the attempt to reach conclusions about matters of fact by *a priori* demonstration. This was the main point of protest in the seventeenth century, as it stood in the way of the natural sciences. But they are also attacking the claim to direct insight: and it is about this, under the name of intuitionism, that they seem at present to be most concerned. They dislike it because direct insight claims to be final and is not shaken by the ordinary rules of public evidence. They even regard it[18] as a main cause of intolerance and all the evils which derive from it.

The difficulty is this. On the one hand, the claim to direct intuition is the setting up of a private conviction against the crowd; it is based on a blinding vision which owes more to immediate experience, and less to authority or argument, than the prevalent public convictions. It is the product of a determination to rely on one's own reaction to life. That is to say, it is tied, on one side, to the empirical complex. If 'empiricism' is the name for that complex of ideas and habits which is opposed both to authoritarianism and to rationalism, intuitionism is empirical through and through: as indeed has often been recognized in the case of 'conscience'.

On the other hand, the man who claims direct intuition is usually supposed to be claiming finality. This is what sets him in opposition to the empirical scientist, who claims only to provide such explanation as the shifting data permit.

In fact, the criteria for 'empiricism' are: (1) the appeal to experience; (2) the admission of corrigibility. 'Intuition' qualifies under (1), but not under (2). Whether we call it 'empirical' or not depends on the weight we attach to these factors respectively.

The following observations may help to clarify:

1. When we talk loosely about the appeal to experience, the question presents itself, whose experience? Often enough, the appeal is to some allegedly common human characteristic: *anyone* could have the experience. It is in this spirit that Kant talks of the 'categories of the understanding': they belong to

---

[18] Cf. P. H. Nowell-Smith, *Ethics*, Pelican edition, 1954, p. 47.

man *as man*; that is how they tie in with the programme of the French Revolution. Such ascriptions should be made cautiously; 'man as such' has been loaded with a number of transient attributes, such as self-interest (man-as-such = economic man), sexual repression (man-as-such = Viennese Jewry at the beginning of the twentieth century), philosophical curiosity (man-as-such = the entourage of Plato and Aristotle); for that matter, a disposition to religion (man-as-such = the prevailing set of attitudes and habits from the Vedas to Voltaire). These examples show how easy it is to represent as common to humanity what may well be, sociologically speaking, the habits of an epoch. Nevertheless, in the case, e.g., of thinking causally, the ascription is as valid as any ascription can be; *any* sort of man in *any* situation will be found to think causally, however preposterous his view of what causes what. We may, then, admit common human characteristics, which are part of all men's experience to date, with the solemn warning that they must not be used to smuggle in as universal the particular and corrigible insights of particular persons or epochs.

2. As already indicated, though we may all think the same way, we notably do not think the same things. But intuitionists frequently claim to know what is true universally. Now if the subject-matter is seven plus five equals twelve, the issue is purely academic. Whether this great truth is known by direct insight or synthetically *a priori* or is reported by exhausted empiricists who have combed the universe unsuccessfully for exceptions, it is still common knowledge, and anyone who fails to act on it will be quickly disillusioned. But if it concerns (to select instances of which we are unlikely to approve) the self-evident merits of slavery, or child marriage, or warfare as a way of life (and all these things have received immediate moral approval), many of us would protest that the allegedly self-evident is plain error. And there are other plenary inspirations which many people would wish, if not to reject, at least to qualify (for example the cradle-to-grave philosophy of the welfare state). In these fields, the claims of intuition, though intensely personal and based on experience, appear to admit of falsity or exaggeration. The appeal to experience can never be conclusive and it can often be mistaken.

3. Why, then, is it so often asserted that the experience is not corrigible? The word intuition has something to do with this. It was originally used in Latin, *intuitus*, by the schoolmen to denote the direct insight of angels as opposed to the sense-bound thinking of men. It was secularized by Descartes, who used it to describe the clear and distinct ideas independent of all sense which are the vehicles of human thinking, thereby committing what M. Maritain justly called *le péché de l'angélisme*, the sin of posing as an angel.[19] Since the seventeenth century it has been used to distinguish direct from indirect modes of apprehension, with the suggestion that the direct is infallible and the indirect subject to error, and not least by Bergson, who thought all intelligence to be indirect and extolled intuition interpreted as other than intelligence as the way past appearance to reality.

Finally, in ethics, it led ultimately to the extreme position of Prichard, for whom moral insight was its own justification so that all one could do about it was to examine its implications. There is thus good reason for suspecting intuitionists of claiming incorrigibility, and in that case the fact that they also based themselves on experience and not on demonstration or authority would not suffice to earn them the title of empiricists.

But in this traditional account of intuition there is a simple confusion. Immediate apprehension is not incorrigible.

One may illustrate with a case of moral intuition. One can be never so clear that one ought to tell the truth come what may, and yet afterwards discover, like Gregers Werle in Ibsen's *Wild Duck*, that it ought to have been withheld. The fact that the deliverances of conscience are immediate is no reason for supposing them infallible. As Sir David Ross recognizes, our moral intuitions from time to time are very fallible, but they are the best we have.[20] He says:[21]

> We are quite incapable of pronouncing straight off on its rightness or wrongness (of an act) in the totality of these aspects; it is only by recognizing

[19] In *Trois réformateurs*, 1925, p. 78.
[20] That is, concerning duties absolutely. *Prima facie* duties are a matter of knowledge from the start. That is indeed to claim infallibility, but not in respect of moral insights in any particular situation. The incorrigibles are possibles. Actualities are as corrigible as ever.
[21] *Foundations of Ethics*, 1939, p. 84.

these different features one by one that we can approach the forming of a judgment on the totality of its nature; our first look reveals these features in isolation, one by one; they are what appears *prima facie*. . . . But an act may be right in one respect and wrong in more important respects, and therefore not, in the totality of its aspects, the most right of the acts open to us, and then we are not obliged to do it; and another act may be wrong in some respect and yet in its totality the most right of all the acts open to us, and then we *are* bound to do it . . . obligation or disobligation attaches to it in virtue of the totality of its aspects.

It will be instructive for our later examination of religion if we recall his reasons. Intuition appropriates a particular facet of a connected whole and not only can but must be corrected as further intuition appropriates other facets of the same truth. The picture is like maps of Australia before Cook's voyages: a number of loose ends with the whole beginning to show up behind, and, of course, the hinterland uncharted.

Thus the frequent criticism that the claim to direct insight is a claim to incorrigibility may be shown to be mistaken, and what is commonly called intuition may be placed on the empirical side of the dividing line on which, but for misunderstandings, it would naturally fall, as only one insight, however illuminating and important, of an individual human person. With this last disclaimer, empirical philosophy is reunited with its old partner in the complex, empirical religion. The next phase of the argument is to show that religious assertions and practices are corrigible and that if they were not they would not be properly religious. That, however, is a controversial story, and it is hinted at in conclusion in order to show why it is important to rescue empiricism from its misadventure.

6. *On Avoiding Further Misadventures*

We have noted that the interpretations of empiricism which set it in antagonism to belief in God do not represent the total empirical complex, and rest on dogmatic assumption, limiting the testimony of actual experience. We have now to suggest how they should be corrected, so that misadventures shall not recur. We advance the following suggestions:

1. Awareness is of things-in-relation.
2. Awareness is of the continuous.

3. Awareness is not a fact in its own right; it is 'intentional' and directed to objects.
4. It has to discover the objects to which it is directed.
5. It is inseparable from valuations.

Some of these points have been made, negatively, in passing; and by no means all self-styled empiricists have denied all of them. But many have denied some of them; and it is only if all of them are accepted that the road is clear for the empiricist approach to God.

1. Things are experienced in a system of relations. Empiricists tend to fight shy of the admission, because the term suggests the tightly drawn totality of Absolute Idealism. But one of its main proponents was William James, to whom Absolute Idealism was anathema. He challenged the 'loose and separate' school in the following terms:

> Intellectualist critics of sensation insist that sensations are disjoined only. Radical Empiricism insists that the conjunctions between them are just as immediately given, as the disjunctions are, and that relations, whether conjunctive or disjunctive, are in their original sensible givenness just as fleeting and momentary . . . , and just as 'particular', as terms are.[22]

Indeed, James argued (and I think rightly) that atomism and absolutism give rise to each other: if the given is intrinsically unrelated, the experience of relatedness can be supported only by going beyond the given, just as, if relatedness has to be read into the given to account for the facts, that must be because the facts have been atomistically conceived. Both the opposed errors arise from the same source: the assumption that what is given is atomic sensations. James, on the contrary, presents it as a finding of experience that 'fact is all shades and no boundaries'.[23] If this is so, empiricism not only was misrepresented by the atomic sensationalists, but can be corrected within its own terms of reference. That is a matter of importance for the philosophy of religion, first, because the belief that what is real is atomic is the heart and soul of atheism (it is far more radically atheistic than metaphysical or dialectical materialism,

---

[22] *A Pluralistic Universe*, 1909, p. 280. On the same page, he calls his doctrine 'radically empiricist', 'in distinction from the doctrine of mental atoms which the name empiricism so often suggests'.
[23] *Op. cit.*, p. 288.

in which the religious impulse is often as active as it is mis-directed, so that they are not so much atheistic as idolatrous); and secondly, because the slogan 'all shades and no boundaries' may also be found to apply to the dealings of God with the world.

2. The same arguments which hold for relatedness hold also for continuity. It is not a question of re-connecting atomic experiences; it is a question of falling into step with a continuing experience. Here again, James empirically reinforces the traditional empiricism and concludes: 'If we do not feel both past and present in our field of feeling, we feel them not at all.'[24] His exposition of the theme is linked with an attack on 'conceptual systems', and an appreciation of Bergson's appeal to 'intuitive sympathy'. Experience, he tells us, does not give atemporal blocks connected by temporal succession; it gives succession directly as it occurs. 'What exists is not things made but things in the making.'[25] 'Reality *falls* in passing into conceptual analysis; it *mounts* in living its own undivided life – it buds and burgeons, changes and creates.'[26] Whether the view that the datum is continuous in time need carry with it the anticonceptualist consequences drawn by Bergson and James is a matter for debate; the concept might well be part of the burgeoning. But by firmly insisting that what is given is the continuing, they achieve in respect of succession as well as in respect of coexistence the separation of empirical and atomic which, as has been argued, is essential to an empiricist inter-pretation of religion.

In this case there may be complications; the generalization of the temporalist approach may lead to a temporal God. At this stage it need only be said that to describe God as being 'from everlasting to everlasting' means not that he is timeless but that he is coeval with all possible time, and to be coeval with all possible time presupposes time to be coeval *with*. That is certainly the conclusion drawn by James, and he commends it to the ordinary believer as more familiar than the 'monistic perfections' of 'conceptual substitutes' for God devised by 'remote professorial minds'.[27] That is as may be; it will be

[24] *Op. cit.*, p. 283.
[26] *Op. cit.*, p. 264.
[25] *Op. cit.*, p. 263.
[27] *Op. cit.*, pp. 311f.

discussed in detail later. For the moment, we may be content to note that if the given is continuous, God remains what he cannot be under the atomistic formula, a live option, entirely congruent with the first premisses of an empirical philosophy.

3. Still keeping as close as possible to experience, we note that awareness may be treated either as a fact in relation to other facts, or as 'intentional', in Brentano's sense, as pointing towards other facts. Either way of taking it is permissible; but the first way of taking it is a heuristic device, proper enough for purposes of natural science, but the product of deliberate abstraction, and therefore improper for metaphysics and especially for empirical metaphysics, for it manhandles experience in the interests of theory. What we actually notice, in ourselves and in others, is the *directedness* of mental processes: not only of plans for action but of thought and feeling also. So much so, that when it is apparently absent, we are puzzled, and turn to psychoanalysts, or re-examine situations with a view to finding what has escaped us. Once again, directedness does not in itself establish theism; *what* our mental processes are directed *to* depends on our environment and on the mutual adjustment of the processes themselves. But if there were no directedness, theism would be impossible; even if there were a God, we could not possibly know it; mental processes would be exactly like any other processes, and the only logical – and very unempirical – terminus is metaphysical physicalism. On the other hand, once directedness is admitted, it is natural to proceed from one directedness to another, with some hope of finding a more inclusive or explanatory object at each stage of the process. After all, Brentano began by writing on Aristotle.

4. In case the defence should seem at this point to be swerving into rationalism, it must be stressed that there the objects of human awareness have to be *discovered*. When we direct ourselves in inquiry, the object of the directedness is not fixed, even to the extent that it is in action. It is in fact in some way misleading to talk about knowing; once we know, a mental process has died, in the happy way that such processes do die, at the moment of achievement. The living process is *getting*-to-know – a point stressed by Plato in a sceptical-cum-mystical passage at the end of the *Phaedrus* (278c) – and the object of its

intense directedness appears only when the process is over.
Thus, as metaphysicians, we do not start with God; we may
start with the *idea* of God, the content being taken for granted
and the reality held in suspense; but, as Bergson pointed out,[28]
that method puts too much weight on the idiosyncrasies of
the assumed content: if the world does not present them, God
will be non-existent. 'Now who can fail to see,' he adds, 'that, if
philosophy is the work of experience and reasoning, it must
follow just the reverse method, question experience as to what
it has to teach us of a Being who transcends tangible reality as
He transcends human consciousness, and so appreciate the
nature of God by reasoning on the facts supplied by experience.'

5. James' dictum that 'a fact is all shades and no boundaries'
applies not only as between what everyone would agree to call
facts, but also (more debatably) between facts and what some
people call 'values'. No *experience* is value-neutral; the neutrality
of science is an abstract from experience, and even then the
scientist finds in it a certain austere satisfaction. Every *ordinary*
experience is, however slightly, pleasurable *or* painful, exciting
or depressing, a fulfilment or a disappointment. To consider
experience as epistemologists do, as a colourless transaction
between subject (if any) and object (if any), is not to listen,
but to manipulate – again, a laudable proceeding, but the
reverse of metaphysical, and also the reverse of empirical.[29]
The element of valuation may be as simple as delight in the
scent of a flower, and as complex as astringent satisfaction in a
disagreeable duty honourably discharged, but it is an integral
part of the situation, and to exclude it is to substitute for
experience one's own intentions or explanations. This is something which philosophers cannot afford to contemplate; it is
their heavy responsibility to the world to miss out on as little
as possible.[30]

Now it is fair to say that of all the prerequisites for an
empirical approach to theism this is the most indispensable.

[28] *The Two Sources of Morality and Religion*, trs. R. A. Audra and C. Brereton,
1935, p. 225.
[29] That is why no student should be let loose on epistemology without
working, at least concurrently, on aesthetics.
[30] Though they will stand in a queue for hours to watch what Bradley
called the 'unearthly ballet of bloodless categories' from the back stalls.

The other four have a negative significance only: if they are denied, theism is a non-starter; but if they are accepted, it is by no means certain to win. The one and only sure thing about religion in all its forms is that it rejects out of hand the dichotomy of fact and value. The present frantic dissociation of 'is' and 'ought' is evidence of profound disbelief. Religion carries to a higher point an association which belongs to experience from the beginning. If we can get rid of this last abstraction we are in a fair way to 'follow the common' to the vestibule of grace.

APPENDIX TO I

Professor Braithwaite, Empiricism and Religion

OTHER DAYS, other ways. In recent philosophy 'empiricism' is not so much a modest and probabilist theory concerning the knowledge of things, as an exacting and undeviating theory concerning the meaning of statements. Those which in principle cannot be verified in experience are not described as untrue; they do not even come up for discussion; they make no sense. Religious statements are frequently so classified. In the foreground is a highly polished and sophisticated logical doctrine; its appeal is to the large number of practising secularists who have not even revolted, but have never known anything else. There is today a greater ignorance about religion than at any time in our history, and it is the sense of its irrelevance among the uninstructed (including graduates) which gives power to the elegant and technical attempts to discredit it.

This is the background for Professor R. B. Braithwaite's famous Eddington Lecture, *An Empiricist's View of the Nature of Religious Belief*. It raises the question of *Theism and Empiricism* in its acutest form. Claiming to be an empiricist, Braithwaite refuses to subscribe to any kind of statement about God; in the sense in which we have used the word, he is therefore not a theist. Philosophically he is as hard-boiled as any. Yet he is a practising member of a Christian community, and is therefore concerned to show not that religion makes no sense, but that it does not depend on the unverifiable statements which *do* make no sense.

There have been many criticisms of this position: I restrict myself here to his use of the word 'empirical'.[1]

[1] In general, the point of view adopted in this work is closer to Braith-

In a move which might easily be mistaken for a diplomatic compromise, Braithwaite takes advantage of a recent concession, under which the theory of meaning as verification is softened down into a theory of meaning as use. He insists, however, that under this change 'there is no desertion from the spirit of empiricism'.[2] His salvaging of religion, minus statements, does not depend on the comparative tolerance of the word 'use'; the tolerance has been read out of it by definition. Just how empirical these manœuvres are may be left to the reader to decide. What is certain is that, allegedly in conformity with use, he reduces statements about God to statements about moral intention (which allegedly *can* be verified), supported by illustrative stories the edifying character of which does not depend on their literal truth. This, he says, is the way 'to explain, in empirical terms, how a religious statement is used by a man who asserts it in order to express his religious conviction'.[3]

Two points emerge from the above review. Use *is* different from verification; but, like verification, it pins us down to the observable. It will be argued that if it is *significantly* different from verification, it does *not* pin us down to the observable; and even if it did, it should not compel us to reduce religious statements to moral statements. It will further be observed that to some verificationists moral statements are as objectionable as religious statements, and it will have to be seen whether Braithwaite's reductive methods might not be used against moral statements also.

That 'use' is different from verification has seemed to some philosophers a significant departure; they have felt warranted in talking about 'different logics', and have allowed that the logic of religious discourse is not quite the logic of experimental

waite's than that of many of his critics. Like Braithwaite, I shall treat action as the chief test of religious concern. Like Braithwaite, I have personally been influenced, in a Christian sense, by the novels of Dostoevsky, and am hardly likely to overlook the role of fiction in inducing faith. The difference is that on my view there are *grounds* for religious belief other than the practices by which they are *tested*, and I for one should not be moved as I am by fiction if it did not incorporate something of reality.

[2] P. 59. References throughout are to the reprint of the lecture in *Christian Ethics and Contemporary Philosophy*, ed. I. T. Ramsey, 1966.

[3] *Ibid.*

science. It is clear that Braithwaite has no such intention. What is not so clear is why he should favour a change which on his showing would appear to have little importance. It involves him in this difficulty: that the *use* of religious statements is, amongst other things, to make affirmations about states of affairs. If he wishes to exclude this reference, he has to appeal over the heads of those who *use* religious language to his own method of verification. It is certainly not the case, as he asserts, that 'the religious assertion is used as a moral assertion'. If it is to be presented as a moral assertion, it has to be manhandled by philosophers in the teeth of religious usage.

But in fact Braithwaite has no call to be mealy-mouthed about verification, and his Christian critics have no call to fight shy of it. In one sense, Christians are hardened verificationists: 'by their fruits shall ye know them'. But what they find verified in the appropriate action is the presence of God, which in Braithwaite's version is unverifiable (and presumably meaningless). He has his reply to that, too: 'almost all statements about God as immanent,[4] as an indwelling spirit, can be interpreted as asserting psychological facts in metaphorical language'.[5] But, as such, they are corrigible, which the theistic interpretation will not admit.[6] Theists are caught in a 'double-think' position: 'they want to hold that religious statements both are about the actual world (i.e. are empirical statements), and are also not refutable in any possible world, the characteristic of statements which are logically necessary'.[7]

Let it be made clear at once; if God does not run the risk of falsification he is not verifiable either. There *are* conditions which would lead me to disbelieve: if, e.g., the world were known to be an irredeemable chaos. Only these are not the conditions which happen to obtain. Even in its natural state, we shall argue that the world is fundamentally right-side-up; if God is in Christ, the anticipation broadens into a certainty. But in one sense Braithwaite is quite right; we know, to our cost, when we lose touch, what a world without God would be

<hr />

[4] Statements about God as transcendent are presumably beyond all possible verification. Even that may be disputed, as we shall see.
[5] 'An Empiricist's View of the Nature of Religious Belief', p. 56.
[6] *Op. cit.*, p. 57.   [7] *Ibid.*

like. 'If there is a personal God, how would the world be different if there were not? Unless the question can be answered, God's existence cannot be given an empirical meaning.'[8] This is not only to be conceded; it is to be underlined. Even losing the feel of there being a God makes important differences to human behaviour: how much more difference would it make if there were no God at all! Take the difference it would make if there were no government at all, and the difference it would make if there were no poets at all, and add them, and the total would fall incomparably short of the difference it would make if there were no God at all.

Still, as Braithwaite says, the test of the difference is in action. 'I cannot pass from asserting a fact, of whatever sort, to intending to perform an action, without having the hypothetical intention to do the action if I assert the fact.'[9] This is true and important, and will be developed in chapter IV of this work. But what it shows is not that asserting the fact is irrelevant, but that only as appropriated in intention can it pass into action and receive verification. Indeed, 'asserting a fact' is where the whole thing starts. Braithwaite wishes to support a Christian morality. Good luck to him, but is his choice entirely at random? If the world were not built that way, it would be what well-wishing pessimists declare it to be, a desolating impossibility, for ever imprisoned in the formula, 'too good to be true'. The intellectual component of Christian faith cannot be analysed away into its moral content, for Braithwaite's own reason: that it makes a difference to the moral content. The difference between religion on the one hand, and history or science on the other, does not consist of the absence or presence of appropriate tests. It is simply that in religion one tests with one's life, instead of looking up references or doing experiments.

Part of the trouble is Braithwaite's moral theory; to be precise, his sharp distinction between 'asserting a proposition' and 'subscribing to a policy of action'.[10] To 'subscribe' to a policy is not to defend it. Does it make no difference what policy one subscribes to? But the gambit is even less promising in religion than it is in ethics. Truth-claims, implicit in moral

[8] *Op. cit.*, p. 56.   [9] *Op. cit.*, pp. 62f.   [10] *Op. cit.*, p. 60.

discourse, are open and explicit in religion. Braithwaite recognizes the difference but accounts for it by representing the surplus as 'entertaining of stories'. But again, what sort of stories? Only those stories will do which make a point, and that point is not a story, but an affirmation.

In his role of empiricist, Braithwaite recognizes only observables and scientific hypotheses. The point to be made against him is not that he is mistaken, but that both have their analogues in religion, though they appear differently, and behave differently, because of their peculiar context. Religious discourse abounds in observables; it is concrete through and through, far more so than, for example, the discourse of science. If it claims to observe, through a glass darkly, that undivided concentration of structures and values which it calls God, it should not, if only because of the blanks in the chart, be called unempirical, any more than Captain Cook should be called unempirical. What it is trying with difficulty to discover is entangled with the world, and the entanglement provides some of the clues. Certainly no historically grounded religion would stand if its empirical basis, namely its historical assertions, were removed from it. Christians are empiricists who *find* in Christ ordinary human nature, and God besides. They *find* it, and cannot make sense of ordinary human nature on any other terms.

Religious discourse, following and interpreting the life of religion as a whole, also resembles scientific hypothesis. The last thing we should say about our religious life is that it is already perfected. Like hypotheses, it has to be improved upon. Like science, though diffused over the whole of life, it springs from a venture of faith, in the progress of which disposition and belief and conduct are constantly being disturbed and reformed. That is the way God comes at us. We go on from one formulation to the next – or fall back, as the case may be. And the main cause of falling back is trying to stay where we are. It all bespeaks, in fact it is the nerve and centre of, what we have called 'the empirical complex'.

The trouble, then, is in the limited use of the term 'empirical', which Braithwaite inherits from thinkers far less susceptible to religion than he is himself. He thinks observation and experiment have no application to deity, even deity conjoined with humanity. This cramping limitation is very far from being due to insensitivity; it is in fact due to dogma. Our business with it is to insist that experience should be understood in its full extent, and not in terms of sensory observation alone. In fact, sense experience, taken contextually and not abstractly, never *is* alone. It certainly is not so in the case, crucial for Braithwaite's argument, of moral intention.

The point of this note is not to contest Braithwaite's 'empiricism', but to welcome and extend it. It is an important part of our own thesis that God is made known through discernible structures and concentrated in a discernible event. As a protest against Neo-Platonist 'henology' and the Neo-Hegelian Absolute, Braithwaite is on the side of the angels. Moreover, he is concerned to retain ritual observance and scriptural story; he retreats from religion not over the whole front, but on the intellectual sector only. But before he starts he takes for granted the assumptions of a clique describing itself as 'contemporary man'. Under this impossible handicap, he has sincerely done his best for the Christian religion.

II

PROLEGOMENA TO AN EMPIRICAL
PHILOSOPHY OF RELIGION

1. *Where to Start?*

HAVING disposed of some unempirically motivated definitions of empiricism, we proceed to examine those empirically presented factors in the world which might justify the belief in God. A modern writer might begin with 'religious experience'. Our ancestors would have appealed to something much more definite: miracles and immortality. In both cases there are difficulties in applying the ordinary empirical tests; a miracle cannot be repeated to order under laboratory conditions, and extra-sensory perception does not require the hypothesis of departed spirits. But in both cases we are asked to consider specific occurrences which are not in principle immune from verification: e.g. by reference to the character of the testimony, or possible observation in the future. As long as these supports are maintained there is no basis for the charge of 'vacuity', which figures so largely in recent criticism. It is with the decrease in their power to move that religion has sometimes seemed to be suspended in the void.

In his famous essay, 'Gods',[1] John Wisdom draws attention to their reduced efficacy, and proceeds to consider the religious way of looking at things as one of many – illuminating, no doubt, but no more illuminating than its opposite, because there is no feature of the things we look at which requires, or even favours, either of them. In the absence of empirical tests, no illumination is mandatory, and any is permissible.

There is a candour and a reverence in Wisdom's essay which set it apart from much modern treatment of religion by philo-

[1] *Philosophy and Psycho-Analysis*, 1953, pp. 149–68.

sopher-critics. But it starts from the same assumption. Now that (as he thinks) God can no longer be grasped by the *old* empirical fringes, he cannot be grasped empirically at all. He is no longer something we can approach, or feel to be approaching us; he is not part of the given at all, he is one of a number of imaginative constructions. He does not figure in the world; he is presented as a possible way of responding to what *does* happen in the world. And the other way is just as possible. The parable of the invisible gardener leaves us guessing, and was devised with that intention.

But if God is not prefigured in the world, he can make no difference to anything that happens in the world. If that were so, Antony Flew[2] would be right in arguing that he is wholly vacuous.[3] Unfortunately certain ways of speaking among believers make the charge of 'vacuity' look plausible: as when they say that no evidence whatever would make any difference to their beliefs.[4] But if God is hoisted as a point of piety beyond the reach of this world, it is not surprising that, as a point of impiety, he should be held to be irrelevant to the world. To keep the argument going, it is necessary to revert to the empirical factors which engender religious belief.

At this stage, some might prefer to reinstate the traditional empirical supports of religion which Wisdom believes (perhaps rightly, as a matter of sociology) to be obsolescent: miracles and immortality. I do not wish to rule these considerations out; but I propose to make my case without them. The belief in immortality is denied by some theists (e.g. Aristotle, and the Sadducees), and maintained by at least one confessed atheist (J. M. E. McTaggart), and it is not evident that either of these combinations is self-contradictory.[5] As for miracles, these

[2] In *New Essays in Philosophical Theology*, 1955, ed. A. Flew and A. MacIntyre, pp. 96–9.

[3] Cf. the welcome admission of this point by William A. Christian, *Meaning and Truth in Religion*, 1964, p. 25: 'if a thing cannot be negated consistently it has no significant consequences'. He writes as a believer.

[4] Belief in the unlikely is not vacuous. Newman thought it more *likely* that observers should be mistaken that Lazarus should rise from the dead. Nevertheless, on the authority of Church and Scripture, he *believed* the less likely proposition.

[5] And if the *reason* for believing in God is the hope of immortality, it is a self-centred reason and not a godly reason.

spectacularly draw attention to the difference God makes in the world, and there could be no more convincing reply to the charge of vacuity: moreover, if 'laws of nature' are empirically established on the basis of custom (as Hume avers), a particular and unusual action of deity need not be a transgression of those laws (as Hume insists): it is rather a supplement – God acting directly rather than indirectly through nature, which is orthodox Thomist doctrine.[6] But as it is proposed to consider revelation as the crown of natural theology, it is a point of scruple not to throw it into action at the crowbar stage. In reinstating the empirical supports of religion, we shall therefore confine ourselves to natural theology, and call as evidence only what ordinary experience has to show.

Unfortunately, ordinary experience is frequently interpreted either as the experience of ordinary men (the appeal to 'common sense', determined by numbers), or, much more misleadingly, as the experience of a fashionable cultured clique, parading as a popular mouthpiece (e.g. Western intellectuals alienated from their religious background). Neither of these senses is here intended. In ordinary experience is included everything, however uncommon, which belongs to the scheme of nature: e.g. mystical states are not to be ruled out because most people do not have them, or are determined not to have them; nor are the normal uncorrupted expectations of the outback chapel or the suburban household, however repugnant they may be to 'advanced' or 'liberated' persons. We use the word to denote whatever can be cited in evidence without appealing to special revelation.

That being understood, we proceed to examine the most pressing candidate, 'religious experience'.

2. *The Assay of Religious Experience*

As a matter of phenomenological description, what is given in 'religious experience' is given as unqualified reality. The

---

[6] Cf. Hume's essay on 'Miracles', conveniently accessible in R. Wollheim's Fontana Library collection, *Hume on Religion*, 1963, esp. p. 211, n. 3, and compare St Thomas, *Summa Theologica*, Book III, ch. 100: *Quod ea quae Deus praeter naturae ordinem facit non sunt contra naturam.*

moment the worshipper suspects that he is contributing to the making of what he worships, he ceases to be able to worship, and with practice he learns to correct the subjective distortions to which he knows he is prone. But when he discerns in himself the difference between a distorted insight and a corrected insight, he admits by implication that there is something there to be discerned. The correcting of an insight is an improvement, i.e. it is drawing nearer to that which the insight is *into*. The growth of religious experience through improved insight is not spun out of the experience itself; it is due to dissatisfaction with the experience and the applying of stricter standards of objectivity. Thus what appeared in the unreformed experience as unqualified reality is later shown to have been imperfect even as an approximation. The very fact that religious experience grows (as it does), proclaims that it cannot at any given time be taken at its face value.[7] To serve as an empirical starting-point for theism it needs to be associated with a definite object.

This, it will be said, is to be found in God. Substitute for 'religious experience' 'experience of God', and the thing is done. Now the substitution is undoubtedly a clarification; it gets rid of the suggestion that religion is simply a matter of feeling; it emphasizes the 'intentionality' of religion – that it is not simply a reaction *to*, but a movement *towards*. And finally it forestalls the objection, otherwise all too plausible, that if 'religious experience' can be cited in favour of theism, 'irreligious experience' can be cited against it – there cannot be an 'irreligious experience' of God.[8] But, for at least three reasons, it will not do.

1. It is a blatant begging of the question. We are asking whether religious experience provides empirical evidence for God. The substitution renders the question otiose, by taking the answer for granted: it assumes that the experience is self-authenticating, as no experience can be. 'Religious experience' does at least leave the issue open.

---

[7] It will be argued later that religious experience is misconstrued if it is taken to exclude the secular excellences; in particular, the drive to objectivity by which it is reformed is part of its own being. What is being stressed at this point of the argument is that it is at no stage self-authenticating.

[8] Or can there? What about blasphemy?

2. That being so, let us try another substitution: 'experience of what we believe to be God'. This robs the statement of dogmatic offence; but by 'believe' must be meant either accepting on faith, and that, by itself, is not weighing the evidence, or 'corrigibly thinking to be God', and that is to admit the need for further interpretation. This second alternative has the advantage of making us face the problem of the 'varieties of religious experience'. Experience is conditioned by the worshipper's interests and convictions. Protestants do not have visions of the Virgin, nor Moslems of Jesus, and Hindus will not have any of it: 'not this, not that'. Even the outstanding religious thinker is thus conditioned, and as for the ordinary worshipper, who moves, however sincerely, in a solid frame of ritual, discourse and edification, his testimony merely reflects a prevailing environment. The ordinary Presbyterian in Inverness or the ordinary Catholic in Salamanca translates anything beyond his compass into the familiar religious language, just like the ordinary Moslem in Mecca or the ordinary Buddhist in Mandalay.

3. There is experience not improperly called religious which is not directed to God at all. This was concealed from mediaeval thinkers, and even from the seventeenth century, because the nearest rival was no further than Islam.[9] A belief in God was common to all known civilizations; Western Europe did not know about Theravada Buddhism, nor was it challenged by an atheism of religious intensity like Communism in its Russian form.[10] It made no sense to talk about being religious without believing in God. Nowadays we are shaken by authorities on the Hinayana, and cannot help recognizing many religious structures, both psychical and ecclesiastical, in the mind and institutions of the violently 'anti-religious' Communist Party. So much so, that a common view of what is meant by religion,

[9] Cf. Descartes, Interview with Burman, *Œuvres*, ed. Adam and Tannery, 1897–1910, V. 159: 'I have so written my philosophy that it could be received anywhere, *even among the Turks*' (italic ours).

[10] Cf. Trotsky, *Lenin*, Eng. trs., 1925, p. 247: 'In each of us lives a small part of Lenin, which is the best part of each of us ... Tomorrow, and the day after, for a week, month, we shall ask, "Is Lenin really dead?" For ths death will long seem to us an improbable, an impossible, a terrible arbitrariness of nature.'

recorded with sympathy and at length by W. A. Christian,[11] is that 'a religious interest is an interest in something more important than anything else in the universe', and that could include art and aeroplanes and success in business as well as political eschatologies.

For all these reasons, 'religious experience' (or even 'the experience of God') does not supply the evidence for theism. Yet it is equally impossible to proceed without it. In its absence, we might conclude on the basis of argument to a cosmological outsize fact; we might recognize in the world qualities traditionally traced back to God (e.g. order, or creativity); but we should not describe as *God* the fact beyond the world, or ascribe to *him* the qualities observed in the world.

But if we cannot start from religious experience or without it, how can we start at all? The answer will be that religious experience is not a separate compartment of life, but includes, amongst other things, an intellectual component.

3. *The Integrity of the Intellectual Component*

Before proceeding to the assay of beliefs, we should note the implications of the word 'component'. It expresses the view that in a satisfactory religion intellectual and other considerations are bound up together. In sociological vein, Professor Leonard Russell has observed[12] that religion has power in society in proportion to the number of activities which are intertwined with it; 'pure' religion being relatively uninfluential.[13] As an account of the decline of religion in our day, the observation is too pertinent to be comfortable: but that does not mean that religion obtains its effects by exploiting alien resources. It means, on the contrary, that 'pure' religion is a ghostly extract from the religious response of the whole man: a religious response which is *merely* religious is not *properly* religious. It is a central and centralizing expression of an attitude which

[11] *Meaning and Truth in Religion*, p. 60. Professor Christian tells me in a private letter that he does not wish to be committed to it, nor his arguments to depend on it.
[12] In a public lecture at the University of Melbourne in 1951.
[13] Cf. W. H. Auden: 'The high thin rare continuous worship/Of the self-absorbed.'

includes beliefs and practices and delight in ritual and music, and also in the plainness of suburban chapels and the stillness of Quaker meetings. Religion, in fact, is a quality not only of special experiences, but also and principally of a whole life, and it takes in not only the moment of contraction and concentration, but also the moment of expansion and dispersion. It does not repudiate other values, it includes them. It is a poor sort of religion which puts, e.g., art and philosophy out of doors.[14] And the great days of religion have been those in which it has circulated most fully through the manifold excursions of the human spirit.

It is in that context, then, that we discuss the 'intellectual component'. What the phrase should signify is the role of the unprejudiced intellect in the total religious response. But what it is frequently understood to mean is the efficacy of belief in producing the total response. The latter interpretation, now that we have accepted the theory of religion *as* total response, gains in plausibility. It used to be said, rightly or wrongly, that the Stoic cosmology was a perfunctory introduction to the Stoic ethic.[15] Are we similarly to say that the point of the intellectual component is simply to minister to the response as a whole? We have just said that the whole man is more than his intellect. In this high endeavour, what more is the intellect than a helpful servant?

The point can be pressed as follows. I have followed as best I can a regime of praise and worship, and I have found that difficulties within and without which formerly defeated me have been reduced to manageable dimensions. I then run into intellectual problems about the existence of the God to whom my worship is directed. Am I to wreck the whole balance of my life for the sake of an academic scruple? Many may be for-

[14] Despite the great impetus given to theological studies by Rudolf Otto, I cannot help regretting his isolation of the 'numinous'. I am not impressed with the attitude of *stupor* before the Wholly Other (*The Idea of the Holy*, tr. J. W. Harvey, 2nd ed., 1950, p. 26), any more than I am impressed with the nun who evinced her saintliness by breaking the crockery (William James, *Varieties of Religious Experience*, 1902, p. 345); and I am very much impressed by Otto's difficulty in re-connecting the numinous with the world, which he undoubtedly wants to do. I prefer George Herbert: 'Who sweeps a room as for Thy laws/Makes that, and the action, fine.'

[15] Modern scholars, I am told, are not so sure.

tunate enough not to experience the tension; but I have to face it, if only, let us say, because intellectual problems are my business.

Of course, I may postpone the issue: I may be at least as sceptical about my doubts as about my beliefs. That was the provisional solution autobiographically described by Descartes in the *Discourse on Method*, Part III:

> To obey the laws and customs of my country, adhering firmly to the faith in which, by the grace of God, I had been educated from my childhood, and regulating my conduct in every other matter according to the most moderate opinions . . . adopted in practice with the general consent of the most judicious of those among whom I might be living. For, as I had from that time begun to hold my own opinions for nought because I wished to subject them all to examination, I was convinced I could not do better than follow in the meantime the opinions of the most judicious.[16]

This is fair enough, so long as a halt is not used as a habitation: and Descartes himself proceeded to reason his way out of his scepticism. But, as a permanent posture, it would demean both thought and worship. The mind being a *servant* of the total response, not a *free contributor* to it, the response is not total; i.e. on our hypothesis, not integrally religious. It is true that the integrally religious response is a counsel of perfection, and to fall short on one side of it is only to display normal human imperfection. Those who are not briefed to sustain intellectual challenges, those who simply do not see the point of them, are not dishonest if they take no notice of them. But for a philosopher engaged in assaying religious experience it would be the worst kind of evasion. For him the intellectual component can be efficacious only if believed to be true. Any provisional commitment he may make is subject to a further examination.

4. *Imagery and the Intellectual Component*

At this point, it may be objected that the natural language of religion is imagery and symbolism. 'It is salutary to remind ourselves,' writes Dr E. L. Mascall, 'that the great majority of Christian people are not metaphysicians, and also that the Bible . . . makes very little use indeed of the language of

[16] Translation by Veitch, Everyman's Library, p. 19.

metaphysics. Its typical instrument of communication is not the concept but the image and this . . . assimilates the method by which the Bible communicates truths to its readers much more to the method of the poet than to that of the metaphysician.'[17] What he says is undeniable; but it is no reason (nor, in the long run, does Dr Mascall suppose it to be) for not emphasizing the role of concepts. Imagery and concept cannot be disentangled; governing concepts run through the imagery unknown to the worshipper but discernible to analysis.[18] Against our own background, we should say that 'creator' is a better transcription for deity than 'consumer', that 'father' is a better transcription than 'landlord' (or 'proletarian'). But 'consumer' would have been a much more appropriate transcription for the gods who hungered for sacrifices, and it is only because we inherit the indignation of the Hebrew prophets, and because the Emperor Julian's massacre of harmless animals was a political failure, that 'creator' seems more appropriate to us today. In general, conspicuous consumption is much venerated in an affluent society, and we ought to be thankful that the church has not re-designed deity to match the environment. But the fact remains that 'consumer' is appropriate to some kinds of religious awareness, and is not excluded by appealing to religious awareness as such. If we find it repugnant, it is because we have come (conceptually) to contrast absorption with creation, and have found creation to be (intellectually) the more acceptable concept.

The same conclusion arises if we consider 'father'. It is better than 'landlord' or 'proletarian' because the family has a care for the individual case and does not think of men merely as functions. But, by itself, it has only half registered with the ex-matriarchal societies of southern Europe, and I remember a horrible story told by a visiting American preacher in Australia of how the description of God as Father awakened hostility at a children's home. The image is useful for us as long as there is a social reality to correspond to it. As for 'landlord' and 'proletarian', God is in fact compared to a landlord in the

[17] *Words and Images*, 1957, p. 109.
[18] Cf. Matt. 13.11: it is not given to the multitudes to know the mysteries of the Kingdom of Heaven; but they can listen to parables.

parable of the unjust steward, and to a proletarian when it is written: the Son of man hath not where to lay his head. In the right context, almost any imagery will do. 'King of Kings and Lord of Lords' is an instructive case: it echoes and imaginatively renews the values of an older society; but God as a carpenter, flushed with a craftsman's skill, is more in the modern idiom.

To sum up: it is impossible to estimate the value of the images except inside a conceptual scheme. To the extent that imagery and symbolism have lasting value, it is because of what they are fit to image and symbolize. Even the great standing symbols, e.g. height and light, though they may be 'a singularly apt illustration of the truth',[19] are suggestive, not mandatory; use can be made in the same sense and with the same conceptual entanglements, of the symbols of depth and darkness.[20] We cannot escape through symbolism from the *symbolizandum*. And if this is so, we are referred, through the imagery, back to the intellectual component.

5. *A Preview of the Intellectual Component*

We shall therefore proceed to review the intellectual component; not as an introductory formality, but as an integral feature of religion. The analysis will be incomplete, pending a further discussion of 'faith' in chapter VII. Here we must content ourselves with the following considerations:

1. The intellectual component of a religion may be either general or specific. As general, it consists of statements not determined by, though congruent with, the inspiration of that religion. As specific, it consists of transcriptions or ideographs of its historical foundations and the personal response of believers. In both cases it will be concluded that the empirical approach is that which theological discourse requires, but the manner of demonstration differs, and they will be taken separately. Contrary to expectation, dogma is more easily amenable

[19] Edwyn Bevan, *Symbolism and Belief*, Fontana edition, 1963, p. 72.
[20] Cf. Böhme's 'Abyss' and Tillich's 'Ground', and an illuminating essay by my colleague Professor Ivan Barko on the frequent inversion of the usual symbolic values by Racine ('La symbolique de Racine', *Revue des sciences humaines*, Fasc. 115, juillet–septembre 1964, pp. 353–77).

to the empirical formula than natural theology, and as it is natural theology that we are here concerned with, and the problem of dogma will arise again in our discussion of faith, we shall deal with it first, leaving the weightier and more difficult discussion to follow.

Specific religious statements (e.g. that Christ is God, that grace alone is sufficient to save, that the Spirit proceeds from the Father and the Son) arise within a single circle of faith. This is true both of the first, which within that circle is all but universal (Unitarians are a marginal case, as are those who decline all intellectual commitments); of the second, which is the subject of conflicting interpretations; and of the third, which some theologians flatly deny. The question which arises is not whether they are true *simpliciter*, but whether they adequately render the experience of believers.[21] Differences in theology reflect differences in experience: grace seems to some more like a rescue operation, to others more like a reinforcement, because some people meet Christ when they are desperate and others when they are still able to try. Even the pivotal specific statements, such as 'Christ is God', are adopted with different emphases and with different degrees of conviction: contrast the whole-heartedness of Athanasius with the entirely sincere reservations of the Arians, or, in our own times, the sway of the balance between the historical Jesus and the Second Person of the Trinity. These are not merely theoretical differences; they express shades of conviction in the response to Jesus himself. It is therefore a mistake to deprecate dogma, and equally a mistake to treat it as unchangeable – unless it is proposed to stabilize the experiences it supports. But even so, the experiences come first, and the need to stabilize them comes from the need for common action.

The general statements of natural theology (e.g. that God created the world, that he is spirit, that he is everlasting, that in him power and goodness are one) are claimed to hold not only for believers, but for all men, and they are less easily subject to verification by collective experience. But even they (unlike the statement 'God exists') commit themselves and are subject, if not to disproof, at least to contradiction. 'God created the

21 Also, but consequentially, whether they are mutually consistent.

world' is indeed a peculiarity of the Jewish-Christian-Moslem family of religions; it is unusual in India and could have no place in Buddhism. 'God is spirit' is denied not merely by Spinoza, but by his Christian contemporary, Henry More, who held that God had a body, and earlier and with less compunction by Tertullian. And there is a constant come-and-go in Western theological history between the Hebrew 'everlasting' and the Neo-Platonist 'eternal'. Natural theology does not and cannot speak with one voice: to suppose that it can is to be stranded on the flatlands of eighteenth-century Deism. How these disputes are to be settled in the absence of direct evidence is one of our main problems; it may be said in anticipation that we have to rely largely on internal consistency, but much will still depend on our ordinary experience of creative activity, or material engagement, or temporal succession; it is from this source that the general concepts emerge and are projected towards God. They are just as much part of experience, and just as far from being vacuous, as any sense-impression.

Thus the intellectual component, while a considerable part of any considerable religion, is still, at one remove, empirically grounded, and inconceivable without its foundation in experience.

2. As was noted in the previous chapter, a claim to insight is neither incorrigible nor arbitrary. Religious insight is no exception. The Catholic Church has been justly suspicious of *illuminati*; a candidate for sainthood has to pass the devil's advocate. Protestantism in its prime relied considerably on the 'assembled testimony' of believers, helping each other with the scrutiny of scripture and making their experiences mutually available. Wise guidance or mutual assistance will help to counter the inevitable risk of bias – a risk which is inherent in human finitude. It is precisely because insights are mutually corrigible that theology progresses – more than it is disposed to allow, or than the outside observer has any idea of. The doctrine of the Atonement, for example, is formally constant, but there are judicial overtones in even nineteenth-century theology which are different from the more strictly ethical overtones of theology today; and I venture to think that this

Theism and Empiricism

represents an improvement. Sometimes we have forgotten things that are best forgotten; we are much less well-informed than Scottish eighteenth-century preachers about the topography and furniture of hell. And no doubt our descendants will speak similarly about ourselves. Our best insights are only snapshots of an encompassing mystery, but perhaps the cameras are improving. It is not only scientists who go on learning. Those who practise the contemplation of God learn also – by experience, by direction, and by communication with each other. But unless our original insights were corrigible, no such advance could be possible.

3. A positive belief with successive variations and a long history is likely to contain some positive merits. Even in matters of science, long-standing beliefs usually contain truth imperfectly formulated; in matters of morals, when testing is looser, it is true, but more inescapable, it is most unlikely that a purely crackpot view of life could survive the centuries; man would have broken it long since, or broken under it. In religion, as long as it is genuinely the centre of a life and not a compensation for it, there is even less likely to be complete incorrigible error; any religion which carries the main weight of human concern in many places at many times must have some latent element of truth. But this is far less than any religion claims. It provides only a negative criterion: if it did not work, it would have to be discarded, but even if it does work, it need not be truer than any other which also works: and many beliefs, not consistent with each other, work over long periods, especially in closed social settings. Thus, to explore the possibilities, we have to use our minds, and as we have only glimpses to go on, the procedure must be tentative and empirical. Religious knowledge consists of lightning-flashes against a background which remains obscure, the highlights and the recesses coalescing in a continuity. Some familiarity with the techniques of Rembrandt may help the imagination.

It will be seen that the elucidation of the intellectual component is not simple or straightforward, and in particular that it demands simultaneous attention to specific features of the secular world and their religious context. Dr E. L. Mascall sets the problem for us when, adverting to the arguments for the existence of God, he observes[22] that their function is 'to direct the attention of the mind to certain features of finite beings which can easily be overlooked and from which the existence of God can be seen without a discursive process', an activity which he describes elsewhere[23] as a '*contuition* of God'. We shall develop it in the next chapter by asking: if the glimpses are said to be of God, must we not somehow be aware of God in order so to call them? – and if they are not said to be of God, how can we spin God out of them? What we are stressing here and now is that in any case, in order to discuss the variations of religious discourse, we must presume that there *is* an intellectual component. Otherwise religion is undiscussible, that is to say, irrational.

6. *The Intellectual Component and Personal Religion*

So far, we have been urging that the awareness of God is essential in religion, and also that it is fragmentary and elusive. But its fragmentation is more radical than imperfect knowledge in science or history, because in religion it is an integral part of knowing that each individual shall know for himself. In a sense, that is true of all knowledge whatever: knowing is an individual act. But in science, history, and even philosophy there is an abstraction from the personal commitments of the knower: he tries, however unsuccessfully, not to be distracted by the non-scientist in him, or the non-historian, or the non-philosopher. In religion, the personal appropriation of what is known is essential; the whole man must enter into it. It follows that religion is not impersonal appropriation of a formula. We cannot just accept God as we accept $2 + 2 = 4$. If we approach him in this flat 'objective' spirit, we shall have no knowledge *of* him at all; at the best we shall have knowledge *about* him. God cannot be apprehended as an object: his subjectivity disappears along with ours. The explicit formulation of this predicament is due to Kierkegaard, and upon it centres the existentialist reorganization of the philosophy of religion. But it is much older than that: 'If any man do his will, he shall know of the doctrine' (John

[22] *Words and Images*, 1957, p. 84.   [23] *Ibid.*, p. 85.

7.17); and it is supported by uncomforting reflections on the disingenuousness of formal profession. You can *think* God, you can *acknowledge* God, but because of the fatal dissociation between thought and action, you don't *know* him. Very few have leaped that gap, and those are the first to say they haven't.

The first reaction to this kind of discovery is to repudiate reason in matters of religion. Luther, for example, described reason as a whore. This is not merely emotive bad language; it brings out a point of fact: all men can use her. He saw clearly that religious knowledge was somehow different, but he assumed that the standard for knowledge was non-religious knowledge, and thus summed up the difference by saying that religious knowledge was not knowledge, but purely a matter of faith. What is wrong here is the assumption, which, indeed, puts him, philosophically speaking, in the same basket as an atheist. The proper correction is to insist that religious knowledge is individual not merely in the general sense that it takes a knower to know, but in the more far-reaching sense that it is the kind of knowledge which nobody else can have. As Whitehead observed,[24] 'religion is what a man does with his own solitariness', and this applies to its cognitive element as to every other.

As soon as this point has been clarified, the objection comes from the other side: each man is claiming infallibility. The issue has been discussed in general terms, and the reply is that when the individual speaks existentially, he speaks at his own risk, i.e. he is not infallible, and knows it. In reporting what his limitations enable him to report, he brings back a partial view which he knows needs to be supplemented. But if he tried to circumvent the limitations, he would not be able to report at all. The knowledge of the greatest things is the obscurest. Not only do we (here at least) see through a glass darkly, but we see what we see darkly only in part.

On the other hand, the report is unmistakable. We know it is not the last word, but we are absolutely sure of it as far as it goes. We profess what we have *known*. The danger we are in is that of supposing that we know more than we do.

Now in our study of the empirical complex we noted that

[24] *Religion in the Making*, 1926, p. 6.

the element of discovery and element of venture go together. The enterprise (including the religious enterprise) is personal and forward-looking. Empirical religion goes thus far with empirical science. 'There is one, even Christ Jesus, that can speak to thy condition; and this I know experimentally.' The words of George Fox are well known; but it is not always noted that they are contemporary with the founding of the Royal Society. The difference is that scientists do not say: 'I believe in the circulation of the blood because I have tried it out in my own person'; whereas Fox does say: 'I believe in Christ, and I commend him to you because I have committed myself to him, and he has saved me.'[25] But in religion, as in science, there is a call for personal discovery; as philosophers would have seen if they had thought as carefully in the seventeenth century about the new kind of religion as they did about the new kind of science.

But is my testimony for God merely a private testimony? In a sense, yes; that is why, at the beginning of the creeds, worshippers say, 'I believe', not 'there is'. But, in a sense, no; for they say it along with others, and they feel they are entitled to impute it to others. In affirming God, e.g. as the source of my being,[26] I indeed affirm something for myself; but what I affirm is not merely for myself, or I could not affirm it even for myself. I give a personal conviction a wider (even a universal) reference. With what right, if my testimony (unlike the scientist's knowledge) can only be my own?

One factor which may encourage me is that other minds work the same way. The believer has *some* evidence for a general imputation of his beliefs: the fact that others receive them gladly. Moreover, if they have given him peace and the energy which goes with peace, he will wish to communicate them as widely as possible – not by way of constraining others, but because he cannot keep such good news to himself. And what he does, others will do also, so that there will be endless cross-testimonies and reciprocities, all building up to a shared

[25] The parallel between experimental religion and experimentation in science is well studied by Richard Hocking, in his essay '*Existenz* and Objectivity', in: *Process and Divinity*, ed. W. L. Reese and E. Freeman, 1964, pp. 1–17.

[26] It must be in some defined capacity: one does not affirm God-in-general; one can only think it.

conviction that each man's God is all men's God. Moreover, the oddities of private inspiration will have been sorted out by the assembling of testimonies; each man's idiosyncrasy of approach is balanced out by his neighbour's. That effect depends on free exchange of experience, such as used to take place among English nonconformists at week-night sessions or in family councils; and the decay of these institutions has left the Protestant witness with no middle way between unreasonable conformity and a privacy all but inaccessible. But with the fullest exchange of minds in the world, a conclusion resting on multiple testimony plus imputation to all men is definitely a risk. There will be some who will deny it and others who will insist on moving amendments.

It may be objected at this stage that religion is nothing like as existentially individualist as it is here presented, and that its personal manifestations fall within the compass of a common norm: in the case of the Christian religion, the authority of church or scripture. Having little taste for gregarious religion, and being mindful of the injunction to lock one's door and say one's prayers by oneself, I have stated what I believe to be a common conviction in a more than usually individualist manner; but it comes in the end to the same thing. The issue concerning authority is not whether religion is based on witness or not, but whose witness is to count. As for scripture, the late Professor John Baillie argued in his Gifford Lectures *The Sense of the Presence of God* that it '*becomes*' the word of God only in so far as it brings about an '*encounter*' with God.[27] He was anticipated, in blunter language, by a 'maid named Isabel', testifying in the Baptist Church at Fen Stanton, Huntingdonshire (Cromwell's county), in the mid-seventeenth century.

A maid named Isabel said, the Spirit assured her she had Christ. It was demanded how she knew it to be a true spirit? She answered, by the effects and not by the scriptures; for she tried the scriptures by the Spirit, and not the Spirit by the scriptures.[28]

Thus, in their different ways, ecclesiasticism and funda-

[27] Italics ours.
[28] Quoted from the *Records of the Churches of Christ, gathered at Fen Stanton, Warboys and Hexham*, by G. F. Nuttall, *The Holy Spirit in Puritan Faith and Experience*, 1947, p. 30.

mentalism presuppose the individual witness; without it the church would be merely an establishment, and the Bible a varyingly valuable collection of books. That is why they are properly considered as outgrowths or deposits of individual experience.

7. *Corrigibility and Faith*

This, it may be said, is all very well; this may be how religious people feel about it individually and collectively; but can we take their word for it? The classical philosopher-theologians, reinforced by the Encyclical *Pascendi* (1906), insisted that the existence of God can be known by the 'light of nature'; and even if this does not amount to Thomist demonstration, it means, at least, conforming to the standards of objective argument. Yet in the very act of stressing the intellectual component, we are reducing objectivity, in respect of religious knowledge, to intersubjectivity plus imputation. Surely the apprehension of a divine object does not follow from the assent of subjects, but vice versa.

The objection is well taken, and it affords us an opportunity to explain. As we understand it, exchange of views is not a substitute for awareness of the case, but a means of achieving it. It can never amount to proof, but it is the best that finite beings can do. Those who demand proof themselves make a distinction between knowing God and knowing that God exists, and not only admit but insist that here in this world none of us knows God at any time. They hold, as we do, that knowledge of God has to be completed by faith. In that case, one would expect them to be diligent in searching out amongst themselves such evidence as has come their way. They have in fact done so, and the evidence figures in the minor premisses of the traditional proofs. Where the difference arises is that they are talking not about God, but about the existence of God. This they believe they can know. Our trouble throughout has been that one cannot know whether God exists if one has no idea what he is like. Even if he existed, he might not be God; he might (as Thomas Hardy suggested in *The Dynasts*) be wholly indifferent, and at times seemingly malignant. The

reason why this alternative does not suggest itself to believers
is that they believe; from their faith they carry over attributes
of the God whose existence they purport to prove. But that
means that they are drawing on the resources of their faith
while appearing to argue from scratch.[29]

We return, then, to the more modest and chancy and faith-
provoking enterprise, perhaps better suited to creatures conscious of their finitude, of building up a tentative and corrigible
knowledge of God (not of his existence) from the sifting of
indications and counter-indications brought forward from their
consolidated, though still open-ended, individual experiences.
That is why we insist on taking evidence, both from the masters,
and from ordinary worshippers who prevent religion from
volatilizing into expertise. We grasp as best we may at the
empirical fringes of God, and what we impute to others is not
what we have grasped ourselves, but the expectation that all
comers will grasp at that which from their angle can be grasped
most effectively. But neither the groping nor the imputation
would make sense if there were not something there to be
known. Any honest opinion refers back to the state of the case,
and the high-level interpretations of the church and the inter-
personal pattern-weaving of individual worshippers merely
continue the process. Religious knowledge is empirical knowledge (imperfect, but growing) of something which is. It is an
empirical knowledge of the non-empirical.[30]

[29] The same applies to the attempt to deduce the attributes of God from
his existence. They are put in at one end and come out at the other. From
mere existence one can deduce no attributes whatever. See chapter V.

[30] See S. Alexander's words on the frontispiece about philosophy in
general. We still have to distinguish between religious knowledge and the
philosophical understanding of religion: at this stage we are concerned with
religious knowledge, phenomenologically, as the subject-matter and starting-
point of the investigation.

III

THE EMPIRICAL FRINGES

1. *The Need for Metaphysics*

DESPITE what has been said about the ambiguity of religious experience, if we are to maintain an empiricist posture, we must somehow start from the fact of that experience. All the theologies and philosophies in the world would not make us talk about God unless they issued from the central activity of worship. That has to be affirmed at the outset, lest the rest of this chapter should be out of focus. But, as we have noted, religious experience itself carries an intellectual component. Its claim to truth is an integral part of it. If that could be refuted, the rest could survive for a time as ritual or feeling, but only at the price of avoiding even the most casual intellectual contacts. Some whom it is impossible not to respect might like it that way; but for a philosopher it would be simply unprofessional.

Once this has been admitted, the fact has to be faced that different religions make different, and sometimes incompatible, truth-claims, which cannot all be sustained. There is no inclination among believers either to whittle them down or to lump them together. What is common to all religions (and it is not much, not even God) is not the centre of any religion. Neither the highest-common-factor God of eighteenth-century Deism, nor the lowest-common-denominator God of twentieth-century syncretism is in the least worshipful. They are outsize facts, or political contrivances, and as lacking in red corpuscles as Esperanto. Contrast Peter's self-portrait as one of those 'who through him do believe in God who raised him up from the dead, and gave him glory' (I Peter 1.21), and Dostoevsky, whose 'hosanna burst forth from a huge furnace of doubt', and

who, if he had not been a Christian, would quite certainly
have been an atheist. Or contrast, for that matter, the educated
Hindu, who does not define himself by doctrine, but still feels
spiritually naked without *Karma* and *Moksha*. In the face of
these luminous intransigences, it is no good trying to reach a
working conception of God either by eliminating the differences
or by pulping them together. Open dialogue may help all
parties, and there is therefore a religious as well as a political
case for its encouragement. But it is the particularities of
particular religions that strike the sparks. It may be significant
that there is so much sense of religion in such diverse quarters,
but these disparate visions cannot be consolidated into a
coherent pattern.

Within any one circle, it is possible to refine more accurately.
But that is because there is a common experience at the centre
(e.g. the experience of an incarnate God). Moreover, there is
less variety in the surrounding secular assumptions, and sometimes a recognized way of settling differences which might
interfere with an effective common witness. In this case it is
possible to build up a congruent and collective picture of God
and his dealings with the world. The discipline which does
so is called theology. There is a tradition that theology is for
good and all. As a matter of history it has evolved, and even
when doctrine is formally unchanged, its content is subtly
transmuted: significantly, in accordance with developments in
secular thinking. But behind all theology is a persisting experience; and though the transcriptions vary it is the experience
that matters. Peter's exclamation, 'Thou art the Christ', was
not a theory; it was forced out of him by what he saw. What
he saw was so extraordinary that ordinary concepts were unable
to catch it. Experiments were made with various combinations;
some came nearer to catching the experience than others, and
those which refused to tone down the extraordinary were,
providentially, the most successful. But it all starts from experience, and the aim of the conceptual deployment is to fix
the experience in the minds of believers as well as in their
hearts. Whether the interpretation is conducted at the top
level and filtered down by edict, or publicly discussed and
settled (for the time being) by the sense of the meeting, is not

here relevant; in either case dogma is an interpretation of experience as well as a guide to it, and in either case (in the former case more slowly, for good or for evil) interpretation changes.

Thus the Christian theologian (to take the most familiar example), meditating on experiences which vary with the peculiarities of the worshipper but not in the object of worship, can present, no doubt with gaps and aberrations and against a background of ineffability, an outline of the Christian God; and if he is asked 'Is there a God?', he will know what to look for. As Dr E. L. Mascall observes, 'The Christian was able to ask this question because he knew, as the Greek did not, what he meant by the word "God".'[1] To proceed in this way breaks the dilemma: how can we set about finding *that* God is without knowing *what* he is, and what is the point of trying to piece together *what* he is without knowing *that* he is?

It will have been noted that in the last few sentences we have passed from theology proper, i.e. the intellectual elaboration of the experiences of particular religions, to what may perhaps be called philosophical theology, i.e. the examination of their associated truth-claims. Theology proper is recommended as making it clear what kind of God truth is being claimed for, and so far, so good. But along this road one must travel with caution. In the first place, we have no right as philosophers to take for granted the experiences or the interpretations of any one religion. In the second place, the experiences, let alone the interpretations, themselves embody philosophical assumptions, not attended to at the moment of worship, but disclosed in subsequent retrospection. Without philosophical inquiry, these assumptions are unprotected; they must run the risk of rational examination, or remain isolated from the main stream of culture.

It is for these reasons that we propose to go back, for a time, from theology to metaphysics. It is important to understand what this means. It means that we have to station ourselves outside the circle of faith in order to understand it. That is just what most philosophers of religion who are also believers are currently pressing us not to do. That admirable collection,

[1] *Existence and Analogy*, 1949, p. 16.

Religion and Understanding (ed. D. Z. Phillips, 1967), is peopled almost entirely with writers who believe it to be impossible. It is easy to understand why. Religion is not the sort of thing one can merely contemplate and be uncommitted about. No one who is not deeply involved in it has a hope of understanding it. But the same is true about art, or morality, or even science. In all these cases, and also in the case of religion, the philosopher has to have the feel of the thing from the inside as well as the view from the outside. But the one does not impede the other. If he is a believer, he has to put himself in brackets; if he is an unbeliever, he has to imagine himself implicated. Thus – to return to the point – metaphysical detachment is possible, and, if it is possible, necessary – if only in order to pursue theology in a secular society without schizophrenia.

By metaphysics we shall understand not a study of categories of thought, and still less a sort of overweening metalinguistics, but a study of the most general structures of the world. The phrase suggests a return to Plato's *Sophist*, and in so far as it takes us behind theory of knowledge to theory of being, the reminder is to be welcomed. If we remember also the conclusion of that dialogue (249ab) that souls are as real as Forms, and how it provides a link between the supremacy of Forms in the middle dialogues and the supremacy of God in Book X of the *Laws*, we shall have still further cause for encouragement. But the inquiry must take its own course. Theism is a possible answer; but just for that reason it must start level with the others. It has been argued that it characterizes the more advanced religions, and that religion should be measured by its more perfected manifestations. But apart from the perfectedness, in its own style, of Theravada Buddhism, if the theistic interpretation is to have metaphysical credentials, it will not merely have to characterize the more perfected religions, it will have to be true; and perhaps being true is a chief mark of being perfected.[2]

In any case, we must not expect finality. That is settled for us as soon as we insist that metaphysics is concerned with the structures not of thought but of things. Kant may have been

---

[2] This will hold even if the standard of truth does not reach the level of necessity required by the classical natural theologians.

wrong in interpreting metaphysics as the study of categories, but he was entirely right in seeing that only so could it retain its traditional claim to necessity. If we go behind his back and revert to the ontological model, we are forced into a role which he never contemplated, that of metaphysicians who, because they are metaphysicians, are also empiricists.

Even so, believers may find the role assigned to philosophy excessive. They may even ask, with Tertullian, 'What has Athens in common with Jerusalem?' In their interests, being one of them, I add the following explanations:

1. Wittgenstein wrote: 'God does not reveal himself in the world.'[3] If that is true, he does not reveal himself at all: the world is just what it would be if he did not exist. But in fact any alleged revelation of God is also a revelation of something else. As Norman Kemp Smith observed, 'We never experience the Divine sheerly in and by itself: we experience the Divine solely through and in connexion with what is other than the Divine.'[4] And, if that is so, it is to that other that we must direct our attention if we want to gain a glimpse of the Divine: as Christians, centred on the Incarnation, well understand. And that other, together with its divine affiliations, falls within the scope of philosophical inquiry.

2. If there were no such overlap warranting philosophical scrutiny, the quarantine would work in both directions. The study of religion would indeed be an inside job, unencumbered by secular pressures, but conversely religion could contribute nothing to the understanding of the world. Much of the protest against philosophy starts from the conviction that religion is not something to be discussed but something to be lived. The trouble is that unless it penetrates the regions which philosophers can discuss, and is thus itself discussed, it cannot be lived: it is wholly impotent.

3. It is not being asserted that God is available to intellectual effort alone. It is only too possible to believe that he exists, and not effectively to believe *in* him. But without such an effort the utmost devotion might be attached to an utter nonentity,

---

[3] *Tractatus Logico-Philosophicus* 6.432, Eng. trs., 1922, p. 187.
[4] 'Is Divine Existence Credible?', in: *Religion and Understanding*, ed. D. Z. Phillips, 1967, p. 120.

and we should be none the wiser. 'There is no understanding of religion without passion.'[5] Right. But the passion must have an object, and many sincere people insist that there is no such object. In dealing with intellectual objections intellectual methods are not only in order, they are mandatory. And passion, even more than intellect, needs to be rooted in reality. Disillusioned thinking runs to scepticism; but disillusioned passion runs to despair. Nowhere, and least of all in the case of God, can passion shape its own object. There has to be a God if we are to love him.[6]

In conclusion, it may be asked whether it would not be much simpler to practise the philosophy of religion in the mode of clarification rather than of metaphysics. In that case, all we should have to do would be to tidy up religious concepts: to state truth-claims in coherent form rather than to raise the question of their truth. Simpler, yes, but evasive; and possibly disastrous. Evasive, because the question of truth has been raised anyhow, and it cannot be silenced by the improved arrangement of our own assumptions. Possibly disastrous, because clarification is frequently used to dissolve concepts inconvenient to secularist ways of thinking. In fact, clarifiers practise metaphysics under their hats; and we have a right to insist that it be done in the open.

So we turn to an inquiry into those general structures of the world with which belief in God has most commonly been associated, in the hope that there, if anywhere, the overlap, and the distance, may be brought to light.

---

[5] D. Z. Phillips, summarizing Kierkegaard, *Religion and Understanding*, p. 79.

[6] Samuel Alexander made the point admirably in the two following passages (*Space, Time and Deity*, Vol. II, pp. 342, 353): 'Religion leans on metaphysics for the justification of its indefeasible conviction of the reality of its object; philosophy leans on religion to justify it in calling the possessor of deity by the religious name of God.' 'A philosophy which left one portion of human experience suspended without attachment to the world is gravely open to suspicion; and its failure to make the religious emotion speculatively intelligible betrays speculative weakness. For the religious emotion is one part of experience, and an empirical philosophy must include in one form or another the whole of experience.' One does not need to accept the whole of Alexander's explication of deity to endorse these methodological preliminaries.

2. *Prolongations*

In searching for 'the most general structures of the world', we are not abandoning the empirical enterprise. We are making no assumptions about absolutes or necessities. We are looking for those features of the world that have the greatest persistence and constancy. We are *looking*; we are not inventing, or asking what *we* are contributing to the interpretation of things. We are looking, in fact, not for categories but for structures: or, if we prefer the language of Samuel Alexander, for categories interpreted as structures. We are adopting the stance of epistemological realists. As has often been observed, realism and empiricism go together.

It follows that our account will be incomplete. We shall glimpse the structure of the world at the end of innumerable avenues and in the most intricate contexts, and only after a long apprenticeship of submissive meditation shall we even be able to say what is structure and what is content. In principle there is no difference. What is there is structure if it is found continuously, it is content if it shifts and varies.

Now if this is our approach, the knowledge of God will on the one hand be as immediate as realists claim knowledge of the external world to be, and on the other opaque and discontinuous. There is no inconsistency between these two conditions. Our knowledge of the external world is a patchwork of glimpses and we should expect our knowledge of God to be still more elusive. Even when it seems clearest, it is misleading to talk of an intuition of God. The most we can say (but that is something) is that there is an enigmatic inward illumination of the world by the presence of God. But this is something we *receive*; we do not arrange it, and it often comes when we least expect it.

The traditional way of recording these impressions is to say that we know God through his effects. That is to sacrifice the factor of immediacy, and requires us to envisage God, not as presence, but as cause. We shall study later in detail the attempt to recover the cause from the effect; here we simply remark that if the effect does not in some sense *overlap* with the cause, no such recovery is possible. What is called an effect is a presence, not merely a proxy or a signpost. I propose to describe it as, from the Godward side, a prolongation,[7] and our approach to it, from the worldward side, as a grasping for fringes. A few explanatory remarks are appended.

1. In speaking of 'fringes', we use the word in the plural. There is no one shape of God in the world. Nor will it be surprising if, within the limitations of our experience, some of the fringes look like being incompatible, or that some of them are specially transparent (or opaque) to some of us, and others to others.

2. There is much in the world that is alien, or at least alienated, from the presence of God. Nothing that has been said should be allowed to diminish this sense of discrepancy. But, as we present it, the discrepancy between God and the world is revealed in the world. The ensuing problems are discussed below, p. 72.

3. 'Prolongations' are also perfections, and when the world fails to receive them, there is defect. Perfection, and defect, are present throughout the universe, and the segments from which they appear to be absent are the result of deliberate abstraction. This is so not merely in human affairs, but also in respect of what is commonly called inanimate nature. Leibniz held that 'there is a world of created beings – living things, animals, entelechies, and souls – in the least part of nature',[8] and Whitehead found in the simplest physical structures at least an analogue of what, in men, we should call feeling. The seeds of perfection are there at all levels. Consequently, as Leibniz saw, the separation of factual from perfectional considerations, or the limitation of the latter to human issues, is a mistake – one with serious consequences for theism, which must entertain and defend the final coalescence of perfection and being.

4. In the next section, we shall take as instances of 'presence' or 'prolongation' the order and the creativity observable in the world. Here, in anticipation, we note that they are pre-

---

[7] The term 'prolongation' I find to have been used before me by Lucien Laberthonnière: cf. *Essais*, p. xxvi, where he writes of the 'prolongation of the divine life into the life of man'. I owe the reference to John Macquarrie, *Twentieth-Century Religious Thought*, 1963, pp. 183f. I am encouraged by the coincidence.

[8] *Monadology*, ch. 66.

requisites for action.[9] For example, if there were nothing in things corresponding to the constraint of order in our minds, confusion would spread through everything we do. Expecting it, and relying upon it, we should have no grip on things if it turned out to be merely a human idiosyncrasy. According to the best empirical principles, the dichotomy just could not be accepted.[10]

5. On the other hand (and this also is essential to our thesis), order as we experience it is incomplete. It is true that the better we do our grouping, the better we shall understand. Even the failure of some things to group helps us to understand; exclusions and adhesions throw light on each other. The effort to stretch our minds to cover negation widens the view and takes us nearer to totality. The progress, however, is asymptotic; Kant was right when he affirmed totality to be an *ideal* of reason. There is no point at which thought can rest and claim that a perfect order lies open to its view. And if that is true of thought, it is even more true of action, which manœuvres in a packed archipelago of particularity and, by definition, deals with situations one by one.

6. In what follows there will be some approximation to the cosmological argument and the argument for design. The difference is that in the classical arguments the distinction between the imperfect and the perfect coincides with the distinction between the world and God, whereas in our version the distinction is revealed in the world through the prolongation of God into the world. We do not assume that everything in the world is necessarily imperfect. In this we are in accord with the kind of religious apprehension which recognizes individualized perfection at a point of time.[11] For Christians it comes to a head in the Incarnation, which is perhaps after all

[9] The consequences will appear in chapter VIII. What is said here about order applies differently to creativity. See below, pp 70f., 78.

[10] It could of course be entertained, and by philosophers it must be entertained, if only to go along with, and outrun, those who make it seem plausible by failing to consider action. For the rest, 'methodical doubt', as practised by Descartes, was intended to show that if the sceptic is given enough rope he will hang himself.

[11] As H. D. Lewis perceptively remarks (*Our Experience of God*, 1959, p. 116), there is in religion 'a content peculiarly its own and yet made up of the features of finite experience'.

the crown of things rather than their reversal: but it is also a
feature of the religious approach to nature.

> Epitomized in thee
> Was the mystery
> Which shakes the spheres conjoint:
> God focussed to a point

as Francis Thompson wrote of a blade of grass. The little things
of God are as good as the big things; and they grow up all
round us, piecemeal and in profusion. His presence in the
whole rises out of presences smaller and more intimate; the
one is built out of ones and not out of fragments. That, indeed,
is how it is variously available to various beholders. So the
contingent may well be a prolongation. Some contingent
things, of course, are horrible; but that is a different issue.

7. We have spoken about the 'presence' of God. As experienced in religion, presence is undivided; it cannot be
parcelled out into constituent attributes. That such a presence
envelops me, both inexorably judging me and bringing me
peace, is so much part of me that I have to turn myself inside
out to align myself with those who miss it. How to convey it
to them is like trying to convey to an autistic solitary that there
are other people. It is a case for poetry or parable rather than
for argument. Yet it is possible at a lower temperature to
distinguish in it two features which are fused in it, but from
the outside can only be depicted as successive and alternative.
It is prolonged, in nature and in man, as order on the one hand,
and as creativity on the other. In both equally the presence is
made known; they pull in different ways, and for that very
reason they belong together. It is precisely because they are thus
divided and yet need each other to stay in position, that they
put pressure on us to look behind them for a presence in which
they are united. We shall see that there are at least some
significant human analogies.

3. *Order and Creativity: the Drift to Order*

The most significant prolongation is to be found in the moral
life, which exhibits in the highest degree both the overlap and
the deviation. For the moment, however, we shall keep to the

more universal structures of the world. We do not wish the God at the end of the story to be presented as a purely human requirement without standing in the cosmos. That is precisely how the reduction of religious to ethical assertions begins.

By 'structures' we do not mean 'universals'. For example, 'One' and 'Many' occur in all situations in the world, but in our sense they do not structure it. What structures it is 'One' made concrete, namely order. In the same way, but in more complicated fashion, the concrete rendering of 'Many' is 'being created' – more complicated, because 'many' in itself does not directly refer to 'creating'. Yet 'many' has no point except in the context of 'one', and only when considered as created is it compatible with order.

To the exploration of order and creation we now turn. We shall consider them in the first instance as constituents of the world, and proceed to show that, taken as such, they insist on pressing beyond their boundaries. Hence we shall come to see them as prolongations of God, to whose nature they jointly belong: but only at the end of the discussion.

And, first, let us take the fact of order.

There is order wherever differences are set in a framework of unity. The differences become more significant as their place in the order emerges. That is why there is in the nature of things a drift towards order. We say 'drift' rather than 'purpose' or 'nisus' because no drift goes on to the bitter end. It is a term used by Professor J. N. Findlay in *Values and Intentions* to describe what 'necessarily tends'[12] to happen – a tendency which runs laterally into by-ways, goes forward deviously and intermittently, and in no way excludes incompatible tendencies. The drift to order is only one of our pieces of evidence, and, as we shall see, if it excluded other drifts it would fail to provide the evidence we require.

We can trace the drift to order in the history of cosmology. The more we know about nature, the more it presents itself as one world. There used to be a qualitative, even an axiological, distinction between the heavens and the earth: now they are integrated and seem to exhibit the same uniform behaviour – a fact which is described by the use of the term 'law'. The

[12] Findlay's phrase, *op. cit.*, 1961, p. 212.

discovery that there is nothing odd or privileged about the heavens is in a sense a religious discovery: it is a move away from arbitrariness and idolatry. Popular religion preserves the distinction, mainly as illustrative imagery. The results are unfortunate. It encourages the belief that God is in a material place called Heaven, rather than anywhere else. On that kind of religion, the Russian cosmonaut who reported that he had found no God in outer space made the appropriate comment.

The drift towards order can be illustrated even more forcibly in the economy of human nature. There appears to be a sort of inbuilt sanction against division: as Plato said, 'injustice' (i.e. the subversion of the economy) 'renders a man incapable of action' (*Republic* 352a). The drift can be expressed in the act of will, which forces unity on recalcitrant inclinations: in that case imperfectly, because unity is achieved by mutilation. It is expressed, negatively, in the chaos of a divided mind: to the extent that order is lacking, the structure breaks down: and this holds both of indecision on the level of consciousness and deep-seated repression. It is expressed best of all in the unforced unity of heart and mind which in a Christian are the fruits of grace. But, positively and negatively, to be at one in oneself brings energy and happiness, and to be at war in oneself wastes energy and brings unhappiness. The drift to order asserts itself both in harmony and in sanctions against disharmony.

The drift to order is thus vindicated in the growth of our knowledge and the improvement of our behaviour (and by the sanctions which, in either of these respects, follow failure). This is the lasting truth in Absolute Idealism, and it is too easily forgotten in the contemporary litter of scraps and snippets. But we have illustrated from *our* knowledge and *our* behaviour: can we argue from the way *we* understand things, or conduct our dealings with them, to the structuring of these things themselves?

A preliminary point is that in an order supposed to have been hammered out in the struggle for survival, it would be strange if our tendency to group things together in thought had no factual foundation. It is not logically impossible, and that is the point on which sceptics have fastened; but it is, to use a convenient expression of Professor Nowell-Smith's, 'logically odd'.[13] The issue here is not whether things can be grouped wrongly; of course they can, as when whales are classed as fishes. The issue is whether the attempt to group the intrinsically ungroupable could be of any use in the business of living. If there were no order in things the ascription of order to things could only result in failure. The presumption is that in grouping we are not inventing, but on the way to understanding. Any doubts on the subject arise from an artificial separation between knowledge and action.

4. *Order and Creativity: the Drift to Creativity*

It is part of what is meant by order that it requires not only unity but variety. If unity stood alone, there would be no order: there would be the One of Parmenides, devoid of any specific characteristics whatsoever. It will be replied that unity does not exclude differences, and that is how there is order. This is true; but unity carried to the end, unity which should include all possible differences, overrides, by a cunning act of appropriation, their character as differences. What is missing from this picture is the note of tension between the constituent characters of the world.

The other major character is creativity.

In human affairs, any important revision breaks up order as previously understood: 'I came not to send peace, but a sword.' Less obviously, any individual decision has the same effect: even if it helps to sustain an existing order, it is an originating factor not merely to be subsumed under that order. If God is identified only with order, there can be no source of initiative for decisions to flow from. It is because order has been considered the only requirement that history and individual development have been reduced to predetermined chains of events.

The same applies to the significant breaks in the order of the cosmos sometimes gathered up under the name of Emergent Evolution.[14] The question is not whether new qualities emerge causelessly: that is a phantom wished on their opponents by

---

[13] E.g. *Ethics*, Pelican edition, p. 83.
[14] See C. Lloyd Morgan's book of that name, published in 1923, and Vol. II of Alexander's *Space, Time and Deity*, 1920.

uniformitarian determinists. The question is whether, when they emerge, for whatever reason, they make a difference to the 'go' of events,[15] whether a new qualitative simplicity ensues from increased quantitative complexity. This is the question to which determinists of all sorts, theological and materialist alike, insist on answering 'No'. But I have still to find any reason for this view except an *a priori* determination to unify at any price.[16] Anyone as intent as an empiricist ought to be on savouring things as he finds them should call for caution. He will not deny the drift to order, but he will find in the world also the operation of creativity, and not only will his forms of order show an 'open texture', but they themselves will be subject to significant revision. And if I am threatened with Occam's razor, I shall reply that a beard is quite in order, and I do not intend to shave the skin off my face in order to get rid of it. To the hard-boiled 'principle of economy' I oppose the principle of luxuriance. Perhaps this is one of the differences between philosophy and science. Science needs the most economical theory because it works within defined terms of reference and aims at solving specific problems. Philosophy needs luxuriance because it is its overriding duty not to miss out on anything. That it will not succeed goes without saying; but it will approach success more nearly if it keeps itself as receptive as possible to the range of possibilities. This range is what the scientist particularly hopes to reduce; quite rightly, so long as he does not carry the mental attitude over into metaphysics.

I accept, then, with the 'natural piety' commended by Alexander, and at its face value, the phenomenon of origination, and propose to ask whether it might not be attached to an attribute of God always in tension with his unity, namely his creativity. Here, again, is a possible prolongation of God into the world.

There is, however, a complication about creativity which there is not about order. Order, as we observed, is the concrete expression of the drift to unity. It cannot be similarly said that creativity is the concrete expression of the drift to multiplicity.

---

[15] The phrase is Lloyd Morgan's, *op. cit.*, p. 27.
[16] Natural science was born in a Calvinist environment, and has never recovered.

Multiplicity is just presented to us, and in itself is not creative at all. It is, in fact, the raw material of order. It is not, however, the opposite of order, which is chaos. Creativity is not chaos; it only looks like it to minds accustomed to traditional kinds of order. It is invention, initiative, an excursion into the unforeseen. So far from being resistant to order, it depends doubly upon order. Order is the springboard from which it leaps, and order is what (in a new pattern) it creates. The relation between order and creativity is therefore asymmetrical.

Consequently, they are not opposites. In human experience, there are creative organization (e.g. when a staff officer so disposes the members of his institution as to elicit the best they have to give) and organized creativity (e.g. the control of the creative artist, who holds his material together and shapes and reshapes it till it forms an organized whole). But they are frequently poised against each other, particularly when each is functioning at a low level. It is bad order that is uncreative, and bad creation which is disorderly. It is almost a law among values (if we may here anticipate the following section) that they are far apart at the base and converge as each approaches its climax. But, in any case, the opposite of creation is not order but torpor (or sloth), which is not ordered, just as the opposite of order is not creation, but chaos, which is not creative. Asymmetrical they certainly are, in tension (often a fruitful tension) they may be; but there is nothing to prevent them from belonging together, and not least in virtue of the tension which holds them apart. We might even say of them what the Lebanese poet Kahlil Gibran said of marriage:

> You were born together, and together you shall be for evermore.
> You shall be together when the white wings of death scatter your days.
> Aye, you shall be together even in the silent memory of God.
> But let there be spaces in your togetherness,
> And let the winds of heaven dance between you.

5. *The Constitutive Factors and their Limitations*

It will be noticed that, taking order and creativity as examples, two constitutive features of the world are really in conflict with certain other things in the world. Right down the middle of

the world runs the opposition between order and chaos,
creativity and torpor: the constitutive features are opposed, in
the world, to their own antitheses. Yet these constitutive
features are in fact, as far as they go (certainly not in scope),
identical with two of the outstanding attributes of the traditional
Christian (or Jewish, or Moslem) God. That is to say, if there
is such a God, there is an overlap of divine and cosmic characters, and a split down the cosmos. In that case, in respect of
those characters, God and the cosmos are continuous, even
though in the cosmos they are scattered, and in God they are
concentrated. It follows that if there is a God, he will not be
'wholly other': he will have in this world, irrespective of
revelation, channels of activity, and a home.

It will be noticed also that the two constitutive factors, and
their opposites, fall within a scheme of valuation. Order and
creativity, in their several ways, are good things, and chaos
and torpor are bad things. This may be considered mere
anthropomorphism: why should we call things valuable because we value them? But try to think away our preconceptions:
if the physical constituents of the world behaved anyhow, or
not at all, there would *be* no world, only fragments, or a mere
lump. Order and creativity are *mutatis mutandis* for the physical
world what they are for us: the condition of its being what it is.
It is possible for us to renege on the whole enterprise and to say
that what we are is a bad thing; it is even possible to give this
depressing conviction an odour of sanctity. But such perversity
can only occur on the level of consciousness. A disorderly or
torpid world simply would not go, whether we are there to
see it or not. For the physical world, its viability is a sort of
value. If this is so, the world is never what is called, euphemis-
tically, 'value-free', and when segments of it appear to be so,
as in the natural sciences, it is because value has been read out
of them, for the special and laudable purposes of scientists,
who are sustained in their labours by their passion to discover
the truth, but diminish the truth, and belie their passion, by
preoccupation with the 'value-free'.[17]

---

[17] In case these comments seem unappreciative, let it be said that the
scientist is concerned primarily with lines of communication, not with total
strategy. He does his work; we do ours.

Evidently, neither of the two constitutive factors goes the whole way.

1. In the happily mixed constitution of things, they are balanced against each other, and the excellence we find in them draws entirely from their mutual limitation. Undisturbed, each would develop into the opposite (i.e. the polar defect) of the other: order would become torpid and creativity chaotic.[18]

2. The two constitutive factors are not exhaustive: they have been selected because they are both ubiquitous and concrete, and also because they are disclosed to us without aid from revelation. Later, in a more explicitly religious context, but in relation to order and creativity as facts of secular experience, we shall consider the constitutive power of 'the divine concern'.

3. No possible constitutive factors, or combination of them, can go the whole way, because limits are set by that which they have to constitute. Order and creativity have a transitive force; they presuppose something to be organized or made. If that were not so, and there were a God, he would be everything. But the presence of God in the world is not an omnipresence: there are recalcitrances and rejections which cannot be assigned to him, even though he may overrule them. That there should be something about the world which does not express the constitutive factors which are to be represented as his prolongations should forestall the charge that the theory of prolongations issues in pantheism.

4. But the simplest and most fundamental reason why the constitutive factors must be taken as incomplete is that there can always be more of them. They are identified as constitutive by their constancy and not *a priori*. Their status is that of very high-grade empirical facts; and they can hardly ask for more, as anything that is *a priori* is not a fact but a supposition or a train of argument. The constitutive factors are incomplete because they have a future, and they have a future because they exist in time. How this bears upon the way we talk about God will appear later.

[18] A human illustration: conservatives bury their heads in the sand and radicals theirs in the clouds.

6. *More Here, Less There?*

We have noted two structural elements of nature and of human experience, which are also traditionally listed among the attributes of God; and we have suggested that by following them up, in their various quarrels and reconciliations, we may discover that they are expressions of God hidden from us by their very familiarity. We are encouraged in this course by recalling that both figure, in varying proportions, in standard religious experience, and that the one thing religious experience is firm evidence for is 'something beyond itself'. All these points must be borne in mind as we face the first major objection.

It can be argued that the more the ancient attributes of God can be located in the world, the less we need to look for their explanation to a God beyond the world. If the world in its own right exhibits order and creativity, it can do without the supernatural supplement which it would require if it were intrinsically torpid or chaotic. It is paradoxical, but true, that a materialist view of matter kept God in the picture for the greater part of the eighteenth century. If the world was a mechanism, there had to be a mechanic.[19] The test came when Hume artfully suggested that the world was more like an 'animal', with its principle of growth inside itself.[20] When the adjustment which God had been called in to explain was shown to be a self-adjustment, the explanation was superfluous. The same thing happened, on a larger scale and with more sensational repercussions, in the debate over evolution. So, when we find two of the characters most commonly ascribed to God already pervading the world, why should we have to look to God to account for them?[21]

Thus, to establish our case, we have to show that the con-

[19] Cf. C. D. Broad, *The Mind and its Place in Nature*, 1925, p. 90.

[20] *Dialogues concerning Natural Religion*, Part VI, ed. Kemp Smith, 1935, p. 211. The suggestion is accompanied by a reminder that 'according to almost all the theists of antiquity', 'Deity is the soul of the world'. This is a dexterous device for giving the believer a spurious and temporary support while knocking the foundations from under him: a tactic of which Hume was a master.

[21] Why, indeed? asks Kierkegaard. The moment you throw down the drawbridge, the world will storm the castle.

stitutive structures of the world are neither mere effects on the one hand, nor wholly autonomous on the other. If they are considered as mere effects, we should have to argue (dubiously) from effect to cause. If they are understood as autonomous, the reference to God is unnecessary. If they are discerned as unfinished but demanding fulfilment, we can best make sense of them if we see in them the continuation (not simply the effect) of a divine presence, the approach to which will be more like the extension of a view than a transference of the mind from one thing to another.

How, then, is it possible to show that order and creativity are in this world exhibited incompletely, and in what way do they demand a supplement?

There is one sense in which they are obviously incomplete: they require each other. This we have admitted and emphasized and we have shown that the imperfections of each taken separately are at least diminished when they are taken together. Now it could be argued that they are entirely removed, and, taken in conjunction, no longer point to a completion in God, but to a completion in each other.

There is one sense in which, even together, they are incomplete: there will always be more of them. They have an indefinitely continuing field of operations. If they were complete, they would have no further scope. But is time, in this instance, the essence of the contract? They will, no doubt, have further achievements to their credit; but will they be any more order and creativity than they are now? Is there anything about them, at any time, in respect of which they are less than what they have to be?

One answer, common in many religious traditions, is that they must be less than what they have to be if they operate in time at all. That convenient way out is not open to us. We shall say here dogmatically what we shall later have to argue:[22] that non-temporal order and creativity are inconceivable. Order is of temporal things, and creativity requires time to move in. What is unsatisfying about order and creativity as they stand is not their temporality or even their particularity (as we have seen, there can be perfection in detail), but that

[22] See chapter IX, pp. 242.

order and creativity are *not quite* what their deployment in the
world nevertheless requires them to be. What we are in search
of is an order and a creativity which shall be wholly what they
are, and deny nothing of what they are: for example, their
involvement in time. [23]

It will be asked how, if we do not already know what they
have it in them to be, we can recognize the lack of it. If we
answer, as we are expected to answer, 'We can't', we are back
in the position of assuming God in order to argue for him.
That, we repeat, is to shirk the issue. But, in general, recognition
of defect does not presume previous knowledge of the appropriate excellence; indeed, in matters of policy it is usual to hit
on the right solution by first becoming aware of what is wrong. [24]
So far, the recognition of 'not-quiteness' as the first step towards
God is entirely in order. [25]

But, if the 'not-quiteness' of order and creativity as we know
them is due neither to their mutual interference nor to the
alleged limitations of time, what kind of a thing is it? This is
the climax of the argument, and what follows is central for the
whole work.

1. The *experience* of incompletion is well known to us: there
can be no adequate analysis of experience without it. Love,
we are told in the *Symposium*, is the child of Power by Poverty:
to desire, to aspire, to estimate, to control – all these activities
spring from incompletion, and are poised on the edge of it.
Not to take this experience seriously would be entirely unempirical.

2. That there should *really* be incompletion is not surprising.
It is the consequence of an unfinished universe, in which there
is always more to be done. Those only should be surprised
who expect God to fix everything for good and all. That kind
of God is 'too small', he is not equal to the next occasion.

3. All the same, incompletion is incongruous; it suggests the

[23] It is not, we repeat, a question of scale. As L. P. Jacks once remarked,
'you don't cure a man's squint by enlarging his face'.
[24] That is why protesting students cannot be expected to produce
blueprints. Even God started by saying 'Thou shalt not . . .'.
[25] There is no need to exaggerate it into total alienation. That way there
is no passage in either direction; not even from God to man, because there
would be nothing for God to lay hold on.

Platonic paradox of 'both being and not-being'. We may have to put up with incongruity, and it is only intelligent to recognize it for what it is; but it descends from, indeed it almost carries with it, a demand for completion.

4. Yes, but why should the demand have to be satisfied? Our feelings about it put no constraint on the facts. The basic reason for pressing the demand is that the actual and observable incidence of order and creativity in the world is less than what is nevertheless in terms of their own constitution demanded of them. Both order and creation are most efficacious, i.e. most themselves, when they exceed their own average. They would be most themselves if they held the ultimate reserve power over chaos and torpor, and were wholly in tune with each other. By the same token, even their restricted operation points back to the unrestrictedness of their source. By following the empirical indications, we find ourselves drawn to look beyond the horizon.

5. What we glimpse there is something which is indefeasibly what here and now (or at any here and now) is exhibited sporadically and tied to circumstance. The intimation does not draw us wholly out of the world; it confronts us and directs us to something not limited to the world, but continuous with the world, and capable of indefinite expansion in the world. Exposed to the grip of sloth and the list to chaos, the world is 'not quite'; but at its peak points it coalesces with something strengthening and disturbing which we can only dimly identify. And, in that context, the 'not-quite' is revealed as not incongruous but perfectly natural.

6. At this stage, we are presenting evidence, and arguing that it points beyond itself. Empirically and as philosophers, we can trace its direction but cannot conclude to its destination. For one thing, we still have to reckon with the counter-evidence. Still, as we proceed, the sense of incongruity diminishes; and it is permissible to hope that *if* we could pursue the course the whole way, it would wholly vanish. Thus far an empirically based philosophy can take us. To go further we should need a historical revelation of the perfect instance; and that is something which no philosophy can supply.

7. Hitherto, with some difficulty, we have kept order and

creativity in parallel columns. But, as has been noted, they are related asymmetrically. Order does not produce creativity; creativity does produce order. If we press order alone back towards its own perfection, all we shall find is more and better order. If we similarly press creativity, we shall find more creativity, and order besides. So it is at least a possible speculation that at the far end, where each merges with the other in its own perfectedness, creativity brings about the order of the world, as well as giving rise to its own image in the world. In that case, creativity assumes a certain precedence, and the world would issue from the tension between its product, order, and its own continuance.

Thus, in general terms, we have prepared the way for the view that there is an overlap of God into the world; that from the side of the world there is a grasping of fringes of God in the world; that from the side of God the overlap is a prolongation: and that there is something about the prolongation which requires to be traced back to its divine hinterland.[26] Starting from scratch, and without religious assumptions, this is the direction in which the analysis of structures seems to call us. But that is only a beginning. It needs to be supplemented by reference to specific situations and especially the human situation; structures may pass over into *attributes* of God, but only situations can reveal his *presence*. In the next chapter these points will receive attention, and the whole theme will, it is hoped, appear more compelling as the context expands.

But there will still be reservations. In the first place, the world, on our own showing, is structured imperfectly, and the imperfections are as much evidence concerning the world as the structures themselves. In the second place, all that philosophy can provide in these regions is an increasing probability; sometimes receding as the imperfections are found hard to account for, but even without that complication not to be transmuted into certainty. At this exciting moment in the dialectic of the spirit, faith takes over; and with it so many

---

[26] There is this resemblance between our approach and the cosmological proof, that both take their start from incompletion. The difference is that we do not have to invoke the causal axiom to bring together what should never have been separated: God, and the shapes of God in the world.

things become clearer which in the philosophical ascent are no more than reasonable anticipations. That, as we shall see, is how faith and empiricism join hands.

IV

VALUES AS FRINGES

1. *Religion and Moral Autonomy*

WE HAVE tried to show in general terms that the perfections of the world are continuous with a beyond to which they are pointers, and at the same time and for that reason not complete in themselves. In this chapter we are to trace the same features in the structure of human values. Because it exhibits the problems most clearly, we shall concentrate on the evidence from ethics.

In human behaviour, structure and defect are accessible to consciousness. There is a gap between performance and possibility which the best man never quite closes. The drift to order and creativity (and morality is both) has to reorganize itself in the face of obstacles; it has to appropriate its opposite.

From one point of view, the transition from this-worldly structures to their continuation in God is easier in the case of values: easier, because it is forced upon us. The gap focuses attention on the absences of God from the world which, in our amazed contemplation of order and creativity in nature, it is easy to forget; and it thus incites us to pursue his presence on the far side of nature. From another point of view, the transition is more complicated. Through experience of obstruction, the moral agent acquires a self-standingness which is often in tension (fruitful though the tension may be) with the specifically religious mood of adoration: and this is true not merely of hustlers and reformers, but also of humble conservatives exerting themselves to plug dykes and to keep their own souls in order.

Thus only if we are conscious of the gap are we sufficiently disturbed to explore new shapes of God beyond our knowledge;

but in endeavouring to cope with the gap we keep ourselves so consciously erect that we sometimes do not think about God at all: and that goes not only for atheists, with whom the posture is constant, but also for believers in moments of in-attention or practical emergency. And so the gap which was to lead us to look for new shapes of God is interpreted as a break within the world to be mended by our own efforts.

The first way of meeting this challenge is to accept the description of morality as an assertion of will against resistances, and to argue from the defects of morality so defined to its completion on another plane. This was the point made by F. H. Bradley: 'The end, sought for by morality, is above it and is super-moral.'[1] It is particularly pertinent here to refer to Bradley, because he finds a resolution of the moral contra-diction in the attitude of religion. If what he says is true, we have found what we were looking for, an activity which leads out from nature and on to God. If we were *completely* to mend the break within the world, we should be taken beyond morality and beyond the world at the same time.

But this way of meeting the challenge will not do, because morality is not simply overcoming obstacles. Moral action can be easy and gracious without ceasing to be moral. In fact, if the obstacles are moral obstacles, the morality which has over-come them is more assuredly moral than the morality which is still beset with them. We have said before that the more order there is in the world, the less one has to go beyond the world to account for order. In the same way, the more there is in the world of a sort of secular grace, the less, it could be argued, do we have to receive grace from outside it.

The ethics of the Stoics and Epicureans can be cited as a case in point. Both *apatheia* and *ataraxia* testify to a spiritual victory in which the strain has abated. Similarly, the Buddhist ethic has all the marks of a hard-earned tranquillity. Yet the

---

[1] *Appearance and Reality*, 1930, p. 437. That he also finds religion to be similarly divided against itself does not here concern us, but is due to his logical theory about relations: religion, as a relation between man and God, is self-contradictory because it is a relation, not because it is between man and God. As our view of the attributes of God involves tension, that the expressions of religion (effort and adoration) should also involve tension is neither surprising nor disconcerting.

Stoic religion is fatalistic and this-worldly. The Epicurean pantheon is admittedly indifferent (the gods are side-tracked before the business of living begins, because, as Lucretius has told us, they get in its way), and the Buddhist religion (at least in its purest form) is humanist and non-metaphysical. The implication would seem to be that the vanquishing of obstacles does not take us beyond morality but takes us into it for the first time, and without recourse to God: though, in the case of Buddhism at least, not without religion.[2]

It would appear from these instances that morality does not necessarily require to be transcended in religion: the required amendment of the obstacle-race theory can be effected within its own resources. So much must be taken for granted as we approach the second attempt to meet what may be called the humanist challenge: namely, by blurring the boundaries between religion and morality. From the point of view of religion, such a blurring is necessary anyhow, because religion without its ethical moment is defective as religion; if the same can be shown to hold of the moral life (i.e. not that it is transcended in religion, but that it runs over at the far end into religion), we shall confirm, in this new sphere, the doctrine set out in the last chapter, that there is a continuity between the advancing finite and the incorporating infinite, as well as a difference of scope and power.

It is very difficult, in such a case, not to start back to front. Once we take note of what happens when God is brought into the picture, it is so clear that morality gains in stature and independence by belonging to religion; but at present we are trying to follow the drift of moral experience, and moral experience seems to be telling us that it can attain the disengagement produced by religion without resorting to religion. The only way to proceed is to test it further, and the only way to test it is to compare what it has so far told us with what it tells us when it speaks from within religion. To that end, we shall have to allow ourselves a preview, anticipating the disclosure which properly occurs only when secular morality is pressed to the limit and fails to satisfy its own criteria.

[2] But there the religion wells up inside the ethic; there is no advance from ethics to religion.

It is perhaps significant that Christian morality[3] has one characteristic which distinguishes it sharply, not only from obstacle-morality, but from Stoic or Epicurean models. It is not merely without strain but is positively joyful. Both Stoics and Epicureans, in their very different ways, tried above all things to avoid inward disturbance. They would have thought it improper for divinity to swing into the orbit of human weakness, like Jesus in Gethsemane: 'My soul is exceeding sorrowful, even unto death' (Matt. 26.38), but they would also have thought exaggerated the canticles of joy in heaven over the one sinner that repenteth. Everything that could be contrived, Stoics and Epicureans between them accomplished. But there is one thing that cannot be contrived, and that is spontaneity. 'The wind bloweth where it listeth . . . So is every one that is born of the Spirit.' It is not an accident that this infinitely flexible kind of morality is one that has a religious backing; it can happen only if the agent no longer has to consider his stance and with complete unselfconsciousness expresses a constant concern in variable types of action moulded to the occasion. A morality belonging to a religion does not have to set itself against the world; it does not have to clench its fists or strike attitudes; the world is with it, and secular moralists with many of the same things to say would affirm them more happily and less defiantly if they were able to view them in their proper context. The peculiar note in Christian morality is one of liberation from strains and stresses. It justifies the emphatic comment (John 10.8), 'All that ever came before me are thieves and robbers'; what they stole was life and spontaneity. And so the text continues: 'I am come that they might have life and that they might have it more abundantly.'

We have gone beyond our terms of reference; but it is interesting that the one genuine breakthrough from Bradley's moral impasse occurs when action is reinstated in the current of being, i.e. replaced in a religious context. So, in a sense, Bradley was right: there is a dialectical progression from morality to religion. But in a sense he was wrong, for to make that progression it is not necessary to leave morality behind;

[3] Christian morality; not in all respects identical with the morality of Christians.

on the contrary, the progression having taken place, morality becomes more adequate *as morality*. And yet there is no break between the old morality and the new. They are both moralities, and apart from a few sublime outgrowths they figure mostly the same virtues. Christian morality (or any morality conscious of the presence of God) exhibits an excellence not wholly other than that of secular morality, but without its strain and its indignation – the whole thing, not annihilated, and not merely added to, but incorporated and raised to a higher power. It is not because secular morality breaks down that we look to God; it is because it works as far as it goes, and bears witness in itself that it has not reached the end.

This description gives us exactly what the argument requires: a secular excellence doing its job better for taking on a religious character. But (as we have so often found) the prospect stands out clearly only when it is viewed from the top. What we still have to explain is how secular morality fails to satisfy its own needs, without invoking God to decide the issue beforehand.

2. *The Moral Frontier*

We shall first establish and illustrate a general theory about outstanding moral performances in any style, and later apply it to the case in hand. *When any morality reaches its own peak, it moves forward into another dimension.*

Take, for example, the case of Regulus. His sacrifice was a supreme exhibition of city-state morality, fulfilled punctiliously and heroically. But by virtue of its sheer sublimity it soars far beyond his own style. It rests on a sense of obligation to a public enemy far beyond anything shown by competing ideologists today. In his act, Roman virtue was extended beyond *Romanitas* in favour of the perfidious and uncongenial Carthaginians. It anticipates Locke's pronouncement that 'the keeping of faith belongs to men as men, and not as members of society'.[4] By carrying *Romanitas* to the limit, he outran it. He may even be said to have prefigured the Categorical Imperative. In his decision to return to Carthage, the Lares and Penates

[4] *Second Treatise of Civil Government*, Book II, ch. 2.

to which he paid his devotions put on universality. He was building up gods better than he knew.

The case of Regulus illustrates the general principle; but it does not take us from secular to religious morality. It rather expands to rational and international proportions a traditional city-state morality *and* religion. Let us take another case, from which the religious overtones have been scrupulously eliminated: the case of justice in a modern community.

Justice is (rightly, as far as it goes) a particular favourite with secularists; it is upright and self-standing and prescribes its own standards. There is no nonsense in it about supererogation. It deals in rights and with generalities. It is its business not to make distinctions; so much so, that it sometimes fails to make relevant distinctions, and when it does, it states them in terms of groups or classes of people. I do not deny that this way of transacting certain aspects of public business is entirely necessary; I ask only if it meets the whole of the situation which it confronts so adequately on its own level. I intend to show, in the spirit of the above argument, that if it is pressed hard enough it opens the door to something else.

If justice is to be done, the circumstances and personal contexts of each action have to be taken into account. This is just what a broad characterization of actions and persons in terms of types and standard situations cannot do. The system of public justice is meticulous, but it is de-individualized; it has to be, but for that very reason the attitude which it expresses cannot be contained within its boundaries. It has to be supplemented by social workers and psychiatrists who explore precisely those personal factors which public justice excludes as a matter of principle. Justice, in the end, takes into account the kinks and excrescences which it formally eliminates. As a matter of history we have been (and in left-wing circles still are) so obsessed with eliminating privilege and bringing all members of society to a common level, that we have not sufficiently regarded the infinite variety of situations in which actions occur. It has been customary to say that such consideration is not a matter of justice, but of mercy or supererogation. But in fact there is no such opposition: it is in trying to work out the implications of justice within the framework of justice that we find ourselves compelled to consider the situational factors which it has excluded. Justice breaks its own shell.

Consider how justice can be done in individual cases not quite conformable to the average. Only, to be sure, by means of the finest individual perceptions. And does not this require us to go out beyond the rules and identify ourselves with off-beat problems and predicaments? Along these lines, by pursuing justice we fall into the frame of mind in which we do not stop at justice. We meet in the middle of the road those who are committed to more than justice and have to take heed that they do not overlook justice in the process. That is why it is written both: Till heaven and earth pass one jot or one tittle shall in no wise pass from the law, till all be fulfilled, and: Except your righteousness shall exceed the righteousness of the Scribes and Pharisees ye shall in no case enter into the Kingdom of Heaven.

A good example is provided in scripture: the example of the 'second mile'. Experts explain that the reference is to the duty of guarding caravan convoys: if a man is ill or in trouble, the guard for the first 'mile' will replace him on the second, and so undertake a double responsibility. To *prescribe* the second mile on a primitive roster-sheet would be positively unjust. For the individual to *undertake* it is an extension of justice. The second-miler, considering both the enterprise and his fellow human being, thinks he *ought* to do what he cannot be *expected* to do.[5] In biblical language, he both fulfils the law and exceeds the law. Again, justice, at the far end, passes over into personal concern without loss of content, but only of its claim to finality. It moves into a realm in which its equity and punctiliousness are strictly preserved, but there are no limits to love and service. The dialetic of justice goes right to the edge of Christian morality; and there are no guards on the frontier.

It will be said: these considerations force us back from mere justice to agapaistic morality,[6] but agapaistic morality, though part of the Christian religion, is not limited to it, and may be

[5] Incidentally, the example disposes of the theory that 'ought' is merely legal or social.
[6] I prefer 'agapaistic', as a matter of etymology; I believe 'agapeistic' is more usual.

practised by atheists on purely humanitarian grounds.[7] As a matter of history, except for Jewish anticipations, it belongs to the Christian dispensation, and is practised today outside Christianity mainly by ex-Christians living on their religious capital; but on our own showing it could be re-invented by unsentimental secularists realistically appraising the alternatives. We have therefore to show, in a last and most difficult application of our principle, that agapaistic morality, into which, at its peak, justice passes over, itself 'necessarily tends' to pass over into religion.

We may note, first of all, the remarkable *freedom* which it introduces into the moral order. 'The wind bloweth where it listeth; so is every one that is born of the Spirit.' As A. D. Lindsay observed,[8] 'there is a touch of the infinite about it'. What distinguishes agapaistic ethics from any other kind is precisely this spaciousness, this inexhaustibility, this absence of finalities and strictures, in short, this freedom from the limitations of which, for good enough reasons, ordinary moralities are compounded. Is there not a pressure to say at this point: here is God impinging on a closed world, and making all the difference to it by opening it up?

Secondly, agapaistic ethics assign absolute worth to the human creature, sometimes in the teeth of appearances. This is natural enough; where the infinite is, there is reverence. Reverence, in the first place, for persons in their manifold simple relationships; reverence is the inward hold we have on their reality. But it cannot stop there: men are not the sum of things, and we have only their word for it that they are the summit of things. Any reverence we have for each other both leads to and derives from the reverence we have for the whole of nature. Kant very properly bracketed in the act of reverence 'the moral law within' with the 'starry heavens above' – viewed, as the context shows, not astronomically but aesthetically. It is wholly relevant to agapaistic ethics, which encompass not only the just but the unjust, that the sun shines and the rain falls on the evil as well as the good. Reverence, then, once

---

[7] Non-theistic Christians whose whole religion is *agape* are a case apart. But their practice testifies against their theory. See below.

[8] *The Moral Teaching of Jesus*, 1937, p. 91.

operative, is apt to spread, and cannot be contained on the human level. And its essence is to point to something beyond itself. Both man and nature fit naturally as prolongations. Of a scene which is infinite and evokes reverence, God is the sense and the direction.[9]

In the above argument, it has been assumed that agapaistic morality is humanly possible, and also a pointer to the divine. In a darker mood, especially after reading M. Sartre, one might wonder whether agapaistic morality *was* humanly possible. Love, he tells us, is the destruction of the other by the appropriation of his freedom, and mutually. After all he has said, I would not care to bet on my own or anyone else's total immunity from *mauvaise foi*.[10] But, as Fr H. Paissac points out in his brilliant little book, *Le Dieu de Sartre*, in that case God is not merely the implication of agapaistic ethics, but the condition of its possibility. If God were *autrui* as another person is, he might well be destructive of human freedom; it is only because he is not, because in loving us he is not engaged in diminishing us, because we have learnt, more or less, to move in a religious context, that we are able to love our neighbour without the *mauvaise foi* which otherwise engulfs us. We do not need, of course, to accept the Sartrian mythology of consciousness, but as it is extremely plausible it is interesting to note how, if we do accept it, the passage to God is effected by another route. One way, agapaistic morality leads up to God; the other, agapaistic morality is stranded without God. In neither case is it independent of God. If we prefer the first, it is partly because cynical insight is not the only kind of insight (if we follow Sartre, even sincerity is a pose), and partly because we are better able to do justice to the gradations of moral development, which are both vertically and laterally of great complexity. In any case, we should remember the difference between *believing* in agape and exhibiting it, and note that it may be exhibited by those who disclaim it. We should also note that their behaviour is the best witness against them. And,

[9] As Fr Paissac observes (*Le Dieu de Sartre*, 1950, p. 75), 'Les choses veulent dire Dieu, elles ne le disent pas.'

[10] Readers of Sartre must be irresistibly reminded of St Paul: 'there is none righteous, no, not one'. The parallel does not seem to have occurred to him.

finally, either way and every way, the signpost points over the boundary.

3. *Morality and the Will of God*

In attempting to show how secular excellence points beyond itself, we have tried to avoid certain standing misconceptions. In the first place, we are not only not saying, we are denying, that the excellence of secular or indeed any kind of morality consists of obedience to the will of God. It grows up to meet the requirements of the world and points to God – which, if God has had anything to do with the making of the world, is not surprising. In the second place, however, we are also denying the counter-affirmation, often regarded as the only alternative, that morality is complete without reference to God. It is true enough that pagans and atheists have 'values', and that whole tracts of behaviour can be satisfactorily organized without going a step beyond them. But those same tracts are reorganized in a wholly different and more gracious spirit by men who have refreshed themselves with worship and contemplation: and there is no barrier between the two worlds. Indeed, atheists who have found it impossible to live in a permanent attitude of cynicism or defiance, particularly if they are given to meditation, are already teetering on the brink. In a sense, morality without God is perfectly in order: but it does not reach the high point on which it is itself set. These conclusions anticipate the argument; but we shall lead back to them in due course. Even without the prior recognition of God, and indeed as part of the evidence for believing in him, we can observe the pressure on the boundary of a morality which it cannot contain.[11]

In the third place, we are not forced into the position adopted by Professor W. G. Maclagan, of securing morals by depersonalizing God.[12] His argument is that the moral agent

[11] In an article on 'Morality: Religious and Secular', *Journal of Theological Studies*, 1962, reprinted in *Christian Ethics and Contemporary Philosophy*, ed. I. T. Ramsey, 1966, pp. 113–26, I have tried to show that under the heteronomy of morals the moral agent is more autonomous. Those who declaim on the autonomy of morals are cosseting an abstraction.

[12] In *The Theological Frontier of Ethics*, 1961, p. 170.

must reach his own decisions; that current doctrines concerning grace involve the encroachment of God on the making of decisions; and that this would not be the case if God moved us as an impersonal principle. What impinges on our freedom is the notion of God's *activity*. With much of this protest I am in sympathy, particularly with the emphasis on decision and the deprecation of Calvinist doctrines of grace. If this were the place to do it, I should enlarge on the virtues of Pelagius (a decent Britisher caught in a web of North African intrigue) and on the perceptiveness of the seventeenth-century Jesuits in distinguishing between the 'sufficient grace' which sets us on our path, and the 'efficacious grace', ensuing on the right use of the 'liberty of indifference', which has power to save. But this approach does not compel us to treat God merely as a magnetic point of reference, and still less to treat him as a set of principles. The exercise of our power is actually enhanced by the power of God working in us. Even in human affairs, autonomy is not abolished or even diminished by the adoption of good ideas from other people. If I decide to act on sound advice from my wife, I am more autonomous in respect to my environment than if I were to make mistakes on my own. To call this gain a loss of independence is to confuse independence with isolation. In the same way, to take counsel of God is to have at one's disposal the best possible advice, and to adopt it (which it is only too easy not to do) is a decision: a better decision, I venture to think, than I could have achieved alone.

These reflections, however, lead us to the next open frontier: the frontier of personality. Here, again, we shall try to show that at its highest point human experience reveals an incompleteness which points on to something of the same order but relieved of the limitations.

4. *Interpreting Omnipotence*

We may begin by reflecting on the theological doctrine of omnipotence. There is no doubt that for many sincere spirits this is the major lion in the path. There is also a standing danger to which in this case theologians appear to have yielded, in allowing the devices fit to explain the mysteries to one genera-

tion to persist, inappositely, into the next, which they are apt
to confuse. In the case before us, an explanatory device has
been identified with the mysteries themselves. The result is the
identification of power with absolutism, and the disinclination
of those who dislike absolutism to accept power. This is bad
enough in politics, but it is doubly unfortunate in religion.

The natural way of getting the subjects of oriental despots to
understand the majesty of God was to deck him up as an
oriental despot. The theologians who coined the imagery had
to display him as one and supreme, different from all the little
particularist godlets, with power reaching not only somewhere
but everywhere. They did the best they could, and they have
been helped by the repetitions of history: for instance, by the
incidence of absolute monarchy in the theologically formative
seventeenth century. It would, moreover, be unfair to conclude
that absolutist conceptions of God entail absolutist conceptions
of politics. They may coalesce, as in the France of Louis XIV;
on the other hand, they may collide, and most of our modern
Western freedoms are the products of the collision. The worshippers of the absolutist God summoned up the courage to
challenge the absolutist state. But, however fortunate the effects
at the time, the absolutist God is not at home in the world which
his worshippers helped to build. In the administrative structures
of a democracy, we are inclined to ask: which is easier, mani-
pulating puppets or exercising authority among free men? Any
little godlet with a little dexterity can manage the puppets:
the truly godlike activity is to manage free men. In fact, it
takes God to do it; for it is part of the contract that they
remain free, and the best administrator has to compromise
with necessity. That is why omnipotence, properly understood,
and delivered from its load of inapplicable illustration, goes
with freedom: freedom requires from God (to put it vulgarly)
more of what it takes. It is also why so many things happen
which a divine autocrat might not have chosen. The open
texture is not permissive; it is part of the divine ordinance,
and the test for power is not the absence of limits, but the
extent to which it elicits freedom.[13]

[13] These thoughts go back to conversations with my former tutor at
Oxford and professor at Glasgow, A. D. Lindsay (later Lord Lindsay

The habit of thinking that God can do anything at all is not restricted to theologians. It assumed philosophical form in the Scotist tradition, and in the eccentric theory of Descartes that God is supreme over the eternal verities – which, taken seriously, would include the possible annihilation of the multiplication table, or even of logic. It was an incalculable good fortune for the Western tradition that St Thomas Aquinas insisted that God cannot do the intrinsically impossible, that his will is yoked in equal harness to his intellect. But he still does not hold that God is displayed in the initiatives of the human creature; he thinks of them as permitted, and predictable. He does not affiliate human with divine creativity as he affiliates human with divine intellect – not even under the rubric of the *analogia entis*.[14]

Human analogies are fallible, but when it is at all costs needful to cultivate the imagination, they have a significant place. We may note, therefore, that no good executive tries to do everything himself. According to the analogy, there are many things which happen which are delegated to subordinate creators,[15] some of necessity better performers than others. And this is as it should be, for otherwise we should be perfected automata and not the minor sources of initiative which, in God's image, we are created to be.

All in all, then, the concept of omnipotence needs revising.

---

of Birker). I note that in his posthumously published *Selected Addresses* (1957), they are set out publicly, and reinforced with the authority of Kierkegaard. See pp. 69ff., and especially the Kierkegaard quotations: 'If we rightly consider omnipotence, then clearly it must have the quality of so taking itself back in this very manifestation of its all-powerfulness that the results of this act of the omnipotent can be independent.' 'It is only a miserable and worldly picture of the dialectic of power to say that it becomes greater as it can compel and make things dependent. Socrates knew better: the art of using power is to make free.'

[14] His problem is to reconcile divine foreknowledge with the formal freedom of the faculty of acting: and in France in the seventeenth century the Jansenists jumped one way and the Jesuits the other. The dispute would never have arisen if he had not unduly circumscribed divine foreknowledge. Divine foreknowledge should encompass not all possible actualities, but all actualizable possibilities.

[15] In Rodgers and Hammerstein's *Carousel*, God is depicted as dealing with the problems of newly arrived spirits not personally, but through agents: mainly, if my memory serves me, country doctors. The suggestion is imaginatively satisfying.

And, by way of final comment, the traditional doctrine suffers from a theory of choice akin to the discredited wage-fund theory of nineteenth-century economists: it assumes that the more power God has, the less man has. But if men are engaged on his business, even unknowingly, the more they have, the more he has.

It has been necessary to discuss omnipotence because the traditional pre-Kierkegaardian interpretation would obstruct the passage from personal existence to its completion in the existence of God. To this theme we now return; with some trepidation, because it is too large a subject for the passing treatment which is all that is here possible.

5. *The Completion of the Person*

The conception of personal existence is sometimes stated so as to make the passage impassable. For example, a hard-shelled individualism will define a person in terms of his occupancies and his rights: his security, his freedom from invasion, the proper maintenance of what Bosanquet called his 'hexagonal fences'.[16] The person so defined cannot expand upward, his excellent fences get in the way. Or to take another example: Bosanquet proposes in the place of many-fenced units a single-fenced unit, which absorbs all the upward inclinations of the many, and converts them into the raw material of a civic whole. This is a particularly plausible perversion, for we know that sense of elation which goes with doing things along with the crowd: but civic excellence is not religious excellence, unless religion is reduced (as by Rousseau in the *Social Contract*, though not in *Emile*) to 'civic religion'.[17] Yet again, a person may be defined in terms of an agency directed unilaterally and unreciprocally towards the world – including other agencies. In that case, any possible rolling back of the frontier of personality will have been forestalled. Fortunately for our argument, the definition is untenable: each agency would be

[16] *Philosophical Theory of the State*, third edition, 1920, p. 78.
[17] It does not alter the principle of the thing if the unit is expanded, as Bosanquet was prepared to expand it, to international proportions (*op. cit.*, Introduction to third edition, p. xii). World citizenship does not in itself qualify for the Kingdom of Heaven.

absorbed in every other agency, i.e. each would be an agency and not an agency at the same time.

From these intrinsically unsatisfactory attempts at defining a person, we turn to more promising attempts, and we note with interest that they lend themselves far more easily to our purposes. What is common to them is that they stress mutuality as opposed both to separateness and absorption. For example, A. A. Bowman tells us that 'it is a distinguishing mark of persons that other persons can and should exist for them not as objects but as subjects';[18] and John Macmurray:[19] 'Personal individuality is not an original given fact. It is achieved through the progressive differentiation of the original unity of the "You and I".' Now this mutual process of person-making is never complete; and its incompleteness does not have to be brought home to it from the outside: it makes itself felt in the heart of the process itself. As Bowman observes: 'Man does not qualify his claim to personality; yet the restrictions of his nature do not entitle him to assert it unconditionally.'[20] Following up the clues to personality as given, empirically, in experience, the distinction of subject from object, the difference between subject-subject relation and subject-object relation, the inevitable gaps in the communication between subjects, together with the decent reticences proper between finite persons but establishing them as finite, we are brought to see that being persons is something we cannot achieve, and yet it is being persons that is our special *mode* of being. If any finite existent ever called for completion in its own idiom, it is personality.

But it cannot be completed in isolation, or by aggregation, or by unilateral initiation, nor even in finite mutualities. If it is to be completed at all (and it certainly calls for it), it must be as participating in a personal existence which is more than human.[21] There is just no other alternative. But participation

---

[18] *Studies in the Philosophy of Religion*, 1938, Vol. II, p. 391.
[19] *The Form of the Personal*, Vol. II: *Persons in Relation*, 1961, p. 91.
[20] *Op. cit.*, II, p. 397.
[21] Note: 'if it is to be completed at all'. There is nothing to prevent a sceptical empiricist from saying 'no'. All that is here adverted to is a drift, and a drift is not a demonstration. The 'must' above is therefore, at this stage, hypothetical. At the same time, the pressure to completeness is a

is not merely a reference back to another world. It involves an overlap; God reaching down to be a constituent of the world, and the world rising to incorporate it. As Whitehead observed, alluding to one of the said constituents, 'creativity is not separable from its creatures'.[22] This is the picture which will be elaborated later: at present we merely reaffirm, concerning personality, the open-endedness of the finite creature, and his testimony that, if he is to be what he is, there must be somewhere something which is in greater measure what he is, with which he is somehow continuous.

6. *Overlap and Distance*

The drift of the argument is now sufficiently clear to provoke objections. The first is that continuity is stressed at the expense of distance. We have been looking for affinities rather than cleavages, for God-overlapping-into-the-world rather than God-beyond-the-world. But, it will be argued, the sense of utter transcendence is essential to religion; as Kierkegaard might have said, where there is no gap there is no God. Incompleteness is a feeble rendering of alienation. Adam and Eve were not settled on sub-divided paddocks within Eden, they were thrown out of the garden altogether. Those who report 'encounter' with God appear to be at least as much disconcerted as reassured. Francis Thompson, converted after and through the difficulties of his early life, wrote, one suspects autobiographically:

> 'Tis Heaven that lies beyond our sights
> And hell too possible that proves;
> For all can feel the God that smites,
> But ah, how few the God that loves.

In the face of this testimony, can we talk about continuity and affiliation and ignore what makes religion stark and real – the infinite distance and the desperate failure of communication? Ought we to be preparing the way for a religious viewpoint in

---

strong one, and stronger grounds should be provided for resisting it than a mere determination to apply to persons as subjects ways of thinking appropriate to the abstract operations of natural science.

[22] *Religion in the Making*, p. 79.

which the great gap between God and his creatures is smoothed out into a graded highway over an unguarded frontier?

Again we have had to anticipate, but open-endedness and incompleteness in the human person are associated with one kind of religious response and alienation and total depravity with another; and it is well to be clear of our direction. In stating the case for gradualism, we are preparing an empirical foundation for faith. Under the opposite approach, we can only proceed dialectically through scepticism and despair. The genius of Kierkegaard was that alone among the practitioners of this approach he saw this necessity and embraced it unflinchingly.

But we still have to answer: and the objection is to be welcomed, for it enables us to avert a misunderstanding. We have no intention of eliminating the sense of distance; we hope merely to assign it to its proper place. In the first place, it is entirely appropriate in those who fall short of God's intention for them; and that means all of us, more or less. But the more or less matters. The perfectionist who thinks he has failed in an examination because he scores, say, only 80 per cent, and who thereby equates himself with the genuine failure who scores a scanty 20 per cent, is doing no justice to the knowledge that is in him. In the same way, the person who knows he could be more of a person but is accepted as a fair working model is further up the scale than one who is hardly a person at all. The word 'person' is value-loaded (like the words 'order', 'creativity', 'morality'), and in all such cases the top-ranking instance is the standard instance. No one, it is true, reaches 100 per cent; in that sense 'there is none righteous, no, not one', and it is well for the higher scorers to be reminded of it. It is in fact good for them, as a necessary exercise in humility, to mark themselves down in those respects in which their failings are better known to them than to the world outside, and not to go about thanking God that they are not as other men. In fact, they themselves are not the best people to do the grading. But it is just not true that they have no merit; in fact, there is a certain subjective merit even in their self-devaluation; and there is a measurable discrepancy evident to many outside between their performance on the one hand and that of the do-no-gooders and couldn't-care-lessers on the other. It is in their serious sense of incompleteness that there is the best evidence of something which surpasses them and overlaps them. After all, how do most of us catch religion, or anything else worth having? By admiring those who have it and following the best we know. It is they who point us to something better.

The sense of distance, then, varies with the degree of imperfection. A. D. Lindsay said of the citizens of a democracy that though they do not all count equally, they all equally count. In the same way, before God men are equally at fault, but they are not at fault equally. Even if some estimable citizens have only papered over the cracks, even that is meritorious; it is better to cover up and carry on with the job.[23] Every room can do with a spring-cleaning, but some rooms more urgently than others. The trouble is not with the generic entity 'man', but with the specific creatures 'men', and differentially.

If this is not orthodox, I cannot help it. And perhaps it is unorthodox only in part. It is no part of Christian doctrine to maintain the *original* depravity of 'man', or the world. They were created in God's image. The question is whether since the Fall the gap between man and God has become so absolute that man can do nothing about it, and only wait for God; or whether we can get to work like men to reduce it, and to show thereby that God is working in us. The empirical approach through the limited excellence of the finite creature foreshadows the second view. The other view, as it disqualifies every kind of human effort, is necessarily anti-rational and though not in itself anti-empirical, is as selective of its facts as it is of its texts.[24] It is only some men who have felt the gap to be uncrossable; and they may need to be subverted in order to be restored. Others, just as sincere in their love of God, and not so handicapped, make progress gradually and think less about being saved and more about him. And they do not deny that they need all the *guidance* in the world.

[23] It is also imperative to seek help from God through clergy and ministers and friends and even through psychiatrists, but that is part of a different story.

[24] On this latter point, cf. Luther's description of the Epistle of St James, with its overtones of 'do-it-yourself', as 'an epistle of straw'.

7. *Involvement in Time*

A second objection to our proposed programme, coming from the different angle, is that through his prolongations God will be involved in time. The statement is undoubtedly true: but is it an objection? If God is not in time, he cannot love, heal, listen to prayer, make differences in the world, engage in encounter, stir, soothe, create; in fact he cannot *do* anything whatever. The timeless God is a legacy from the Alexandrian Neo-Platonists, for whom *doing* anything was far too vulgar. There are timeless things in the world, and we admit, with Whitehead, that they are genuinely structural, though it is easy to think of them as constructs or abstracts. Even so, they are the permanent and repeatable features of the world; the things that enter into every situation, but give rise to no situation. But the living God cannot be compared to a coathanger or a skeleton: if he is a creator, especially one powerful enough to be a creator of creators, he must concern himself with the particularities for which the structures of the world are only common characters and not entities in themselves. Any God it is possible to have dealings with must be enmeshed in time.

One answer, congenial to those for whom metaphysics is a religion-substitute, is that God is indeed involved in time, but that only goes to show that religion is philosophy *manqué*. That which is real is therefore not God, but a truly timeless Absolute, and God is at best its nearest temporal approximation. Such was the view of F. H. Bradley, who greatly disliked anti-religion, but definitely classed religion, which is concerned with God, as second-best to philosophy, which is concerned with the Absolute, and precisely for that reason.[25] In this appraisal, Bradley showed his usual insight. He saw what religion was, much more clearly than some of his orthodox critics; if there is something wrong with his estimate, it must be that there was something wrong with Absolute Idealism as a philosophy. On

[25] In the same way, Plotinus conceived the Divine Mind as an emanation of the One, and attached to the One, rather than to the Divine Mind, the attitude of religious reverence. So A. H. Armstrong, *An Introduction to Ancient Philosophy*, 1947, p. 188: 'In the Enneads it is the One rather than the Divine Mind which corresponds most closely to what we mean by "God".'

that issue, which deserves a book to itself, it can only be said here that Absolute Idealism was, more than any other recent movement of thought, anti-empirical, both in tone, in method, and by declared intention; and we, who are attempting to expound a philosophical empiricism passing naturally into faith, have been working on wholly different lines. What we are able to say on temporality is what any empiricist must say; what will happen to it when the passage into faith has been achieved is another question, but as it will be a main part of our theme that faith does not reverse empirical probabilities but fulfils them, it is not to be expected that one of the first postulates of empiricism will be discarded.

It may, however, be urged, by way of compromise, that in some way not known to us God *combines* the attitudes of time-lessness and inaccessibility with those of activity and nearness. That, in fact, is what much contemporary orthodoxy assumes. In a contribution to the volume *Process and Divinity*,[26] I have tried to show that they cannot just sit side by side: so taken, they are incoherent, and the discrepancy should not be masked by a pious appeal to ignorance. If justice is to be done to the total conception, one must be subordinated to the other; and I have given reasons for treating temporality in God as total, and timelessness as episodic. The volume is a *Festschrift* in honour of Professor Charles Hartshorne; and I can only hope that he will not think that the inspiration I have derived from him has been misapplied. It is Professor Hartshorne, more than any other writer, who has developed the view that in some aspects at least the perfection of God is relative; i.e. it may be surpassed by himself at another moment. He does, however, maintain that in other respects his perfection is absolute: it could never be surpassed even by himself. The respects enumerated are his essence and his goodness, as opposed to his accidents and his aesthetic fittingness. It might then be supposed that as regards his essence and his goodness he retains what Professor Hartshorne calls the 'classical' (as opposed to his own 'neoclassical') characters of impassivity, changelessness, and even timelessness. If that were so, we should have to ask how

[26] 'The Two Strands in Natural Theology', *op. cit.*, ed. Reese and Freeman, 1964, pp. 471–92.

juxtaposed and disparate characters could together constitute
the being of God;[27] or, alternatively, whether the gap which,
according to the classical model, strictly regarded, separates
God from the world, should be allowed to reappear unbridged
within the nature of God. But I do not believe that such is in
fact Hartshorne's intention. In the first place, the whole drift
of his argument is against the view that only absolute perfection
counts. In the second place, if it is replied that it still does
count, he is ready to admit that the 'essence' in which absolute
perfection inheres is not self-subsisting: 'God may depend,
even for his essence, upon there being creatures.'[28] In the third
place, even if God's essence, 'the definable positive characteristic by which we could conceptually identify him', were as
remote as the classical theology avers, his essence is an abstract
of him rather than his fullness: 'the *Thou* could include the it';
'the personal includes the impersonal, not vice versa'. 'My
friend is not an it, but friendship is, and my friend embodies
this it.'[29] And, finally, it is clear that when Hartshorne talks
about unchangeability, he is not talking about timelessness. If
God is always holy and righteous, he is such 'in appropriate
accordance with changes in the objects of his righteousness'.[30]
God is not so much timeless as coeval with all possible time.
Referring to Bergson and Whitehead, he comments: 'it is time
and not thinghood that leads to God as the self-identity of
process'.[31] 'God is always adequate to every state of the world
. . . this does not conflict with, but even seems to imply, a
different state of God for every state of the world.'[32]

It would seem that indirectly, and with more concessions
to the tradition than we have thought necessary, Hartshorne
comes round to the conclusion towards which we are heading:
indeed, the last quoted passage might have been written
specially for our purposes. The difference is that he describes

[27] Tension is one thing: unexplained juxtaposition is another.
[28] *Man's Vision of God*, 1941, p. 108.
[29] *The Logic of Perfection*, 1962; all quotations from p. 4. And cf. particularly
the following quotation from his later work, *Anselm's Discovery*, 1965, p. 38:
'Existence is general and always means *somehow actualized* in a contingent
concrete form, just *what* form, or *how* actualized, never being necessary.'
[30] *Man's Vision of God*, p. 110.
[31] *Ibid.*, p. 269.   [32] *Ibid.*, p. 112.

himself as a rationalist and we are parading as empiricists, and though both he and we are so wide of the type that the difference might appear to be nominal, it must be remembered that he claims to be establishing by metaphysical argument the definitive truth of the matter,[33] while we claim to be establishing an empirically probable position which it is reasonable to crown with an act of faith. What we have to say at the end will in fact be even more like Hartshorne than what we are entitled to say now. As a defence of timelessness in God, resort to Hartshorne as a second line of defence is worse than useless; in the case of God, at least, he drives a wedge between timelessness and essence, thus ending a long and unhappily fruitful misalliance.

We shall proceed with our programme, therefore, undeterred by the prospect of a God moving in time, and convinced that so to depict him makes him more, not less, the master of the world. We shall return to the subject in the course of our final review.

8. *The Counter-evidence*

In the previous section we have tried to show that the concepts of 'morality' and of 'person' are, in their different ways, open-ended, and call for completion beyond their boundaries. The time might seem to have come for an analysis of the act of faith, in which the completion actually occurs. But there are several hurdles to be cleared first. In the first place, we have to examine the claim that in matters of religion the intellect has no standing. In general, we shall try to show that this view is the natural consequence of assuming that it has *all* the standing; in fact, that rationalism and fideism are the right and the left of the same movement of thought. In the second place, we shall have to look at the traditional proofs of the existence of God: not exhaustively, but in order to situate ourselves in relation to other ways of thinking. In general, we shall find that the arguments presuppose what they are intended to prove, but that their 'empirical premisses' serve as pointers, and they

[33] 'Here I am an ultra-rationalist', as he says in the collection, *Faith and the Philosophers*, ed. John Hick, 1964, p. 32.

themselves as an articulate representation of a completed faith. Both these topics will receive attention in the following chapter.

But the most urgent problem, which will occupy us for the rest of this chapter, is that of counter-evidence. We have been building, persistently if hypothetically, on the evidence of what is right with the world. In view of the inclination both of angry radicals and depressed conservatives to show that it is all wrong, the emphasis is, I believe, right and proper. But if we build on evidence, we must allow counter-evidence. Why should evidence one way count and evidence the other way be slighted? If order is evidence for God, sloth (in some ways the most deadly of the seven deadly sins) is very much evidence against him. If we testify to him by our good acts, intentionally or otherwise, we testify against him by our bad acts, again intentionally or otherwise; and who shall say that our good acts outweigh our bad ones? Certainly not those who have been taught by Christianity, long before Freud, to discern the ambiguous springs of goodness.

Now it is one of the main contentions of this book that the evidence does not go the whole way: it has to be completed in faith and verified in practice. It is therefore against its whole tenor to slur the counter-evidence. The only thing to do with it is to turn it into corroboration; and that is not what it is to start with. The last thing we wish, or can afford, to do is to affirm by faith against the facts.

Let us, then, take the most frequently cited, and the most damaging, piece of counter-evidence: the ubiquity and power in the world of suffering and wickedness. There is a familiar dilemma, first devised in the Middle Academy by Carneades: either God permits evil, and then he is not good; or he does not permit it, and then he is not all-powerful. As the combination of power and goodness is held, and I think rightly, to be what is distinctive of God, the dilemma is the most serious problem for religious belief.[34] It was devised by a Greek to meet a Greek philosophical situation, but it applies equally to philosophical

---

[34] That it does not arise for Buddhists has much to do with the interest shown in Buddhism by dissatisfied Westerners who want a religion but see no way of getting past it.

deism or undogmatic modernism. *And there is no general answer to it.* There is a particular answer, given by Christianity, and its efficacy depends on its particularity. All that can be done is to weaken the supports for the argument and thereby to prepare the way for the Christian answer.

1. The first, which is old and respectable, is that in the absence of the divine characters the world, and human affairs, would be unworkable. As Plato insists (*Republic* 613bc), one has to consider the long run. Of course the wicked may begin with a spurt and take the lead, but because of their 'injustice', i.e. the disorder in their souls, they cannot complete the course. In social affairs there is a similar appeal to the pendulum of history. Extremes swing back sooner or later into the orbit of civility. Horrors like Auschwitz bring their own retribution. There is some truth in these observations; but they do not carry the conclusion. In the first place, ice-cold egotism backed by far-sighted policy does not depend on disorder in the soul, and its devices can last a very long time. In the second place, even if evil courses do break down under their own weight, even if everything does come all right in the end, what about the godless interim? Does the destruction of the Nazis cancel out the sufferings of their victims?

2. It will be said, and again rightly, that suffering is not the major evil; to quote Plato again (*Gorgias* 469bc): 'it is worse to do injustice than to suffer it'. This is worth remembering in an age of vulgar utilitarianism; but (*a*) even if suffering is not the major evil, it is still an evil, or its prevention would not be a sign of moral excellence; and (*b*) in human affairs, suffering is the obverse of insensibility or cruelty. Even if suffering were part of the divine intention (which, for Auschwitz, it is difficult to believe), can we find any twisted or inverted blessing in the rubber truncheons of the SS Guards? Again, a truthful observation does not carry the conclusion.

3. It will be said that we must not give to God the lineaments of a man. If a man allowed all the evil that went into Auschwitz when he had the power to prevent it, we should not think well of him. But God is not a person in that sense of the word: the ultimate fact or sanction operates impersonally, and makes or breaks in accordance with the turn of the wheel. There is no

question of kindness or unkindness: the sanction does not produce the situations, it can only judge them, and this it does, grimly if slowly. There is something impressive in this story and in itself it is not unreasonable. It is unreasonable only in a Christian context. If 'he that hath seen me hath seen the Father', God cannot be indifferent. But, in a Christian context, God is already doing something about it; he is meeting the evil in the world in the only way in which it can be met: by identification and sacrifice. This is the point at which God's activity is personal: and it is one of the points at which Christian theology solves a problem where natural theology fails. But, as a defence against Carneades' dilemma, natural theology must not employ concepts which disqualify the Christian answer in advance, especially if they do not serve their purpose. To say that God is grim and faceless is no answer to the charge of indifference to suffering: it is indeed to admit it, and to invite more sensitive spirits to become atheists.

4. It will be said that practice provides the answer to theoretical agony, and it is certainly not unnatural that the fog of cosmic discouragement should descend most heavily on those who are, so to speak, under contract not to act, but to think and feel, the intellectuals and the artists. Evils are not so final for those committed to getting rid of them. The onlooker asks, How could this be allowed to happen? The agent replies, I don't know, but we can straighten it out. If intellectuals were more aware of their professional hazards, they might make more allowance for the scheme of things than they are wont to do. The world is not perfect; but it is good enough to make it worth improving. – All this is true, and when we come to analyse the requirements of practice we shall return to it; but it does not go to the root of the present difficulty. It is encouraging to be told that we can clean up the mess, but why is it there at all? Just ordinary little obstacles, yes; but do we need Auschwitz for our education?

5. It will be said that our sin is the price we pay for our freedom. This issue will concern us further in conclusion. Here we shall briefly anticipate by saying that we shall accept one kind of libertarian analysis, and in consequence do not have to think of God as the direct efficient cause of everything that

happens. It would certainly be better if we used our freedom more sensibly, but it would not be better if we ran on sinless tramtracks. Here we begin to whittle away at one horn of Carneades' dilemma. God, it is said, would not permit an evil. But he would have to if he is committed to freedom. We have re-interpreted omnipotence as the leading of free men; the test for power is not the absence of limits, but the extent to which freedom issues from it. When the time comes, this contention will be all-important: it provides some kind of an answer to the question, why should God permit any evil at all? But the fact remains that he does, and we cannot accept it uncomplainingly unless he provides some way of getting rid of it. That is something for which the Christian tradition is equipped, and the Christian tradition alone. Once again, the objection is well founded, but introductory.[35]

9. *Provisional Summary*

We have groped for fringes, and we have found them. We have done our best to follow the trend of natural religion; we have seen how many of the standard objections do not hold; we may even have been convinced that there are better reasons for believing than for not believing. Nevertheless, we can hardly be satisfied. The power of the counter-evidence is still with us; we have kept the issue open, but it is far from settled. What we have to understand is that, groping for fringes, we can expect no more. We are lucky to have the intimations that we do. We have found that the structures of the world resemble the attributes traditionally ascribed to God; but in human experience, at least, they occur in bursts and patches, and at the best congregate in drifts and do not exhibit a permanent direction. This is the inevitable consequence of an inevitably

---

[35] I have not here thought it necessary to present two standard theological defences: the theory that evil is only privation of good, and the theory that evil is not so evil if it is looked at from some superior point of view. Both these defences manifestly underplay the power and malignity of evil; they are sophisticated attempts to re-interpret the counter-evidence before it has time to speak for itself. The former, with academic gentility, turns a demon into a ghost. The latter is lacking in moral sensitivity: from any possible point of view, Auschwitz stinks.

empirical procedure. It is a commonplace that empirical knowledge is never final; and our knowledge of God is not only empirical, but clouded and hard to come by. This should lead us greatly to revere those whose sight is clearest; but even they present varied and intermittent accounts of him.

Are we, then, because we cannot satisfy the standards of objective necessity, to belittle what evidence we have, or are we to build on reasonable probabilities and look for corroboration elsewhere? The tradition has been to demand necessity: the counter-tradition is to deny that there is any such necessity and then to close the issue. Neither of these attitudes sufficiently emphasizes what predominates in a working religion: the element of faith. We shall have to undertake a careful analysis of faith in chapter VIII; here let it be said that it is a trust displayed in the absence of certainty, a personal commitment filling the gap between reasonable evidence and unfaltering action. If this is so, what is required of those who grope for fringes is reasonable expectation and that is all that the empirical approach can supply. Those who think they can have more make things much too easy for their critics.

Yet the demand for certainty (as opposed to necessity) is not wholly unjustified. For while the intellectual perspective is open, the practical exigency closes inexorably on each successive moment. It is a platitude to say that whatever we do has to be this and not that.[36] And whatever we do we have to back with an assurance out of proportion with its intellectual supports. Yet religion is a matter of doing as well as of believing. The trouble is that at one end it appears to demand a finality which from the other it is unable to provide. There is an open tension between intellectual experimentation and decisiveness in action, and both are essential to any considerable religion. The demand for certainty comes from the side of action. How it combines with intellectual empiricism will appear later in this essay.

[36] That does not exclude compromise, which is itself this and not that.

V

ON PROVING THE EXISTENCE OF GOD

1. *All Proofs are Self-contradictory: the Philosophical Version*

SINCE THE Western religions came into contact with Greek culture their more educated adherents have tried to show that the truth revealed to them by faith can be confirmed, supported, and even proved by philosophy. There has been tenacious resistance, from two quarters. On the one hand, old-guard fideists, with occasional sophisticated spokesmen, object to the deal in the name of religion. One may cite Tertullian, St Bernard, Luther, Pascal, and Kierkegaard; but they are only the eloquent representatives of a tongue-tied majority. For many ordinary believers the philosphers are professional trouble-makers; some philosophers, some of the time, feel like that themselves; and not to feel it at all is to be insensitive to the fruitful tension between philosophy and religion.

On the other hand, philosophers of an 'enlightened' turn of mind object in the name of philosophy. They claim that if philosophy goes about its task disinterestedly it will not conclude to God, either because it concludes to no-God, or because it believes itself unfitted to conclude in these regions at all. In the latter case, the 'modest' philosopher can make terms with obscurantist (but not with rational) religion, as is shown by the temporary alliance between Demea and Philo in Hume's *Dialogues Concerning Natural Religion*, by Mansel's exploitation of Hamilton's philosophical agnosticism in the interests of faith in the mid-nineteenth century, and, more recently, by the notable mutual sympathy of Barthians and Wittgensteinians – again at the expense of rational religion.

The prior issue in these complexities is the scope of philosophy. If the 'modest' view is accepted, neither theists nor atheists are philosophical starters: on the issue between them, philosophy has no means of pronouncing. The atheists can look after themselves; being essentially negative, they are mostly satisfied by philosophical scepticism. The theist, who has to maintain a positive position, is more awkwardly placed. Scepticism, for him, is as fatal as a straight negative.[1] To have no idea whether there is a God or not is an impossible condition to worship in. If that is the conclusion of philosophy, worship can be sustained only by stopping short of philosophy, or going past it.

Our first task, then, will be to consider the classical proofs of the existence of God. Our attitude towards them will inevitably be ambivalent. No empiricist, no matter how far out from base, can agree that existence is a matter of demonstration. So far, we shall find ourselves in the company of the critics. But the critics agree with the demonstrators in thinking that if demonstration is impossible, reason in religion has no standing. This common assumption is what we shall have to challenge. In the first place, even if the proofs are, or must be, inadequate, it would be strange if in the course of what purport to be proofs, there were no significant intimations. In the second place, the empirical philosopher will still be able to busy himself with the 'conspiration of innumerable causes', which produce conviction without imposing finality.[2] We must not allow the deficiencies of particular proofs, or the impossibility of any proof, to deter philosophers from exploring those facets of the world which have led thinking men to espouse a religion.

On that understanding, we proceed to consider two outstanding attempts, one from the side of philosophy, the other from the side of religion, to show that proofs are not possible.[3]

For modern philosophy, the problem begins with Kant: not altogether by intention, because Kant held that the moral arguments for God hold fast where the metaphysical fail; and

---

[1] That is to say, *complete* scepticism: if in the absence of certainty there are still good reasons, that is encouraging as far as it goes.

[2] The phrase is F. R. Tennant's, *Philosophical Theology*, Vol. II, 1930, p. 79.

[3] The proper order might seem to be to set out the proofs first and later to discuss the denial that proofs are possible. We propose here to invert it, to discuss the denial first. Our criticism of the denial will, it is hoped, put our criticism of the proofs into a better perspective.

not altogether in fact, because the moral arguments are conducted in the same manner as the displaced metaphysical arguments, though with nothing like the same sophistication. But, taking account of the history of thought, the *Dialectic* of the *Critique of Pure Reason* is a watershed. Thenceforward rational theology has flourished only in the Thomist revival, and in a few British and French philosophers with obstinately personalist predilections; in both cases against the current, and despite Kant's own morally grounded belief in God, freedom and immortality. The reason why Kant exerted so great an influence is not that he attempted the refutation of individual proofs; his efforts in that sense are impressive but not decisive, if only because he never stated the proofs in their strongest or most persuasive forms. What is in itself impressive, and most influential, is his argument that rational theology is formally impossible. Once that has been established, the refutation of individual proofs follows automatically, whether they appear in their mediaeval splendour or in the scholastic tatters of the German eighteenth century.

Kant's conclusions are much more far-reaching than his distinction between Understanding (*Verstand*) and Reason (*Vernunft*); but it is through that distinction that he approaches them, and by following up what looks like a linguistic issue we can best appreciate the momentous consequences. In the *Analytic of Pure Reason* he has laid it down that phenomena can be subsumed under the categories objectively and necessarily. But that is because they are phenomena. There is no such knowledge of things in themselves. Yet there is an irresistible 'natural disposition of the mind' to carry over to things in themselves the demand for unity under the categories which, in the case of phenomena, is shown to be justified. This is the illusion which gives rise to speculative metaphysics. Yet it is not wholly an illusion. The drive behind speculative metaphysics is the same as the drive behind science: the difference is that it has no empirical material to work on. Provided it is taken as 'regulative', not 'constitutive', it serves as the principle of the complete enterprise:

> Understanding may be regarded as a faculty which secures the unity of appearances by means of rules, and reason as being the faculty which

secures the unity of the rules of understanding under principles. Accordingly, reason never applies itself directly to experience or to any object, but to understanding, in order to give to the latter an *a priori* unity by means of concepts, a unity which may be called the unity of reason, and which is quite different in kind from any unity which can be accomplished by the understanding.[4]

This mode of statement allows of 'rational unity' in the case of morals, and it acknowledges its relevance in respect of knowledge. But it definitely excludes the objective application of what it affirms as an Idea, and therefore it means the total rejection of what Kant (and his contemporaries) called 'rational theology': 'No satisfactory proof of the existence of a being corresponding to our transcendental idea can be possible by pure speculative reason.'[5]

From such passages has flowed much scepticism about God; but what Kant was attacking was not religion, but the intellectualized abstractions of eighteenth-century modernism. The supreme cause, regarded merely as such, is not an object of religion; it is a piece of pseudo-science. 'We might, in strict rigour, deny to the Deist any belief in God at all, and regard him merely as the maintainer of the existence of a primal being or thing – the supreme cause of all other things.'[6] If we ask what Kant is attempting to discredit, we shall find a number of synonyms whose main point in common is their lack of religious interest. 'The ground of the possibility of all things' (p. 493, A.579, B.607); 'complete determination' (p. 491, A.577, B.605); '*ens realissimum*'; 'a transcendental ideal which serves as basis for the complete determination that necessarily belongs to all that exists', 'a conception of a thing . . . completely determined in and through itself, and known as the representation of an individual' (p. 491, A.576, B.604); 'that being which contains primordially in itself the sufficient ground of every effect' (p. 499, A.590, B.618); and, last of all, 'something which exists with absolute necessity' (p. 496,

[4] Translation by Kemp Smith, p. 303, A.302, B.359.
[5] Translation by Kemp Smith, p. 518, A.620, B.648.
[6] The excerpt is qualified by its context, but only to this extent: that the Deist is later admitted not to deny God, but merely to miss the point of him, cf. p. 526, A.633, B.661. But in any case, the contrast between 'God' and 'supreme cause' is significant.

A.585, B.613). Indeed, it might be said that one of Kant's achievements was to rescue the concept of God from these compromising entanglements: and even if it is possible (as I think it is) to find in them, after the event, some religious value, to maintain the religious pre-eminence of a being so described is to subordinate religion to the alleged requirements of philosophy.

It should be noted further that in denying the competence of 'reason', Kant does not exclude *reasons*. He is attacking metaphysical necessity, and he just assumes that the role of reason in respect of religion is to establish necessity. It is natural that he should have done so; the deists of his time assumed the same thing. When it comes to detail, it is only the ontological proof which he regards as wholly *a priori*; the others, and especially the physico-theological, contain empirical premises, and Kant's complaint, as we shall see, is not against these premises, but rather that they require the ontological proof to provide the necessitarian conclusion. Kant himself was impressed, against his will, by physico-theological considerations (p. 519, A.622, B.650); and if he had not assumed, with his opponents, that they laid claim to necessity, he could have allowed them (on his own showing) a certain probabilist persuasiveness.

Enough has been said to show that Kant's intransigence about the proofs arises from the intransigence of their claims. But it is these claims which are the subject of our present discussion. If we say 'reasons' instead of 'reason', we admit that the intellectual component of religion is relevant, but deny that it is sufficient. That is a far cry from eighteenth-century deism, and Kant cannot be blamed for taking the situation as he found it. We have to consider the claim to have *proved* the existence of God, and Kant's *proof* (*a priori*) that such proof is impossible.

On Kant's assumptions his conclusions follow easily. Reason in the ordinary sense produces certainty only within the limits of space and time. Propositions about God do not fall under that heading. Therefore there can be no certainty in propositions about God. In its more exalted sense, reason is only regulative, and rules are not existences. Therefore, there is no knowledge of any *existence* other than the spatio-temporal. The argument is conclusive: the detailed disproofs are only expansions and applications of it. The question is, therefore, whether the premisses are sound.

Kant's first premiss is that natural science is a body of knowledge which acquires its objectivity by being limited to appearances. This is a conclusion wholly favourable to religion, because it admits of religious supplementation. The contrary view, that natural science is of things in themselves, excludes from existence anything that natural science cannot cope with.[7] But if science comes by its necessity through being limited to phenomena, its categories – including causality – cannot be extended to things in themselves. So far there is nothing to complain about;[8] and theists would be wise to acquiesce.

Kant's second premiss is that the drift of traditional metaphysics is necessitarian. Certainly the theory as he states it lays great stress on logical completeness, and very little on perfection. In this it departs from the scholastic model (e.g. the Fourth Way of St Thomas), and does not satisfy the religious consciousness. Nevertheless, Kant appears to have thought the drift to be unavoidable. On no other terms can there be the complete intelligibility which is the paradigm even for science. At the same time that he pronounces the rationalist claim unsatisfiable, he insists on maintaining it as a criterion. It is here that he was perhaps at fault: being of his age and time, though he saw beyond them at so many points, he accepted the standard account of metaphysics in the eighteenth century, instead of questioning it, and on that basis concluded that metaphysics as a positive enterprise was impossible.[9] His test for metaphysics was completeness. He saw it to be incompatible with freedom, but he rejected metaphysics, not the test. That remains rationalist to the end.

To conclude. Kant has shown that *proofs* of the existence of

[7] It could still be true. But in favour of Kant's view we may cite his own clear conviction that it is incompatible with moral freedom; and this I, at least, should not wish to question.

[8] Many people will complain, indignantly. But they will be anti-empirical materialist reductionists.

[9] He also claimed to be introducing a new kind of metaphysics, concerned with the implications of knowledge in the sciences: but it has no application to the knowledge of God and therefore does not concern us.

God are impossible. It is in that spirit that he claims to 'abolish knowledge to make room for faith'. What he objects to is not God but the itch for demonstration. It might well be concluded that reason has no part to play in religion. But that is not Kant's considered view. As we shall see, he allows some persuasiveness, short of demonstration, to the physico-theological proof, and when it comes to 'practical reason', the containing of religion 'within the bounds of pure reason' is even exaggerated. What emerges from this cursory examination is that demonstration involves extending to the world as a whole the ways of thinking suitable to natural objects – a procedure which (we repeat) leads in the end to physicalism; that Kant was unable formally to think of metaphysics in any other terms; that his suspicions (given his premises) were justified; and that there are traces in him of an empirical approach to metaphysics which he rejects as inadequate, but on which others may work with profit. In the meantime, his criticism of all cast-iron demonstrations may be regarded as conclusive.

2. *All Proofs are Self-contradictory: the Religious Version*

Before examining the traditional proofs in detail, we shall consider an alternative presentation of the view that the existence of God cannot be proved; this time from the side of religion.

We have noted Kant's conviction that religion will not suffer from the disappearance of theological metaphysics. The view we have now to consider goes further. It affirms that as long as religion is entangled in theological metaphysics, it loses its authentic character as religion. The sophisticated formulation of this view is due to Kierkegaard, and it is to be found in the *Philosophical Fragments* and the *Concluding Unscientific Postscript*, the works in which, under the pseudonym of Johannes Climacus, he staged the struggle between religion and philosophy. As a habit of mind, it is much older and very widespread; what is interesting about Kierkegaard is that he does not merely contrast philosophy and faith and then opt for faith; he tries to show how philosophy intrinsically *cannot* discover God, and how in its despair it turns over, dialectically, *into* faith.

As a preliminary, we should note that *in any case* we should not expect a practising Christian to be interested in deist metaphysics. A practising Christian worships God in Three Persons; a concept not to be contained in that of a First Mover or of God-in-general. Moreover, the central doctrine of Incarnation has unquestionably an air of paradox. How can that which is infinite also be finite? How can that to which birth and death are irrelevant, be born and die? Kierkegaard, as we shall see, makes the most of the paradox; he stresses it vehemently, and kicks aside the stepping-stones which might diminish it. But it is certainly there, and the metaphysical deist does not grasp it at all. Even classical Thomism, distinguishing sharply as it does between the sphere of philosophy and the sphere of revelation, confines the paradox to revelation; and indeed what happened between St Thomas and (e.g.) Wolff was that the philosopher's God quietly dropped the particularist elements of Christianity and made religion look like adhesion to a rationalist philosophy. If Kierkegaard's reaction seems violent, these things must be borne in mind.

Moreover, as Kierkegaard pointed out, we should not expect a practising Christian to be interested in Hegel's correction of deism. The whole effect of 'The System' (as Kierkegaard derisively called it) is to link the elements laterally together instead of linking each of them vertically to God. Kierkegaard may have carried his passion for solitariness too far. 'How,' he asks, 'can a man communicate the conviction that the God-relationship of the individual is a secret?'[10] But it is also true that the individual in his relation to God is not simply a well-placed item in the world-historical succession. As such he is deprived of the 'subjectivity' which is the essential feature of religion – to use a later idiom, he becomes entirely 'he', not 'I' or 'thou'. Philosophy being essentially 'The System', and the system being such as to make the God-relationship impossible, again we should not be surprised that Kierkegaard regarded rational theology with suspicion. In fact, it is surprising that he was ready to go along with it as far as he did.

With this preparation, we proceed to the argument. There can be no proof of the existence of God, because proof is objective and God is not an object.

[10] *Concluding Unscientific Postscript*, D. F. Swenson, 1941, p. 72.

An object, by definition, is something which is thought or contemplated. It does not need to be 'existentially appropriated'. It does not matter who thinks or contemplates it: the paradigmatic cases, such as $2 + 2 = 4$, reduce every thinker to the same anonymous level. In more complicated cases, e.g. historical research, there is room for individual opinion, but no demand for it, and the point of it, where there is doubt (e.g. about the purpose of Caesar's invasions of Britain), is to find reasons which would reduce the scope for it in future historians. Objectivity, anonymity, psychical distance, impersonality: these are synonymous, and what they describe is the standardization of the individual by his outward interests. Some might say that this kind of selflessness is a good model for the understanding of religion.[11] But Kierkegaard finds in it an indifference, an uncommittedness, which is fatal to religion. God cannot be apprehended in this impersonal spirit. The 'leap' to God must gather up the whole of a man's 'passionate inwardness'; it must spur him on and leave him panting before the throne of Grace: above all it does not allow him to relax, or create in him an unproductive equilibrium. That way, the subject vanishes, and God with him.[12] God cannot be proved, because what can be proved, if it could be proved, cannot be God.

The contention is of particular concern to us because Kierkegaard bases it on an empirical conception of being. 'The knowing spirit is an existing individual spirit'[13] (unlike Hegel's Absolute Spirit, in which individual existence has been transcended), and is finite, limited, and incapable of embracing truth as a whole. 'Truth is at once transformed into a desideratum' – Kant's 'limiting conception' – 'and everything must be understood in terms of becoming, for the empirical object is unfinished and the existing cognitive spirit is in process of becoming.'[14] To prove the existence of God we should need a God's-eye view: we should have to be able to encompass God by sheer force of intellect; as finite creatures building up our small if growing

[11] See above, p. 44.
[12] Cf. *Concluding Unscientific Postscript*, p. 173: 'The way of objective reflection makes the subject accidental, and thereby transforms the subject into something indifferent, something vanishing.'
[13] *Ibid.*, p. 169.   [14] *Ibid.*

store of knowledge, we cannot rise to this infinite occasion, and (as noted above) if we could, we should have moved out of the possibility of a God-relationship. An empirical philosophy such as befits finite individuals cannot encompass God: only a Herr Professor can do that.[15] And by encompassing God, he denies God. He encompasses God abstractly and ideally, i.e. not at all.[16] But a proper empirical procedure maintains the distance between God and man, within which alone the apprehension of God is possible, and which makes the search for him that of a subject seeking his source in a pre-eminent subject, with the whole force of his being.

As we have in mind a comprehensive reconciliation of empiricism with theism, it is impossible not to be impressed by these considerations. It is important, however, to make distinctions. Kierkegaard does not mean that God can be empirically apprehended by direct inspection. Still less does he suppose that he is disclosed at the end of a long 'approximation process'.[17] What he is saying is *both* that the objective quest must be empirical, not comprehensive, *and* that the empirical quest, being 'approximative', cannot succeed. The advantage of the empirical approach is that it does not pretend to deliver the cosmos (as the 'System', does), and that it admits of complementation (as the 'System' does not). It preserves the subjectivity of the inquirer, and faces over the gap to a subjectivity literally past imagining. The empiricist does not always experience awe, but when he does he does not contradict himself. The rationalist system-maker has everything so well in hand that there is nothing left to be in awe of.

Our present concern with Kierkegaard is that he presents us with reasons why proving God's existence is impossible. At a later stage, we shall return and gather up the many intriguing suggestions that he makes in the course of discussion. At present, however, we have to consider the basic theme: 'subjectivity'.

[15] As a Dane not in academic employment, Kierkegaard snipes with great enjoyment at both Germans and university staff.

[16] Cf. *Concluding Unscientific Postscript*, p. 558, 'The misfortune of the present age is not that it is one-sided but that it is abstractly all-sided . . . the one-sidedness of the intellectual creates the illusion of having everything.'

[17] *Op. cit.*, p. 178.

'The objective accent falls on WHAT is said, the subjective accent on HOW it is said.'[18] It looks as if sincerity were being commended at the expense of truth. But no, truth is being estimated by the standards of sincerity. Consider the following passage.[19]

> If one who lives in the midst of Christendom goes up to the house of God, the house of the true God, with the true conception of God in his knowledge, but prays in a false spirit; and one who lives in an idolatrous community prays with the entire passion of the infinite, although his eyes rest upon the image of an idol: where is there most truth? The one prays in truth to God though he worships an idol; the other prays falsely to the true God, and hence worships in fact an idol.

Now it might well be said that the fervent idolator is the better man; he makes the utmost of what he has, while the self-deceiving Christian has everything and lets it slip. But is it nothing to have a *true* conception of God? If so, intensity of devotion is the whole of religion, and intensity of devotion may be shown in the pursuit of what is false and even wicked. If we reject this consequence, there must be *some* place in religion for an *objectively* true conception of God.

Once again, we must keep our bearings. To admit the importance of an objectively true conception of God is not to say that God can be clearly and distinctly known, or that his existence can be proved. But to deny the importance of an objectively true conception of God is to lend ourselves to any imposture which can stir our depths. It is because he takes this point, and because he wants to present Kierkegaard in the most reasonable light (not, perhaps, a very Kierkegaardian thing to do) that the Rev. James Brown writes of him: 'The highest passion of subjectivity is called forth by an Object, by the very highest and greatest possible Object, by God himself.'[20] But as he quotes Kierkegaard in the next sentence to the effect that in the leap of faith 'reason is set aside',[21] it is evident that the Object is not comparable to any other object; it is rather that to which the subject stands as a Subject. A possible if treacherous analogy would be the relation of a friend to a friend: there is

[18] *Op. cit.*, p. 181: capital letters, Kierkegaard's.
[19] *Op. cit.*, pp. 179f.
[20] *Subject and Object in Modern Theology*, 1955, p. 79.
[21] The reference is to *Philosophical Fragments*, tr. D. F. Swenson, 1936, p. 50.

at least the same distinction between knowing him and knowing about him. But, for what the analogy is worth, what it teaches us is that in knowing a friend, one knows a good deal about him as well, and that this knowledge is not separable from the more intimate business of knowing him. In the same way, though God cannot be sought out by syllogisms, his being an Object is essential to his subjectivity; it is what makes his subjectivity unique of its kind. Whether Brown is right in supposing that Kierkegaard saw this point seems to be doubtful, in view of what Kierkegaard has to say about 'subjective truth'. It is certainly what Kierkegaard ought to say if he is to save his position. But if he does, reasoning about God is at least relevant.

The same conclusion follows if we consider the structure of the sentence, 'God is not an object'. If objective truth has no standing, this statement, which is objectively intended, has no standing either. If it is to register, it must rest on an *objective* distinction between subject and object, each of them with discernible characteristics. Only the discriminating intellect can mark off the sphere of the objective, where it is at home, from the sphere of the subjective, with its 'passionate inwardness', which it does not master, but can readily discern, *because it issues from it.*

This brings us to the final difficulty. When we reflect on the distinction, we find it is not absolute. Philosophy is one expression of 'passionate inwardness' – that expression which is directed to objective discernment. It is one without which 'passionate inwardness' would be impoverished. Kierkegaard could see this in the case of Socrates, because Socrates thought with his life; his thinking and his mission were inseparable. What he disliked about the System was its impersonality; thinking it out did not commit its sponsors to anything. 'Intercourse with the world-historical tends to make individuals unfit for action.'[22] They get the impression that they are grist in the teleological mill, and behave accordingly.[23] It is perhaps

[22] *Concluding Unscientific Postscript*, p. 121.
[23] Unfortunately Kierkegaard was wrong: those who identify themselves with the world-historical process, Marxians, for example, are untiring and unscrupulous.

unfair to belabour the philosopher for the alleged shortcomings of the Herr-Professoriate, and it is perhaps significant that Kierkegaard aims no shafts at the succession of non-professorial philosophers from Descartes to Hume. Even the Herr Professor has his peculiar sense of honour and professional dedication. No philosopher of any standing has been lacking in 'passionate inwardness', and least of all Hegel. The second-raters, perhaps; but that is because they are second-raters, and not because they are philosophers.

We have, therefore, in an important sense to qualify the concept of 'subjective truth'. There is indeed a propensity to self-deception, remarked upon by existentialists from Kierkegaard to Sartre, and it is only too true that there is a fatal gap between understanding and performance. But though objectivity (in Kierkegaard's sense) does not guarantee personal integrity, personal integrity does require objectivity, as the thinker understands it. This is so in all contexts, and not least in the supreme context of religion. There is a crucial passage in italics in which Kierkegaard all but admits it, only to sheer away violently at the last moment. As it brings the whole matter to a head in a short space, I take the liberty of quoting it in full:[24]

When the question of truth is raised in an objective manner, reflection is directed objectively to the truth, as an object to which the knower is related. Reflection is not focussed upon the relationship, however, but upon the question of whether it is the truth to which the knower is related. If only the object to which he is related is the truth, the subject is accounted to be in the truth. When the question of truth is raised subjectively, reflection is directed subjectively to the nature of the individual's relationship; if only the mode of this relationship is in the truth, the individual is in the truth even if he should happen to be thus related to what is not true.

In this passage there is explicit reference to a 'truth to which the Knower is related', i.e. objective truth is a kind of truth, but instead of being incorporated, it is put decisively on one side; if the relationship is 'in the truth', no matter what one is related to, all is well. Either there is here a plain linguistic ambiguity ('true' in English = either 'constant' or 'the case', and the translation reads as if there must be a similar ambiguity

[24] *Concluding Unscientific Postscript* p. 178.

in Danish), or concern for what is the case is held to be of no account. This doctrine is death to philosophy, and in so far as religion has an intellectual component, it is at least an amputation of religion. It is a pity that the zeal of Kierkegaard in unmasking fraudulent intellectuals should lead him to downgrade the intellectual enterprise as such. He draws attention to a standing temptation to which idealists have been peculiarly prone – that of supposing that one can master the material world in the act of thinking about it; and he has not noticed how much of the philosopher's task consists in bringing this congenial error under control. The misrepresentation is only partly attributable to his preoccupation with 'the System'. It is also a symptom of overstrain in Kierkegaard's religious consciousness – the good is always an enemy of the best.

The doctrine of 'subjective truth' makes too little of the element of insight in religion; it allows none of the overhangs and loose ends of divinity which have seemed to us to be so significant; it repudiates the ladder of approximation by which so many decent ordinary souls make their way towards God, without the cataclysm of conversion from despair; in short, it is too much anchored to the uncompromising formula, Either-Or, which is magnificent in a crisis but too abrupt for the graces of a continuous culture, or the subtleties of intellectual endeavour. But the underlying conviction that being a subject is something which can only indirectly be represented as an object remains, is important, and is a warning against expecting too much from the traditional 'proofs'. Elsewhere[25] I have suggested the analogy of a photograph of a three-dimensional object: it misrepresents, but according to a pattern, and it is possible by following the inadequate translation (e.g. through the accentuation of light and shade) to gain some impression of the three-dimensional contours. In any case, on any showing, there is much about God which remains a mystery: but *that* there is mystery would never be guessed but for what can be known.

In what follows, we shall examine the proofs in order. We shall expect to find that they fall short of demonstration, but contain pointers and indicators which, taken together, con-

[25] *Sophia*, Vol. V, No. 2, 1966, p. 8.

siderably enlarge our understanding. Kant and Kierkegaard between them have established the first point, but, thanks to their all-or-nothing frame of reference, have underestimated the second. It is to this mast that a religious empiricist must nail his colours.

VI

THE TRADITIONAL PROOFS

1. *The Ontological Argument*

THE ontological proof of (or argument for) the existence of God is the earliest in modern Christian history in point of time, and raises the most fundamental issues. It has had a chequered career. Propounded by St Anselm in the *Proslogion* (chapters 2–4), it was criticized by St Thomas Aquinas, reiterated by St Bonaventura, reinstated by Descartes, developed, with important logical additions, by Leibniz, utterly discredited by Kant, generalized into ineffectiveness by Hegel, treated with contempt or condescension by both Thomists and empiricists over the last century, and within the last decade resurrected in the USA by Norman Malcolm and Charles Hartshorne. This is an intriguing story, and bears witness to the fascination of the argument itself. Even those who eventually decide against it have wondered from time to time whether it might not be valid, and have mulled over it in amazement and exasperation. But nearly everyone – Professor Hartshorne is a notable exception – has treated it as the rationalist argument *par excellence*, containing no empirical premises or references. It is therefore central to our thesis to consider it in detail, and in particular to consider whether the orthodox interpretation is correct. If it *is* correct, and the argument is valid, there is a cast-iron non-empirical demonstration of God, and empirical pointers do no more than confirm where no confirmation is needed.

The argument as stated by Anselm is to be found in two versions, in *Proslogion* II and III. In the first version, it runs as follows: God is that than which nothing greater can be thought (*id quo maius cogitari non potest*); but that which exists in itself is greater than that which exists by way of thought; therefore, God, if thought, exists.

The classical objection, clinched and vulgarized by Kant, is that there is no passage from thought to existence. On this, we offer the following observations:

1. It is not being suggested that the passage from thought to existence (if that is what it is) applies in general terms. It applies only to the special case of God, than whom 'nothing greater can be thought'. The contemporary reference to 'perfect islands' (Gaunilo), and Kant's sneer about the merchant adding noughts to his cash account, are therefore beside the mark. Anselm was not an idealist; nor, despite the impetus given to idealism by his theory of perception, was Descartes.

2. The first premiss of the argument is undoubtedly defensible. It is not possible to think of God except as that than which nothing can be greater. To affirm God is to affirm such a being: to deny God is to affirm that there is none.[1] In the Fifth Meditation, Descartes makes this point clear by separating the two phases of the argument; and the conclusion of the first, namely that the *concept* of God entails the *concept* of existence, is one which might be accepted even by those who deny that the concept has any application. And the *concept* of God is in this respect unique: of no other concept could it be said that existence is contained in it as the equality of its interior angles to two right angles is contained in the concept of a triangle. As Anselm says: 'That-than-which-a-greater-cannot-be-thought cannot exist in the mind alone. For if it exists solely in the mind even (*vel in solo intellectu est*) it can be thought to exist in reality also, which is greater.'[2]

3. The obvious retort is that while it is true of the *concept* of God that it uniquely includes reality, it does not follow that he really exists. One may argue, as Descartes did, that if he does not, there is a radical discontinuity between concept and existence from the top downwards, such as makes nonsense of science and of everyday discourse, but if a confirmed sceptic

[1] One reason, if I may stray over the borderlands of revelation, why Christ is God, is that if he were not, there would be something greater than God, which is absurd.

[2] *Proslogion* II, translation by M. J. Charlesworth, *St Anselm's Proslogion*, 1965, p. 117.

merely shrugs his shoulders and says 'So what?', is there anything more that can be said to him? Anselm replies: 'If that-
than-which-a-greater-cannot be thought exists in the mind
alone, this same that-than-which-a-greater-*cannot*-be-thought
is that-than-which-a-greater-can-be-thought.'[3] It is at this
point that one is particularly tempted to open one's mouth,
and swallow it whole. But the argument is only pushed one
stage further back along an infinite regress of receding concepts. The breakthrough from concept to reality is a break-
through in concept only.

4. Both Anselm and Descartes, at this point, escape by
locating themselves at the Godward end, thus helping the
argument to its feet by taking its conclusion for granted. In
Proslogion IV Anselm turns from the distinction between
thought and existence which he has been trying to bridge, to a
distinction between two senses of thought: 'In one sense a
thing is thought when the word signifying it is thought; in
another sense when the very object which the thing is, is understood.'[4] In the latter sense, there is no gap between thought and
existence, and if God is thought, then of course he exists. But
that is not the sense in which 'concept' is used in chapter II,
where it is contrasted with reality, and the mere 'word' (*vox*)
does not enter into the picture at all. The original feature of
Anselm's thought fades out into a Platonic realism – which
would not have permitted his problem to be raised.

In the same way, Descartes, in the Fifth Meditation, having
made the undoubtedly important point that it is as repugnant
to conceive a God who lacks the perfection of existing as it is
to conceive a mountain without a valley, turns round and
objects to himself that 'my thought imposes no necessity on
things', but adds that whereas there need not be in reality
either mountains or valleys, there must in reality be existence
if there is God, because in this case 'the necessity which is in
the thing itself, that is to say, the necessity of the existence of
God, determines me to have this thought'.[5] It is true that for

[3] Again *Proslogion* II, *ibid.*
[4] Translation by Charlesworth, *St Anselm's Proslogion*, pp. 120f.
[5] *Œuvres*, ed. Adam and Tannery, VII. 67; cf. for further comment my
Philosophy of Descartes, 1932, p. 140.

Descartes the ontological proof is subsidiary,[6] and that he had already proved the existence of God to his satisfaction by other means, but that is not sufficient reason for closing down his own discussion of concept and reality in such summary fashion from the Godward end.

2. *Anselm's Twentieth-century Comeback*

It is at this point that Professors Norman Malcolm and Charles Hartshorne introduce what they believe to be an important distinction between the argument of *Proslogion* II and that of *Proslogion* III.[7] In his recent work, *Anselm's Discovery*, Hartshorne asks (p. 11): 'Does the reader not see a difference which is more than rhetorical between (1) "that which exists in reality as well as in the mind is greater than that which exists in the mind alone" and (2) "that whose nonexistence cannot be conceived is greater than that whose nonexistence can be conceived"?' The difference is certainly unmistakable, and the lack of attention to it in the main stream of philosophical comment between 1078 (when the *Proslogion* was completed) and 1960 (when Malcolm wrote his article in the *Philosophical Review*),[8] justifies Hartshorne's indignation. In *Proslogion* III the rendering is: 'If that-than-which-a-greater-cannot-be-thought can be thought not to exist, then that-than-which-a-greater-cannot-be-thought is not the same as that-than-which-a-greater-cannot-be-thought, which is absurd.'[9] As Malcolm puts it, existence is not a perfection, but necessary existence is: and that God should lack this perfection is inconceivable. Or, as Hartshorne puts it, the argument is transposed to the field of modal logic. 'Contingency alone makes existence a question of extralogical facts' – and God is not contingent. As Leibniz

---

[6] Cf. M. Guéroult, *Nouvelles réflexions sur la preuve ontologique de Descartes*, 1955.

[7] There is a similar distinction between the Descartes of the Fifth Meditation and the Descartes who replied to the *Second Objections*.

[8] But the citations from St Bonaventure and Duns Scotus in M. J. Charlesworth's *St Anselm's Proslogion*, pp. 4f., show that these writers were well aware of the argument of *Proslogion* III; and Descartes, under criticism, rediscovered it (*Reply to Second Objections: Demandes; en cinquième lieu*; Adam *and* Tannery, VII. 163); for Leibniz, see below.

[9] *Op. cit.*, tr. M. J. Charlesworth, p. 119.

said, 'God must exist if he is possible'[10] – and he is possible if the concept of him is not self-contradictory.

There is, we repeat, much more in *Proslogion* III than in *Proslogion* II; but does it help us? It appears to push the ontological proof more decisively into the *a priori* camp where it has commonly been supposed to belong. Nor, it would seem, does it vindicate Anselm. Like Descartes, when pressed hard enough, he retreats into the simple realism from which he had abstracted himself for the purpose of conducting his proof. If *Proslogion* II is a *non sequitur*, *Proslogion* III is a *hysteron proteron*. The emphasis switches from 'that-than-which . . .' to 'the being (that) so exists that not even in thought can it not exist'.[11] 'Not even in thought' (*nec cogitatione*): thought is where he might most easily not exist (and how right this is); in reality he could not possibly not exist. Yet earlier the impossibility of his not existing in thought has been used as an argument for his *really* existing. In introducing *necessary* existence, Anselm has simultaneously switched to the God's-eye view. This is an insidious temptation for believers trying to understand, and in *Proslogion* III–IV Anselm has not succeeded in avoiding it.

Still, it may be said, Anselm may be confused, but his critics may also be confused, and his argument can be rehabilitated. That is the contention of Hartshorne in *Anselm's Discovery*. The picture he presents is of an Anselm whose intimations are frustrated by the Greek framework of his thought, and requiring, to set him up in business, something like the 'neoclassical' theism of Hartshorne himself. The transaction would run roughly as follows. 'Necessity' has proved a difficult conception in theology (along with impassivity, timelessness, and other Greek adjuncts) because it is thought to hold of God over his whole extent. The ontological proof as restated in *Proslogion* III emphasizes his necessity. Now in one sense we should all agree: it is contrary to what we all mean by God that he should be *merely* contingent; that is why some of us worship, and why others are atheists. But, according to 'neoclassical' theism, necessity attaches to him as absolute, while his commerce with the world shows him in his relative per-

---

[10] *Monadology* 345.
[11] *Proslogion* IV, tr. Charlesworth, p. 121.

fection, i.e. the changing expressions of his nature which exhibit his supremacy in every possible situation. It cannot then be urged against the ontological argument that in favouring necessity it favours impassivity and timelessness; they all belong to God's nature in one aspect only, and no more than their opposites. Now I am sympathetic with this general point of view, provided (see above, p. 98) that the element of timelessness is treated as a subordinate structure sustaining the fullness of life, and I am happy that an overstatement in my article, 'The Two Strands of Natural Theology',[12] should have provoked Hartshorne into accepting the proviso. I claimed that 'the ontological proof runs on purely logical lines and cannot be converted to a temporalist gauge'. Hartshorne has justly convicted me of thinking here in terms of the 'classical' theology, and insists, justly again, that the argument 'belongs with the view that only the bare essence and existence of God, taken as an extreme empty abstraction, is timeless or *a priori*'.[13] 'All else,' he adds, 'is empirical and in some fashion temporal – even for God, and indeed *especially for God*, who does not share the illusions of the ultrarationalists!'[14] He even concludes, 'only a concretely temporalistic theology can rightfully employ the Argument'.[15]

These passages are most reassuring, but they drastically reduce the scope of the argument. On Hartshorne's own showing, it now relates only to the bone-structure of religion; the rest falls outside it. It is on these conditions that he finds the proof acceptable. On these conditions, it is surprising that he finds it important; and no one, I venture to think, would be more surprised than Anselm.

But let us return to the restated argument. It is (subject to the above considerations) what Leibniz made of it: 'If God is possible, then he is necessary.' *Prima facie*, to say that God is possible is to say that he might or might not be. What Leibniz and Hartshorne insist on is that a possible God is absurd; and from that absurdity the argument proceeds. For 'concept' (*Proslogion* II), read 'possibility'. Everything then turns on the various meanings of 'possible'. If 'possible' is contrasted with

---

[12] *Process and Divinity*, p. 488.   [13] *Anselm's Discovery*, p. 192.
[14] The italics and the exclamation mark are his.   [15] *Op. cit.*, p. 193.

'impossible', of course God is possible, but this does not mean either that he is necessary or that he exists. It means, at the most, that he cannot definitely be said not to exist. If 'possible' is contrasted with 'actual', then there is a disinclination to say that God is possible (= *only* possible), and that the concept requires to be filled out by 'necessary,' or at least 'probable' enough to be believed in. Or, finally, 'possible' can be contrasted with 'necessary'. In the first case we have 'possible but not necessary'. In the second case, we have 'not merely possible but necessary (or near enough)'. In the third case we have either 'possible but not necessary' or 'necessary and therefore not just possible'. But in none of these cases do we have, 'possible, *therefore* necessary'. To say that, one would have either to jump from thought to things, or to align oneself with things in advance, and work back to thought.

There is, however, a further sense of 'possible', in which it relates the present to the future. Malcolm argues that God must be necessary because, if he were not, he would 'either have been *caused* to come into existence or have *happened* to come into existence, and in either case he would be a limited being, which by our conception of him he is not'.[16] 'Since he cannot come into existence, if he does not exist, his existence is impossible.' This version of the proof applies, it will be seen, to the whole nature of God, and is not limited by Hartshorne's neoclassical formula. Anselm might have been more at home with it, but on the other hand, if relentlessly interpreted, it would fail to 'save the phenomena' about which Hartshorne is properly concerned. Again, it will be helpful to comment number-wise.

1. It would have to be shown that the concept of God is not self-contradictory. Malcolm's way with this objection is short enough: no demonstration is required in the case of a material thing, and no more is required in the case of God. 'Both concepts have a place in the thinking and the lives of human beings.'[17] As Wittgenstein said, 'the language game is played', and there are times when it would be convenient to be a Wittgensteinian. Malcolm certainly adds that this blanket

16 'Ontological Arguments', *Philosophical Review*, Vol. LXIX, 1960, pp. 49f.
17 *Op. cit.*, p. 60.

sanction does not apply to particular reasonings. These, in either case, have to be considered on their merits. But, even so, there are those who maintain that the concept of God is not merely subject to revision (on this we agree with Malcolm), but intrinsically incoherent. That it is honestly maintained by various people in various forms does not prove that it is not self-contradictory; but it is impossible to say whether a concept is self-contradictory without knowing what the concept is *of*: and to know that it is necessary to descend into detail. It can neither be disposed of nor defended in general terms. As we have contended more than once, it is a question of letting the evidence count.

2. In asking us to take religious language seriously, Malcolm quotes Psalm 90: 'Before the mountains were brought forth, or even thou hadst formed the earth and the world, even from everlasting to everlasting, thou art God', and he adds: 'here is expressed the idea of the necessary existence and eternity of God, an idea that is essential to the Jewish and Christian religions'.[18] Evidently he does not interpret necessary existence and eternity neo-platonically. That being so, he will have to schematize them in time before they will serve his purposes.[19] 'Everlasting' does *not* entail 'timeless', but precludes it. And to fire it off into the orbit of the ontological proof is to suggest that the ontological proof is not as *a priori* as it looks.

3. The suggestion is confirmed by a moving and remarkable passage, confessedly in debt to Kierkegaard, in which Malcolm surmises that the genesis of the concept of God has to do with the admitted fact of an 'unbearably heavy conscience',[20] and that it is by ignoring this and other relevant human phenomena that 'many philosophers believe that the idea of a necessary being is an arbitrary and absurd construction'.[21] The emptiness of necessary being is here filled with a vengeance; it is precisely the kind of evidence that our kind of empiricism relies on. But it takes us further away from 'modal logic', and makes of

[18] *Op. cit.*, p. 56.
[19] I have raised the general issue in my article, 'The Two Strands of Natural Theology', in *Process and Divinity*, ed. Reese and Freeman, pp. 487f., and shall return to it in conclusion, cf. p. 242.
[20] *Op. cit.*, pp. 6of.   [21] *Op. cit.*, p. 61.

necessity itself a fact of experience. This is not necessity in the strict objective sense which the more formal model requires.

4. When all is said, the more formal model does not escape the fundamental defect of the first statement. It introduces complexities, but it remains exposed to the charge that a necessity of thought is transferred to things, or a necessity of things postulated to account for the necessity of thought. Anselm has fairly depicted *fidem quaerentem intellectum*: remove the faith, and the proof is gone.

We are thus forced to deny the efficacy of the argument as presented, both in its simpler and its more sophisticated form. Yet its power to stimulate remains unimpaired. Not only does it conduce (as observed by Thomas McPherson, at the end of an analysis more detailed than is here possible[22]) to the clarification of the concept of God, but, in exploring the distinction and the continuity between thought and reality, it prepares the way for the total conspectus which will be possible only when faith has been reintroduced into the picture.[23] In the meantime, we may note that the proof is not wholly *a priori*. It starts from the notion of that than which nothing greater can be thought. It is surely a fact that somebody *has* this notion; it is not a disembodied entity. There is an empirical premiss here which the rationalism of the demonstrators has concealed. It is the *having* of the concept which sets the whole argument going. In Bernard Shaw's *St Joan*, Act I, the following dialogue takes place:

Joan I hear voices telling me what to do. They come from God.
de Baudricourt They come from your imagination.
Joan Of course; that is how the messages of God come to us.

Joan insists that God speaks to us from the inside through our proper human endowments. Following that train of thought,

---

[22] *The Philosophy of Religion*, 1965, p. 49.

[23] McPherson justly observes, *op. cit.*, p. 37, that the objections levelled against the proof are 'more serious against Anselm's Argument in isolation than . . . in its context'. Kant started the trouble by talking about 'the proof', as if it could be detached from its historical contexts. In Anselm, the aura of faith is never absent and the proof is an effort in deliberate abstraction which was never wholly successful but completely admirable and historically of great importance.

our having the concept of God might be one of the ways that God gets at us. How far the line of argument could be carried is an open question; is there, for example, an argument for the existence of God in the fact of going to church? If there is a God, it is to be expected that he will be refracted in human thought and practice. But the question has been raised, can we show that there is a God? – and until we have an affirmative answer, neither the thought nor the practice can be qualified as refractions. Descartes attempted to provide against this objection by arguing that our having the idea of God could not be caused by anything less than God himself: but, even if he was right, he was going far beyond the bounds of the ontological argument. From the concept as such, distinguished from reality, we cannot conclude extra-conceptually.

Yet, though it does not demonstrate, as the argument is supposed to do, this version of it has considerable suggestive power. If the concept of God is God *in us*, it is not a fragment of pure intellect; it has a personal context in the aesthetic, moral and religious responses of a living creature. What it loses as a proof it gains as a guide. As the pivot of a life, the concept of God is a pointer, though not a guarantee. If we see some of the best people we know living by it and through it, it is hard not to assign *some* efficacy to it as a clue to things, even though its impact varies from almost complete per-meation to almost no influence at all. If even a few forthright testifiers proclaim the concept of God and evince it in their lives, this is evidence to be taken account of, and it cannot be silenced by weight of numbers.[24]

It remains true, however, that the propounders of the ontological argument, in arguing from the concept, have not usually taken into account its personal context, nor have they admitted that it is evocative rather than demonstrative. If there is any virtue, or unwisdom, in our extension of it, they cannot be held wholly responsible. Nevertheless, they have

[24] In this connexion, we must be careful not to confuse *having* the concept of God and *responding* to it. Those who have it may be irresponsive, and those who do not have it may be thoroughly responsive to it provided it is suitably disguised; e.g. atheistic social workers or atheistic artists. They see the radiations of the good though they turn away from its concentrated light. This is one of the triumphs of *Deus absconditus*.

provided the initial impetus; they have insinuated the fruitful suggestion that the concept of God, soberly and responsibly meditated, is a prolongation of God in us.

3. *The Cosmological Argument*

In the *Summa Theologica*, St Thomas Aquinas set forth five proofs (the famous 'Five Ways') for the existence of God. They may be summarized as: (1) the argument from motion to a Prime Mover; (2) the argument from efficient causes to a primordial efficient cause; (3) the argument from the finite to the necessary; (4) the argument from 'better' to 'best'; (5) the argument from the purposiveness of the world to a Purposer. The fourth is the origin of 'moral' arguments, from Kant downwards. The fifth gives rise to, though it is farther-reaching than, the argument from design. The first three, since Kant, have been lumped together as 'the cosmological proof'. Also, since Kant, the third has been regarded as the heart of the matter.[25] The first, to which Aquinas attached especial importance, had slipped out in the eighteenth century as part of the discredited Aristotelian physics.[26] The second, based on the impossibility of an infinite regress of efficient causes, had become precarious since doubt had been thrown on the conception of efficient cause by Hume, and by Kant himself in the *Analytic* of the *Critique of Pure Reason*; and the problem of the infinite regress can be subsumed under the third.[27] Kant was right in bringing the First and Second Ways under the Third Way, and finding in the Third Way the centre of the whole proof. Very briefly, it runs: if everything were capable of existing or not existing, there would be a chance of there being nothing; and from nothing there can come nothing. But there are existing things; therefore there must be necessary

[25] Cf. H. D. Lewis, *Philosophy of Religion*, 1965, p. 162.

[26] Motion, in the argument, does not mean physical motion: it means *l'amor che muove il sole e le altre stelle*, as in the last line of *The Divine Comedy*. But this is just what the physicists and their satellite philosophers in the eighteenth century found most unintelligible.

[27] The Third Way does not occur in the earlier *Summa Contra Gentiles*, and, as M. Gilson has shown (*The Philosophy of St Thomas Aquinas*, trs. E. Bullough, 1924, p. 64), was borrowed at a later stage from Moses Maimonides.

existence. As Copleston points out,[28] this is a complicated formulation, designed to sidetrack the problem of an infinite regress in time. Kant states it more simply, and not unfairly: 'If anything exists, an absolutely necessary being must also exist. But I, at least, exist. Therefore an absolutely necessary being exists.'

In this argument, in contrast to the ontological proof as ordinarily understood, there is an empirical premiss. 'The proof,' Kant continues, 'really begins with experience', but 'abstracts from all special properties through which this world may differ from any other possible world'. The addition shows that the reference to 'I' is purely incidental; he may well have been thinking of Descartes, in whose version of the proof it is central. As a minor premiss, 'something exists', would have been sufficient, and less compromising: nothing that follows suggests that personal existence is more significant for the proof than any other kind of existence.[29] From *any* kind of finite experience or event, not because it is experience or event, but from the mere fact of its finitude, it follows that there must be a necessary being. The alternative is an infinite regress, not necessarily in time, but of possibilities, and there is no meaning in 'possible' except in relation to 'necessary'. There is here not merely extreme elaboration; there is also the existentialist overtone: 'There might be nothing.' The question which echoes through the complexities of the cosmological argument is the simple-minded edge-of-the-cliff question: how is there anything here at all? Only a necessary being can reassure us: and that, as Aquinas says and as Kant repeats, is what men call God.

If it is a virtue in a philosophical theory to produce dizziness, the cosmological argument is most successful. The picture of an endless regress of causes going behind the utmost resources of the imagination leaves one breathless and more than ready to settle for a stop somewhere. But it must be one stop; more than

[28] *Aquinas*, 1955, p. 120.
[29] As we proceed, we learn that the cosmological argument is attempted 'independently of empirical principles' (tr. Kemp Smith, p. 514): but the reference here is to its applying the categories beyond their proper limits: it is still true that it 'presupposes experience in general' (tr. Kemp Smith, p. 508).

one, and the whole process begins again. And unless there is that one stop, all the intermediate stages are only provisional; they demand a ground as much as the last stage from which we start. And the ground must be necessary, because only what is necessary can provide support for an otherwise interminable procession. There is a permanent satisfaction in being first intellectually shaken and then restored to assurance. Hegelians have sometimes claimed a monopoly of this attraction, but Maimonides and St Thomas were well before them.

As part of the Thomist vista, it fits perfectly. But it depends on assumptions which in the eighteenth century were becoming increasingly insecure. Its flank was no longer covered by the Aristotelian philosophy of motion. It is clearly incompatible with the revised notion of cause, either in its Humian form, which subjectivizes necessity, or in its Kantian form, which restricts objective necessity to the connexion of phenomena. It is no longer what it was in the high noon of Thomism, the coping-stone of a philosophy of nature – moreover, it appeared increasingly irrelevant to contemporary religion. It was a continuing philosophical construction with the stones steadily slipping from under it.

Nevertheless, no matter what scientific or confessional props are withdrawn, necessary being is something that philosophical theists are not disposed to abandon. That is why an increasing proportion of the decreasing number of philosophers concerned for religion look to Thomism for a life-line. What, it is asked, could be made of a God who might not have been, or merely happened to be? It is this question, along with less enduring matter, with which the cosmological argument is so properly concerned.

As is well known, Kant put the question aside as unanswerable: 'The concept of necessity is only to be found in our reason, as a formal condition of thought; it does not allow of being hypostatized as a material condition of existence.'[30] What does the theist stand to lose if Kant is right? Not God; only the identification of God with an *ens necessarium*. The cosmological proof purports to provide necessary being. But is this being *logically* necessary? If so, in what sense? Something to

[30] *Critique of Pure Reason*, tr. Kemp Smith, p. 518.

which argument forces us to conclude? But in that case it is the argument which is necessary, not the Being. Necessary existence is not a matter of logic: it is a particular and superlative exhibition of existence itself. It is much *more* existence than any other kind of existence. So expressed, it is not in conflict with empiricism: its necessity is, so to speak, qualitative: it must be *what it is*, and what it is can be explored only tentatively and even experimentally. Where Kant was wrong was in posing the question in such a way that it could only be answered by Yes or No. In refusing to say Yes in terms of the contemporary situation he was completely in the right. And that conclusion is by no means necessarily anti-theistic. If it were, the empirical approach would be disqualified in advance, and its advocates could only consort with sceptics and atheists.

Thus, by way of the cosmological argument, our main theme opens up. The following observations may help to clarify it.

1. There are *things*[31] (not merely connexions between them) which are longer-lasting and structurally more central than others. If we follow our method of expanding implications,[32] we shall find ourselves steadily moving towards a being indefinitely long-lasting and structurally central for the whole world of things, including ourselves. This is only approximation, but approximation means 'getting nearer to', even if asymptotically. It does not afford more than a reasonable hope that there is something to be approximated *to*. But the overlap of the substance and the promise at least suggests that the promise is the centre of the substance. Amazing previews break upon those who are content to work forward step by step.

2. On the other hand, though every trend is intentional (by definition, it is *towards* something), not every intentional object is a real object – as Brentano, who fathered this kind of talk, knew very well. We can think of a world with a more and more sensitive organization, a more and more concentrated creativity; in a way, we can see it coming: but it lurks tantalizingly below the horizon. The proper attitude to it is one of reasonable

---

[31] Events, if you prefer: the distinction does not here concern us.

[32] For the phrase, and the germ of the idea, see my *Philosophy of Descartes*, p. 124.

expectation, but not of certainty. If there were logical necessity in the case, only certainty would be in order.

3. Pulling these threads together, we conclude that the facts justify hope but not complete assurance. But, in religion, the initiate *has* assurance, and even the beginner or the side-stepper feels he might achieve it. Not, certainly, the assurance that things will go his way; rather, the deeper assurance that if they do not, it is still well with the world. That kind of assurance, however, is not based on demonstration. It is easier for simple people than it is for philosophers. It requires an intellectual minimum; it would be incompatible with utter formlessness and chaos; but it does not require intellectual completion.

The proper consideration of this point requires an analysis of faith, together with its companion canonical virtue, rarely alluded to by philosophers – hope. But if anything like it is true, the empirical approach to theism is open, and indeed imposed on us.

We must now return to Kant's objections. In so far as they are objections to the view that the existence of God can be logically proved, we shall have to welcome them, if with reservations. In so far as they claim to disqualify *all* apprehension of God by way of intellect, we shall have to take issue with him.

1. In the *Antinomies*, both sides of the argument purport to be demonstrative; what Kant is asserting is that neither demonstration will serve (First and Second), or, more disturbingly, that both will serve (Third and Fourth). There may be flaws in his expositions here and there, but there is no point in exploiting them. The alternatives are presented dogmatically, without room for manœuvre, and we do not propose to defend even the alternative favourable to theism in this inflexible form. Indeed, the *Third Antinomy*, which presents freedom as both necessary and impossible, is a powerful introduction to the distinction between thinking and practice which is part of our programme, as it was of Kant's. The Fourth, which is directly concerned with the notion of necessary being, and serves as a first instalment of the disproof to follow, is particularly illuminating: commenting on the thesis, Kant remarks that the argument for necessity does not tell us whether what is necessary is something outside the world, or the world itself; and he

suggests that to go beyond the world we have illicitly to introduce the ontological proof. That the *ens necessarium* might very well not be God is a conclusion congenial to those who doubt whether God is best described as an *ens necessarium*.

2. Kant objects to the argument from infinite regress: not because he denies that the regress is absurd, but because he finds equally absurd the dogmatic termination of it in a necessary first cause. He objects particularly that the removal of the conditions without which no concept of necessity is possible is taken to be a completion of the concept of the series. Modern Thomists have seen this point and have rectified it, e.g. Dr E. L. Mascall:

> The point is not really that we cannot have an infinite regress in the order of nature, but that such an infinite regress in the series of moved movers would necessitate an unmoved First Mover not *in* the order of nature but above it.[33]

We may add, whatever may be meant by 'creation', it is not cause in any ordinary sense of the word. There is a decisive difference between cause within the series and 'cause' of the series; and competent theologians have always underlined it. So far we have nothing to complain of, and much to learn.

3. Except in the *First Antinomy*, where the arguments cancel out, Kant does not exploit the special difficulties of regress in time. They are, in fact, covered by his criticism of the argument from regress in general, and they are referred to whenever it is observed that the categories apply only to 'phenomena'. But it is the logical rather than the temporal aspect of the regress which causes him concern. This is in accordance with the original emphasis of St Thomas, who was so little concerned, or, as a philosopher, so much troubled by the temporal aspect of the cosmological argument that he admitted creation in time to be known by revelation only. As we shall again find ourselves in Kant's predicament, again we have no reason to be disconcerted.

---

[33] *He Who is*, 1943, p. 44. He is here discussing the First Way of St Thomas, but the same point holds of the Second and Third. He is also quite certainly stating the intention of St Thomas; Kant has a point against his contemporaries, but they had lost the feel of St Thomas's wonderful balance between presumption and agnosticism.

4. Following Leibniz, Kant described the proof as *a contingentia mundi*. There could be a verbal point here: 'contingent'[34] has meaning only in the context of 'necessary': if there are 'contingent' things there must be some necessary thing. But, as the word is expendable, the point is not *merely* verbal. Both St Thomas in his Third Way, and Kant in his expanded rendering of the proof,[35] contrast 'necessary' with 'possible', and 'possible' differs from 'contingent' as 'might be and is not' differs from 'might not be and is'. Either will do to point the contrast with what self-standingly *is*; and the argument (we repeat) is that unless something is self-standing, there might be nothing at all.

5. The main burden of Kant's disproof (reiterated under several headings) is that what applies necessarily to phenomena does not apply to the totality of things (which includes noümena): the principle of causality is a transcendental principle; the realm of necessity is the realm of the conditioned; the logical possibility of the concept of all reality is not a real possibility. That is to say, the conclusions of the *Dialectic* follow from those of the *Analytic*. If the *Dialectic* is wrong, there is likely to be something wrong with the *Analytic* also.[36] We have the right to consider the whole complex from the side of the *Dialectic* and see if this is so.

6. Underlying the dispute, there are considerations about time which are highly paradoxical, and do not seem to have been given due attention. *It is only at the end of a temporal regress that God is necessarily supra-temporal.* If the regress is conceived not temporally but logically, its rebuttal does not centre on time, and time does not have to be transcended. The 'necessary' to which all the 'possibles' point back keeps all the possibles open. It is not disconnected from them, and is therefore committed in time. And at that point it does not much matter

---

[34] St Thomas does not use the word 'contingent' in the exposition of the Five Ways, but it is habitually used by Thomists; e.g. by Garrigou-Lagrange in his *exposé* of the Third Way: 'contingent beings presuppose a necessary and existent being' (*God: His Existence and His Attributes*, English translation, Vol. I, 1934, p. 385).

[35] *Critique of Pure Reason*, tr. Kemp Smith, p. 509.

[36] Though the development of Kant's thought may well have followed the reverse order.

whether we accept the necessary in principle and then scale it down, or whether we view it as an Ideal of Pure Reason vindicated by approximations. But it is certainly possible to present something like the cosmological proof in a temporalist version. Elsewhere[37] I have described this process as 'schematization', applying to metaphysical concepts as it is applied by Kant to transcendental concepts; and 'necessary existence' then appears as 'existence which is coeval with all possible time'.[38]

From the point of view of a working religion, the change is a great advantage: it makes it possible to think of God as active and accessible, and diminishes the distance between 'the philosopher's God' and the God of Abraham and Isaac and Jacob. From the point of view of philosophy, it breaks the barrier between phenomena and things-in-themselves, and permits a modest discussion of genuinely metaphysical issues. In respect of time, there is a continuity between these two allegedly distinct worlds, and, because of that continuity, the difference between them has to be discussed. It cannot be shrugged off into a void of agnosticism.

But, though from both points of view the 'schematization' of metaphysics has advantages, does it not destroy, rather than adapt, the concept of necessary being? The future cannot be forecast with certainty. If God is not beyond the exigencies of time, might he not persist for a period and then expire?[39] There may be evidence for him of the most stringent kind (we have tried to show that there is), but, as we have also contended, where there is evidence there can be counter-evidence, and in the infinite ages ahead the counter-evidence might multiply. A temporalized necessity is therefore a conditional necessity – unlike the necessities of science, which are de-temporalized

[37] 'The Two Strands of Natural Theology', in *Process and Divinity*, p. 487.
[38] In *Summa Theologica*, I, Qu. X, art. 5, St Thomas, confronted with the gulf between time and eternity, introduces the conception of *aevum*, thus: *tempus habet prius et posterius; aevum non habet in se prius et posterius, sed ei coniungi possunt; aeternitas autem non habet prius neque posterius, neque ea compatitur.* For this clear-sighted attempt to bridge the gulf, he has not always been given enough credit. But his position is not ours; God, as we understand it, *has prius et posterius*, and is master of them.
[39] Cf. Nietzsche, who had a sense of the tragedy, and his insensitive modern imitators, 'God is dead'.

as far as possible. Will a conditional necessity, one resting in
Humian fashion on vivacity and repetition and confirmed by
belief, satisfy the requirements of religion?

If that were all, probably not: but religion is more than its
intellectual component. It is the intellectual component which
is tentative and probabilist; and that is a distinction rather
than a slur, because it comes of keeping close to experience.
If believers proceed on their way unperturbed, it is because of
their total attitude of faith, in which good reasons are transmuted into glowing certainties.[40] As for philosophical theists,
they will be perturbed only if they expect too much from
themselves. St Thomas thought the existence of God could be
proved; Kant denied it. Neither of them saw that the business
of philosophers in the matter was not to prove but to provide
indications. The dominance of Kant in the modern world is due
to the unquestioning acceptance by his predecessors of the rationalist dogma: as usual, radicals succeed when conservatives are
improvident. But if we operate with the schematized concept
of necessity, we can accept much of the content of the cosmological proof and much of Kant's critical comment on it. We
can accept the vertical orientation without the necessitarian
conclusion, and the critique of the necessitarian conclusion
without losing the vertical orientation. Like so many apparently
irreconcilable differences, this one begins to lose its sharpness
when we challenge what both sides take for granted. The
necessity of God is each man's necessity, and not necessity-in-
general. That is how there can be empirical metaphysics. For
the philosopher, it ends an intolerable dualism. For the
believer, it leaves room for faith. For both alike, it makes of
faith a supplement to metaphysics and not a substitute.

It remains to inquire: What is it that is, even in the 'schematized' sense, necessary? As St Thomas said, *à propos* of the
ontological proof, 'because we do not know of God what he is,
we cannot know whether it is possible for him to exist';[41] and
as Kant said in the *Fourth Antinomy*, even if one were to establish

---

[40] For elaboration we refer forward to chapter VII.
[41] This is a much needed supplement to his other contention that we
can be aware of God unwittingly, as we can be aware of Peter approaching
without knowing that he is Peter.

necessary being, it is another issue whether that being is God; the affirmative answer being reached, in his view, only by re-introducing the suspect ontological argument. Necessity is not enough to characterize God. St Thomas was well aware of it; in the Fourth Way he introduces the further concept of perfection (he is careful not to *deduce* it from necessary existence), and with that behind him he can meet the Kantian charge that the philosophers have made of God the final term in a cosmic series: it provides the required sense of distance from the world. Whether the two characters (necessity and perfection) can coalesce is one of the main problems of natural theology. Suffice it to say at this stage that arguments pointing to an *ens necessarium* or an *ens realissimum* do not show that they can. The cosmological argument has therefore either to be supplemented by a moral argument or to fall back on the ontological argument.[42] But as a constructive brain-stretcher, as a destroyer of premature absolutes, and as an insistent pointer to what it does not quite establish, the argument provides a tightly reasoned prelude to that maturer conviction which is fed by other arguments and is vindicated in practice.[43]

4. *Descartes and a Revised Cosmological Argument*

The minor premiss of the cosmological proof is 'something exists', and in principle it does not matter what. For this reason, there is difficulty in tracing the continuity between God and his creatures. If what exists is only something, God might well be anything. If a specific something is the point of departure, serving as such in virtue of its specific character, supposing

[42] Thomists are apt to treat both the cosmological argument and the argument from degrees of perfection (the Fourth Way) as self-sufficient. The impression of a layman in these regions is that the spirit of the text is best captured by keeping them close together, and indeed by making one bundle of the whole five of them.

[43] The view here propounded differs from the now fashionable view that the cosmological argument (along with the other arguments) is best understood as a clarification of Christian belief. It is true that, viewed from the vantage point of faith, its elements fall naturally into place; but it is not (in our view) useless as an argument from scratch. We say that it draws attention, even in the absence of faith, to significant considerations capable of giving rise to faith. It is not only a clarification, but definitely a pointer.

the argument to be valid, one facet of his being will be disclosed along with his existence. The specific something favoured by many modern writers is one's own existence; the promulgator of this specific approach was Descartes. As has been observed above (p. 125), the ontological argument in Descartes is almost an afterthought; he relies mainly on two earlier arguments, the minor premisses of which respectively are: the fact that as disclosed in the *cogito*, *I* exist, and the fact that I have, independently of sensory experience, the idea of God. The major premiss in both cases is: 'the more cannot come from the less'. There are two general features of these arguments, of which one bears particularly on the predicament of Descartes himself, while the other is of permanent importance.

The first is that in proceeding either from my having the idea of God, or from the fact of my own existence, he argues from the presented fact to its only possible source by way of efficient cause: 'The consideration of efficient cause is the first and foremost, not to say the one and only, means we have of proving the existence of God.'[44] It is as a *producer* of me-as-doubter, or of the idea that I have of God, that God is the necessary cause. The point of this emphasis is that the philosopher of science who boasted about 'expelling final causes from the universe' is naturally unwilling to invoke them in the case of human beings, even though in such a case they would not endanger his anti-Aristotelian physics. This approach has the advantage of bringing into the orbit of philosophy the religious theme of creation, submerged in so much mediaeval meditation on the final cause. It does not follow that the God who 'moves by being loved' is not equally authentic, but it does follow that the validity of the idea of God depends not on its representative efficacy, but on God himself as efficient cause. However, as it is the idea of *God*, the efficient causality will ensure its representative efficacy. 'All the reality, or all the perfection, which exists only objectively in ideas, must exist formally or eminently in their causes.'[45]

The second and more permanent contribution of Descartes to philosophical theology lies in his interpretation of the old

[44] Answer to Fourth Objections, Adam and Tannery, VII. 238.
[45] Answer to Second Objections, Adam and Tannery, VII. 135.

dictum, which serves as his major premiss, that 'the more cannot come from the less'. What he means is the 'more and the less perfect'. It is usual for those who think in terms of efficient cause to be lost in the contemplation of power. The argument of Descartes is that the cause of the less perfect must be the more perfect. We have seen that earlier arguments erred in interpreting imperfect as contingent. In Descartes the sense of imperfection overrides, even if it includes, the sense of contingency: and by the same token, feeling for perfection is stronger than the demand for necessity. The argument is thus steered away from purely logical considerations and more nearly approaches the interpretation given by believers of what they themselves experience.

From these general considerations, the argument takes two separate turns. Along the first road, of which we have already allowed ourselves a preview, it proceeds from the idea of God in me to the only cause sufficient to produce it: God himself. Along the second, it proceeds from the fact, and the imperfection, of my existence. Descartes himself says: 'It matters little whether the second is considered as different from the first, or only as an explanation of it.'[46] In fact, they are inderdependent.

1. If the idea of God was not produced in me by God himself, I must have produced it from my own resources. I could have done it (a) by negating by idea of finitude; (b) by extending my own qualities; (c) by making it up. There are no other alternatives.[47] (a) states the issue back to front: I can get to finitude only by negating infinity. Much the same can be said of (b): my qualities could never be extended to the limit of perfection, and my idea of God 'objectively' contains perfection.[48] These are mediaeval objections, anyway. (c) is more in the modern style. Why should the *idea* of the perfect not be less perfect than the *reality* of the imperfect? Here Descartes falls back on the second argument: it is the idea-of-God-in-me that lights up my whole being and gives it what reality it has. How could I be the efficient cause of what makes

---

[46] Answer to First Objections, Adam and Tannery, VII. 106.
[47] Receiving it from others is rightly excluded: the same question could be raised about them.   [48] I.e. as an object.

me what I am? Imagination cannot go higher than its own level. We might add (as we have already seen *à propos* of the ontological argument) that if it does, it becomes a vehicle.

2. *Cogito, ergo sum:* I exist, and so far, nothing else. Indeed, *cogito*, in any positive sense, is an over-statement: *dubito ergo sum* is the better formula. Now, taking it for granted (see above) that I am caused, and that 'the more perfect cannot be a consequence or dependence of the less perfect',[49] I cannot have been caused by myself, or I should have given myself more perfection than I have; or by my parents, for I do not yet know that I have a body, nor were they necessarily more perfect than I am; or by a combination of causes, for the idea of God I have in me, and which informs me, is an idea of unity: and again there are no other alternatives.

Thus, each argument serving as a backstop for the other, the only possible cause of the idea of God in me, and of me as having it, is God.

There are difficulties of detail in these demonstrations. They depend for a good deal of their force on their place in the Cartesian philosophy; they are part of the experiment of supposing nothing to exist but myself in doubt, and on the argument whereby the causal axiom is first placed in doubt and then reinstated. They also depend on the retention in the *idea* of God of the emphasis on bare unity, together with the assertion of attributes incompatible with it. Yet of all the attempts to prove the existence of God, this is the most powerfully persuasive and the most fruitful of disclosures.[50] The reason is that in no other classical writer is the starting-point so concrete and particular.[51] It is not a concept; it is not an undefined finite existence; it is not a system in which the individual is submerged: it is *me* (or, as the French say, more grammatically, *je*).[52] It is not simply the operation of thinking;

[49] *Discours de la Méthode*, Part IV, Adam and Tannery, VI. 34.

[50] I note with pleasure that Professor H. D. Lewis, *The Philosophy of Religion*, p. 173, also finds them 'extremely significant and revealing'.

[51] The concrete personal setting of the second argument prevents the first from tapering off into ideality – the error of 'loving divinity instead of loving God', as Descartes wrote to his friend Chanut, Adam and Tannery, IV. 608.

[52] On this point see the penetrating observations of M. Henri Gouhier, *Essais sur Descartes*, 1937, pp. 117ff.

it is not an 'epistemological subject', like the Transcendental Unity of Apperception; it is an *existing* subject – call it psychological or existential or anything that keeps it particular and free from abstractions.[53] Descartes proceeds from an unquestionable fact and allows it to expand into its implications.[54] In detail, the argument is a variant of the cosmological; but it is revitalized by an affinity with empirical-type personal religion. In its inward and individualist approach to the problem, it is unmistakably part of the empirical complex.

But, from the very virtues of Descartes's presentation, it follows that it cannot be exhaustive. Just because he is more than usually empirical, Descartes cannot prove God from the world without reading him back into the world. All that an empirical approach can do is to meet difficulties and suggest possibilities, some of them rather more convincing than others. What can be said for Descartes is that he puts through this modest programme almost to perfection. He has said enough to leave us permanently dissatisfied with our condition and to show how that dissatisfaction can be removed by meditation.[55] The *forte* of a meditation is to be personal: the method of doubt and the recovery of the doubter from the wreck, is something that has to be practised by everyone for himself. So is the expansion of the primary insight to include the existence of God. It can be recapitulated in the experience of another, and indeed it is in that hope that the meditation is made public; but again, in the experience of that other, it will be a personal adventure. He is called upon to consider the human situation from an original angle. He is first of all forced to recognize the situation for what it is, and then shown that it is not quite hopeless. Thus, whatever defects we may find in the arguments, we shall have had it brought home to us that we need to be supplemented, and that no purely human supplement will do. But if, in

[53] As M. Gouhier points out, *op. cit.*, p. 124, Descartes himself ignores this caution when, from 'je pense', he proceeds to 'une chose qui pense'. 'Une chose' does not develop 'le *je*'; it displaces it.

[54] Cf. again M. Gouhier, *op. cit.*, p. 126: 'La demonstration cartésienne de l'existence de Dieu est le mouvement du *je* approfondissant sa propre existence.'

[55] The title, *Meditations*, is deliberate: the whole essay is a series of meditations, which are none the less so for the intervening argument.

the course of our daily living, we obscurely glimpse a supplement, one which would make sense out of all our fumbling, we should now think it a rational impulse to pursue it; and if, on the whole, experience were thereby enlarged and stabilized, it would be equally rational to treasure our glimpses, and to piece them together till they break into a pattern which both takes up our evidences, and transcends them.

5. *The Argument from Design*

The argument from design was the main highway to God in the eighteenth century. Even Hume took it seriously, and with the aid of liberal theologians built up Cleanthes to such an extent that some interpreters of the *Dialogues* believe him to represent the author's own opinions.[56] Kant, in a well-known passage, wrote that it 'deserved to be mentioned with respect', as 'the oldest, the clearest, and the most accordant with the common reason of mankind'.[57] Historically, it is easy to see why. The argument from design was the contemporary accommodation of science and religion. It found in the laws of nature (which the scientists had asserted against the residual animism of the final cause) the decrees of God. It worked through the newly discovered and amazing evidences of adaptation and found that so far from diminishing God, they added to his glory. It is true, as Thomas McPherson says,[58] that the argument has no particular claim to be scientific; why should it, if it is genuinely metaphysical? But it is (or was) likely to pacify scientists, for its starting-point is one which they had reached after great labour and controversy and in the teeth of the Aristotelian physics.

The argument has often been presented and may be summarized as follows:

There is in the world a remarkable order and arrangement of detail, fit to excite wonder and far excelling the best efforts

---

[56] Wrongly, as Kemp Smith in his edition has definitely shown; but it is a tribute both to Hume's capacity to project himself into another's position, and to the hold that it had on his imagination, that the mistake should have been made at all.

[57] *Critique of Pure Reason*, A.623, B.651, tr. Kemp Smith, p. 520.

[58] *The Philosophy of Religion*, pp. 84ff.

of human craftsmanship. Everything falls beautifully into place, at any rate *as if* it had been disposed by a master planner. It is a common impression that the reference is to the mathematical perfection of the planetary orbits; but, in fact, John Ray[59] and William Derham[60] at the beginning of the century and the better-known William Paley,[61] were all of them more interested in biology than astronomy, and Paley in particular thought astronomy an unsuitable introduction to theism, though an excellent field for its subsequent deployment. Hume was thus getting it too easily when he made Cleanthes talk of nothing but mechanics; but in his general statement of the issue he was right enough:

All these various machines, and even their most minute parts, are adjusted to each other with an accuracy, which ravishes into admiration all men, who have ever contemplated them. The curious adapting of means to ends, throughout all nature, resembles exactly, though it much exceeds, the productions of human contrivance; of human design, thought, wisdom and intelligence. Since therefore the effects resemble each other, we are led to infer, by all the rules of analogy, that the causes also resemble, and that the Author of nature is somewhat similar to the mind of man, though possessed of much larger faculties, proportioned to the grandeur of the work, which he has executed. By this argument *a posteriori*, and by this argument alone, do we prove at once the existence of a Deity, and his similarity to human mind and intelligence.[62]

Cleanthes and Philo agree that this is a fair statement, and so it is.

Comment upon it has been continuous, and mostly critical, though indulgent. But it has been generally assumed that the argument is to be taken as demonstrative. If it is *a posteriori*, as Cleanthes is made to affirm, it clearly cannot be demonstrative. Another use will have to be found for it. One, which is stressed by McPherson, is that it is intended to reinforce the believer and not to convince the sceptic: 'granted that a man believes

---

[59] *The Wisdom of God in the Creation*, 1701.

[60] *Physio-Theology*, 1713.

[61] *Natural Theology, or Evidences of the Existence and Attributes of the Deity collected from the Appearances of Nature*, 1802 (published at the end of the author's life). I owe the point to McPherson, *The Philosophy of Religion*, p. 77. I am also most grateful to him for having shamed me into reading Paley at first hand. As he says, it is a rewarding experience.

[62] *Dialogues Concerning Natural Religion*, Part II, ed. Kemp Smith, pp. 176f.

in God already, it will be of great benefit to him to reflect upon the evidences of "contrivance" in the world'.[63] As far as Paley is concerned, McPherson is able to show by quotation that this was his main intention; though there is, I think a subsidiary intention to speak outside the circle of faith to the world at large. But this is precisely the thesis which all along we have been concerned to deny. It is a religious version of the doctrine that philosophy is no more than clarification. If philosophy is to be metaphysical, i.e. concerned with what is in the last resort the case, it must forgo this advantage (which a philosopher concerned about religion is constantly tempted to claim) and set out from scratch. If it does, it cannot demonstrate; and this was what Hume and Kant between them succeeded in showing. But it can turn up all sorts of predisposing evidence, which helps to lay the *foundation* for faith. The *explication* of it belongs to a different phase of the argument. In fact, much of what is (rightly) rejected as a contribution to *a priori* metaphysics falls into place as an element of empirical metaphysics. This we shall try to show in detail, referring back to our previous discussion of order in chapter III.

1. We shall take it for granted that there is in the world a very remarkable degree of order and adaptation, and that the natural wonder which it elicits is increased by the discoveries of scientists. The question, then, is whether it requires an orderer or designer. The analogy of the architect (more prominent in Paley than that of the watchmaker) is, admittedly, *only* an analogy. Now an analogy is useful as a suggestion, and it should prevent unprejudiced people from concluding to a direct negative without closer argument. It may prove to be a lead to an important discovery. But if it is put forward as a demonstration, it is bound to disappoint. That is why it is tempting to treat it as a clarification; that way it makes sense. We prefer to take it as a hint, to be collated with other hints in exploring the balance of probabilities. Nothing in either Hume or Kant is inconsistent with this policy: and it prevents the failure of the argument as a demonstration from being used to support its negative.

Consider the point about analogy so clearly exposed by

_____
[63] *Op. cit.*, p. 80.

Hume, and so troublesome not only to those who use the argument from design, but also to the expounders of the cosmological argument and the *analogia entis*. If the analogy is pressed too hard, the result is anthropomorphism; if, for this reason, it is relaxed, it leads to an agnosticism within which there is any amount of room for uncertainty and error.[64] This predicament is exactly what we should expect. All analogies waver in this fashion. The way to make them work is to keep the pendulum swinging and to prevent it from swinging too far. But this is a device for stabilizing the imagination, and not for producing certainties. Moreover, it has to be grasped as an opportunity and not accepted unhappily as a disability. What has to be driven out of the picture is the quest for certainty. We can then be properly grateful for such incidental illumination as comes our way.

2. There is a particular difficulty[65] in an analogy between a particular situation, such as a house, and the total situation described as 'the world'. The whole point about 'the world' or 'the whole' is that it is unique; and the mind is thus deprived of its usual advantage of proceeding from past experience. There is a dogma lurking behind this reasonable observation: the dogma that nothing that happens only once, or for the first time, for that matter, can ever be caused, or a cause. The dogma follows inevitably from Hume's general theory of causation, and is a good reason for approaching it with caution. But there are two possible conclusions. The first, which Hume takes for granted, is that there can be no evidence for a cause of the world. The second is to let the dispute about cause slide and to distinguish sharply between cause and creation. In that case our analogies will shift, too. Composing a symphony is much closer to the kind of creation which can be distinguished from cause, i.e. creation out of nothing, than building a house, or even a cathedral.

3. It has been urged frequently, and properly, that the argument from design does not give us God, but only a Demiurge, with enough power to produce the world, but no

---

[64] See especially *Dialogues Concerning Natural Religion*, ed. Kemp Smith, p. 178.
[65] See again, *Dialogues Concerning Natural Religion*, ed. Kemp Smith, p. 182.

more. The only thing we can do with this argument is to admit
it without reservations. As Kant says, 'it cannot hurt the good
cause, if the dogmatic language of the overweening sophist be
forced down to the more moderate and humble requirements
of a belief adequate to quieten our doubts, though not to
command unconditional submission'.[66] And, as Kant also says,
if this is not enough, the 'physico-theological proof must fall
back on the ontological argument', which is, in fact, *the one
possible ground of proof* with which human reason can never
dispense'.[67] Regardless of the merits and nature of the ontological argument, we are not forced back on it, for we lay no
claim to logical necessity. Indeed, the argument from design
has special interest for us because, as McPherson says, it
'implies that empirical evidence is somehow relevant to the
question of proof of God'.[68] Something of what it can contribute is suggested by Kant: 'the physico-theological argument
can indeed lead us to the point of admiring the greatness,
wisdom, power, etc., of the Author of the world, but can take
us no further'.[69] That is all we ask of it.

4. But behind these technical questions there is what might
be called the atheistic intimation: why does order need to be
explained at all? If order were quite as ubiquitous, quite as
free from interruption, as the argument from design seems to
assume, the question might be well directed. It is because the
order in the world is neither wholly established in the world,
nor its only perfection, that there is any reason to look for an
order beyond it. It is commonly supposed that the *perfection*
of the world-order is a reason for believing in God. If so, it is a
chancy reason, as any imperfection would by the same token
be a reason for not believing in God, and the imperfections are
for all to see. It is the need for order, and its imperfect hold
on the world, which together point to a centre for it which is
not the world. The argument from design is too firmly rooted
in eighteenth-century deism to discern the imperfection, as is
evident in the frequent conjunction, 'God and Nature'. It is
also impervious to excellences of the world other than order;

[66] *Critique of Pure Reason*, tr. Kemp Smith, A.625, B.653, pp. 520f.
[67] *Op. cit.*, p. 87.   [68] *Op cit.*, p. 87.
[69] *Critique of Pure Reason*, tr. Kemp Smith, A.629, B.657, p. 523.

e.g. to the creative impetus which the world can display, and in virtue of which a failure of order is not necessarily a calamity. All in all, the argument from design was too much wedded to order, and it is necessary to go far beyond it to meet the objection just raised against it.

It will be rejoined: that is not quite the point. What the ordinary atheist has in mind is that more particularly in the higher ranges of what he refrains from calling creation, there *are* self-adjustments which render the 'hypothesis' of deity unnecessary. As has often been pointed out, the conflict about the evolution of species was not merely due to fundamentalist obstinacy about Genesis; it was due to the discovery that the origin of species could be explained without reference to special creation, that is to say, *from the inside*.[70] Further, the more human beings can be shown to be helping themselves, the less it is necessary to invoke God to account for their performances. As Comte expressed it, 'God has been regent during the long minority of humanity', and humanity has now ascended the throne. Or, to modernize the metaphor, he is like an ageing professional man who keeps on when his ambitious junior, free, white and fifty-one, is waiting to step into his shoes.

Thus, so far from basing his argument on the infallible machine, the atheist begins by drawing attention to the encouraging discrepancies. To re-emphasize them is very far from meeting his case. In fact, the whole discussion, on both sides, has outrun the argument from design. We shall resume it shortly, under the heading of 'cosmic teleology'.

5. But before leaving the traditional argument, it is worth adverting to a point of nomenclature. The 'argument *from* design' might better be described as an 'argument *to* design'. If it is merely *from* design, design being one of the premises, it has its conclusion in its pocket. What is at issue is whether there *is* design. *If* there is, there is obviously a designer. This is not wholly a triviality, for an argument which does not clearly make the distinction may unfairly make the best of both worlds. At its best, it is an argument *from* order *to* design

---

[70] Cf. F. R. Tennant, *Philosophical Theology*, summary of ch. II in Table of Contents, Vol. II, p. vii: 'If the world were a self-explanatory mechanism, a theistic interpretation of Nature's regularity would appear superfluous.'

(and a designer), and it is proper to accept it, and to insist on its being taken, in that limited sense.

6. 'Cosmic Teleology'

In a postscript which he does not amplify, McPherson remarks that 'the argument is not yet dead', and he refers us to F. R. Tennant, as one who has more recently 'attempted this kind of empirical approach to the question of the knowledge of God'.[71] Professor H. D. Lewis commends him likewise.[72] In my considered view, the neglect of his great work, *Philosophical Theology* (1929), by philosophers interested in religion figures with the neglect of Whitehead by philosophers interested in science as one of the most unfortunate and gratuitous refusals of a heritage in the history of British thought.[72a] He concerns us in general because he claims throughout that his approach is empirical: 'coercive demonstration being confessedly unattainable, it is to be inquired what kind of justification for reasoned belief natural theology can afford'.[73] He concerns us here particularly because one of his most convincing efforts in this sense is his reconstruction, in Vol. II, ch. 4, of the argument from design. In what follows I am deeply indebted to him, not, I hope, as a copyist, but as one who has found his way of thinking a sure guide to my own.

   1. The argument from design has to be seen in the wider context of a 'cosmic teleology'. In its heyday, e.g. in the Bridgewater Treatises, it tended to dissipate itself in a number of special applications: to geology, to biology, to physics (but not primarily) and even to technical activities like agriculture and manufacture. Too often, though not always by conscious intent, the operation of God was cited as a proximate cause. Under a theory of special creation, this was quite a proper proceeding: that accounts for the rather special association, already noted, between the argument from design and the interest in biology. The whole point about special creation was

---

[71] *Op. cit.*, p. 83.   [72] *Philosophy of Religion*, p. 140, and again pp. 224f.
[72a] At the last minute my attention has been drawn to its reprinting (1968) by the Cambridge University Press. It is to be hoped that it will now experience a revival.   [73] Vol. II, p. 79.

that God was the proximate cause. But Darwin has shown that, as a proximate cause, God is not needed – however much he might be implicated in the whole process.[74] Those who had thought of God as a proximate cause were naturally disconcerted: but that was because 'their God was too small'. They had to be shown that purpose is not an alternative to a proximate mechanical cause, but operates by and through it. With particular reference to evolutionary biology, the now underrated Absolute Idealists made this subject one of their special concerns; one of them, R. F. A. Hoernle, coined the slogan: 'not mechanism or vitalism, but mechanism and teleology'.[75]

But cosmic teleology, using and appropriating the mechanisms described by the particular sciences, is a far cry from the original argument from design. What holds them together is the vision of divine purpose; but it will have to be differently elaborated. In the first place, it places more demand on the metaphysical imagination. God-as-proximate-cause, provided the effect is sufficiently impressive, is quickly assimilated: that is perhaps why it persists in hymn-books when it is no longer academically fruitful. Cosmic teleology requires a survey of the whole system of things, in their ascending order of completeness. As Tennant observes, 'The discovery of organic evolution has caused the teleologist to shift his ground from special design in the products to directivity in the process.'[76] Directivity, however, entails a direction; and the direction is towards the most complex and advanced episode in the evolutionary story, namely, Man. The conclusion may be criticized as anthropocentric; but Man figures in the story as part of the purpose, and the purposer is his creator as he is the creator of the rest of nature. It is certainly intended to depict Man as part of nature, but that is a direct advantage and should help to counter the charge of anthropocentricity.

It may be asked, however, how this kind of argument can be qualified as 'empirical'. Superficially, attention to 'directivity in the process' is less a matter of experience, and more like taking a stance, than the recognition of 'special design in the

[74] He was even prepared to describe proximate causes as secondary, leaving ample room for the primary. *Origins of Specie*, Worlds Classic ed., p. 440.
[75] *Studies in Contemporary Metaphysics*, 1920, p. 143.
[76] *Op. cit.*, Vol. II, p. 85.

products'. What is there in the *facts* to suggest that there is 'directivity'? Here we come to the second main point: the empirical introduction is contained in the phrase, 'the fitness of the environment'.

In 1913, in a work under that title, Lawrence J. Henderson (a biologist, not a philosopher) observed that the compounding and distribution of the three basic chemical elements are such as to provide the 'maximum of fitness' for living creatures that actually exist. This is a matter of observation, and also for amazement. Other compoundings and distributions, which would not have sustained life, would have been possible, and the odds against a purely fortuitous collocation of all the prerequisites would be fantastically high. Of course, the wildly improbable does happen; but the probabilities are so low that the alternative of purposed fittingness might well be considered, and to rule it out is unscientific in the highest degree.

If this point is reluctantly conceded, the next way of evasion is to locate the teleology inside the process. For us, it is an insidious suggestion, in the literal sense of the word; it waits in ambush to take us off our guard. For it is in a sense *true* that the teleology is inside the process: otherwise it could not be argued that it informs the proximate 'mechanical' (or other) cause. But the question is whether it is *only* inside the process. In terms of our earlier discussion,[77] we should have to say that if it did not point beyond the process it would not prevail within the process. But we might perhaps here comment in general on what Tennant calls *Zweckmässigkeit* without *Absichtlichkeit*, purposiveness without intention. As he points out, men may build more wisely than they know, but they often do not, and later they know the difference; the potency ascribed to nature, however, if teleology is entirely unconscious, must be unerring; in other words, 'must vastly exceed the sapience and foresight of humanity'. 'In fact,' Tennant continues, 'the theory requires us to believe that Nature keeps her head, which is *ex hypothesi* brainless, through all the changes and choices of cosmic history.'[78] This is far too good to be true. If things go better without intelligence and purpose, what are intelligence and purpose for?

[77] See p. 75.   [78] *Op. cit.*, Vol. II, p. 108.

We are therefore driven back on the hard alternative: either design or pure chance. As the adaptations of creature to environment depend on the adaptations of environment to creature, and as these are minute and subtle and detailed, not only, as Henderson saw, as between chemical compounds and living things, but also as between living things and rational beings, we may be pardoned for not preferring pure chance. It is not a certainty, but what is? Only one thing; that this is no place for certainty. That is why, even if theism is no more than a probability, atheism is positively excluded.

7. '*The Fitness of the Environment*'

The third point to consider has just been raised in passing. It relates to the remarkable fittingness of human activities with their natural background. The first case is one to which we have already alluded: the mere fact that *an object allows itself to be thought*. It is not the thinking that is so wonderful; it is the ability to think things as they are. They might so easily have been otherwise: the lines of communication might have been wrecked by Descartes's *malin génie*. This extraordinary adaptation we take for granted, because we are used to it. And when we do notice it, it is to pat ourselves on the back for thinking, rather than to give thanks for the dispensation under which thinking is possible. We shall see later how this adaptation is conclusively illustrated in action; in the meantime, we merely ask that it be read off both ways, and not simply as the subjection of appearances to the categories of the understanding. In view of idealist misapprehensions, it is well to lay a compensatory emphasis on the responsibility of thought to things. 'Nature will open to the right pass-word; but she has chosen it, not we.'[79]

The second case is one which we postponed, and must now take up: the adaptation between man and his environment in his admiration of 'the beauty of nature'. There are few experiences which show man more utterly committed to the world; for some, indeed, it almost takes the place of religion. It takes none of the effort of positioning and re-interpreting which is

[79] Tennant, *op. cit.*, Vol. II, p. 82.

needed to appreciate works of art; it is an adaptation in which we are claimed by what we belong to. For that reason it seems strained and unnatural to interpret it as wished upon the world by our own feelings: at the very least, there must be something specific in the world for the feelings to catch on to.[80] If so, there is yet another subtle adaptation between ourselves and the world we live in: and, like other adaptations, it is both too good and too improbable to have happened accidentally. This is not a proof. It appeals only to what Tennant calls 'alogical probability'.[81] But that (as we have said before) is the most we can ask for. It adds to other adaptations to build up a reasonably convincing picture of a continuous purpose.

To render the picture as complete as possible, we should need to give an account of the adaptation between the course of the world and the moral order. As this has been anticipated in chapter IV and will have to be discussed again in the context of action, we need here do no more than note that if the world had been planned to promote the moral order, it could hardly have been planned better. In particular, if it had been created automatically perfect, it would not have served nearly as well.

At each stage, then, and in all human activities, we note an adaptation which is powerful enough to give rise to the activities concerned, but does not seem to spring from either factor, or from their mutual involvement. The conclusion, to be received cautiously but confidently, is that there is a teleology reaching into the world and working its way through the world in an evolutionary spiral, but not centred in the world, though everywhere manifest in the world. This is a considerable extension of the argument from design, but it brings out what I believe to be its central principle, which earned it the unwilling respect of Hume and the warmer though still conditional respect of Kant: that the order of the world is neither self-generating nor self-sustaining.

In conclusion, it will be objected that both Paley and Tennant reached their convictions before the deluge, Paley

---

[80] For a clear statement of the view that beauty is a 'dependent or consequential characteristic', i.e. that it is in itself subjective but consequent on objective characteristics, cf. W. D. Ross, *The Right and the Good*, 1930, pp. 122f.
[81] *Op. cit.*, Vol. II, p. 91.

in the years before 1789 and Tennant in the years before 1914, and that their estimates are fantastically optimistic. If this were a study in biography or history, we should note that both writers published in the bad times to follow (in 1802 and 1929 respectively), and that Paley knew at the time that he was suffering from an incurable disease; and we should admire rather than rebuke the courage and insight which looked beyond the immediate future to a cosmic vista of conspiring adaptations. But, personal factors apart, neither writer overlooked the difficulties. Paley freely admitted 'defects in the contrivance', insisting only that they are not to be blamed on the contriver: 'Teeth are contrived to eat, not to ache.'[82] Tennant wrote a whole chapter on evil, and near the beginning stands the sentence: 'The fact that evil exists in the world is a primary datum for the empirical theist knowable with much more immediacy and certainty than is the being of God.'[83] The evidence for design does not ignore evil; it is presented in spite of evil. So we shall conclude by turning to the first of the arguers from design, who stuck to his intimations of it through all his seventeenth-century obsession with the Fall: Thomas Burnet, author of *The Sacred Theory of the Earth* (1689), who wrote a style like Hobbes' and had something of his contempt for pretences. His mechanisms may not have been up to date; the geological flaws in the world he attributed to the Flood; the Flood he attributed in turn not to the Tigris and Euphrates, which, he argued picturesquely and earnestly, could not have turned it on, but to a spontaneous eruption of subterranean waters, synchronizing with an outbreak of human wickedness. But, he explained, since these ravages, though 'there is enough of design to prove a Deity', 'the world as we know it is not the world as God designed it, and it is therefore both unscientific and blasphemous to ground our devotion on its alleged perfections'. So writes Basil Willey,[84] who tells his story; and the tone of the argument, suitably demythologized, might suit our temper better than the smoother deistic versions which followed.

[82] *Natural Theology*, 1804, pp. 507, 523.
[83] *Philosophical Theology*, Vol. II, p. 181.
[84] *The Eighteenth-Century Background*, 1940, p. 28.

Thus, from an extended review of the classical proofs, we conclude:

1. that they do not achieve demonstration;
2. that many arguments used against them do not hold water;
3. that they provide good reasons for believing;
4. that they are confronted with counter-evidence which must be faced without evasion.

And at this point we pass from the shadow of the syllogism to the analysis of faith.

VII

AN ANALYSIS OF FAITH

1. 'First Faith'

THE ARGUMENT so far has been that there are good reasons, of an empirical sort, for holding that God exists, and that if there were no such reasons, no amount of devotion, no claim to direct insight, no amount of labour expended, could carry the conclusion. It is possible to build an impressive culture on a series of well-correlated misapprehensions. Before proceeding to consider the relation of good reasons to religious assurance, we have to be sure that the good reasons are there. We believe that they have been supplied and that they include much of the subsidiary argument in the traditional proofs.

At the same time, being empirical, the reasons cannot amount to proof; they can only provide a high degree of suggestiveness. Those who expect demonstration and only get reasons may feel that they have been given nothing. This is short-sighted of them; those who want there to be nothing and insist on proof will be well-pleased. But they have a point: there is a difference between having good reasons (which is all that the philosopher can supply) and the finality of religious conviction. The religious attitude cannot be satisfied with good reasons. The late Lord Lindsay of Birker used to quote the invocation of an over-intellectualized Scots minister: 'O Thou who art our ultimate hypothesis and our eternal hope'. The absurdity of it lies in its juxtaposing of the languages of experiment and assurance. We have been attempting to avoid this confusion by assigning each of the languages to its appropriate sphere. The traditional mistake lies not in insisisting on the assurance, but in founding it on the theoretical concept of necessity: in deriving it from the past and not from the future. In analysing further the nature of religious assurance, we shall suggest that it belongs to an open-ended human situation, and its triumph is not that it limits open-endedness, but that it is completely at home in it. That, in the long run, is why reasons in religion cannot amount to proof: if they did, they would not be religions. The traditional proofs in fact supply good reasons, elevated into proofs by mistaken presuppositions.

It will be noted, however, that good reasons facilitate, but do not constrain. That they should facilitate is essential to any believer with an intellectual conscience. That they should not constrain should be insisted upon by any philosopher with a religious conscience. The demand for constraint can grow up only too easily in a closed religious circle: not only in the interests of an ecclesiastical discipline, but also, and more insidiously, in the practice of a congregational like-mindedness.[1] That it should have been supported by an appeal to philosophy has been equally unfortunate for philosophy and for religion. This category mistake, as unbelievers have gleefully pointed out, leads to intolerance and discourages inquiry. We should not oblige them by acceding to it.

That being so, what are we to make of the assurance which leaps to a personal certainty and leaves even the good reasons trailing behind it? The answer is that this is what is meant by faith, and that the sphere of its operations is in the first instance in practice.

At a later stage, it will be necessary to re-connect faith with its object and its reasons: to discuss, in fact, the already complex phenomena of 'faith in', and 'faith that'. But faith, unlike philosophy, is practised by simple people, and for that reason we shall begin further back: with what might be called 'faith, full stop', and will be referred to hereafter as 'first faith'. The most striking examples are to be found in the Gospels. To the woman who touched his garment in the crowd, and was healed, Jesus said: 'Thy faith hath made thee whole' (Mark 5.34). To the disciples in the storm-tossed boat, he said: 'Why are ye so fearful? How is it that ye have no faith?' (Mark 4.40). To the ruler of the synagogue, whose daughter was reported dead, he

---

[1] Collectivity in religion as in politics may be at least as oppressive as absolutism.

said, 'Be not afraid, only believe' (Mark 5.36). To the father of the boy with the 'dumb spirit', he said, 'All things are possible to him that believeth'; and the father replied, in terms which every believer echoes: 'Lord, I believe; help thou mine unbelief' (Mark 9.23f.). Even the whimsically hyperbolic passage about the mountain (Mark 11.23) testifies in the same sense: the man who 'shall not doubt in his heart, but shall believe that those things which he saith shall come to pass: he shall have whatever he saith'.[2] What is peculiar about all these passages (which are only samples) is that the faith to be displayed is demanded of the subject, and that no mention is made of any object (not even of God, and still less of the existence of God). The basic feature of faith is refusal to accept 'the impossible'.[3] In its absence, what seems impossible really is impossible: in Nazareth 'he could do no mighty work', because of 'their unbelief' (Mark 6.6). He had grown up among them, and they did not believe he could do it. Nothing could show more clearly how first faith, simple faith, depends on the individual who has it, or has it not. What Jesus did with these decent simple folk was to help them to have it. He did not do 'mighty works' in order to create faith; he promoted faith in them and then performed the 'mighty works'.

If these plain facts be accepted, we may now elaborate 'first faith', avoiding for the moment both 'faith in' and 'faith that', while admitting in advance that in the full compass of a matured faith both 'faith in' and 'faith that' find their place.

1. 'First faith' is fastened on the future. It will not admit that the future is tied to the past. That is how it is linked to forgiveness, and a new life. It is more than ordinarily open-ended; it insists on keeping open what tradition and history and science seem to have closed. The Pharisees could make nothing of sinners; the nationalists could make nothing of the

---

[2] To the last passage, there is a prelude in v. 22: 'Have faith in God'. The Greek is Ἔχετε πίστιν θεοῦ. If, as scholars generally agree, the genitive is an objective genitive, here is an exception to the rule and an anticipation of the second and more complete phase of faith. It would be wonderful if the scholars were wrong and the genitive were a subjective genitive: 'Have the faith that God has' – which, as a matter of fact, is offered by King James's translators, in very small print, as a possible alternative.

[3] In the language of faith, that word is allowed only in quotation marks.

tax-contractors; the doctors could make nothing of the woman with the haemorrhages (she had 'suffered many things of many physicians', says Mark, a layman, 'and was nothing bettered, but rather grew worse').[4] It is easy to be overawed by this array of authorities; but if we have faith, we can keep open what fate, circumstances or common sense seem to have closed. It is a complete travesty to represent it as closing issues which intelligence, experience and imagination combine to keep open.

2. Faith is forward-looking: but so is fear. Fear keeps us behind our defences, holding on to what we have, lest worse befall. Faith takes us out from behind them, to remove the evils from which in fear we take refuge. This, at a higher level, was why Jesus attacked the morality of the Pharisees. It is no good being locked up in a model prison; there is no help but to go fearlessly to the heart of the evil. The contrast between faith and fear is the most prominent feature of Gospel ethics; not the contrast between faith and works, and still less the contrast between faith and doubt. '*Be not afraid*, only believe.' Doubt sometimes gives a sort of intellectual sanction to fear: that is why doubt, *in practice*, falls under the same condemnation. But in the earliest Christian records, at the level of 'first faith', there is no trace of concern about intellectual deviation. That does not mean that it has no significance, but it belongs to a more sophisticated stage of development. Not only so: that it should be considered the prime enemy of faith is itself a deviation. Refusal to entertain doubt, to consider issues or interpretations on their merits, is itself a form of fear, and therefore, in the primary sense, a form of disbelief.

3. It will be seen that faith (in the first phase) has nothing to do with the absence of obstacles. On the contrary, in all the cases mentioned, there was every reason for not believing. This circumstance may mount up into an awkward intellectual issue; but there should be no mistake about the facts. The displays of faith recorded in our texts are no doubt spectacular: they are the peak-points of an attitude calmer and more diffused, arising from circumstances less challenging and unpromising.

[4] Luke, a medical man, who otherwise follows Mark in this narrative, suppresses the impertinence.

Moreover, if there were no such diffusion, the concentrations of faith at the points of greatest difficulty would not be forthcoming. But what we cannot say is that faith is a comfortable air ride over problems with which reason and inventiveness are battling on the ground. As those who have made any progress in it know, it engenders peculiar backslidings of its own: 'Lord, I believe; help Thou mine unbelief.' It is rather a demonstration of attachment and confidence in a world full of trials and frustrations.

4. At this ground-floor level, the faith of religion is inseparable from faith displayed in any other forward-looking activity. Intense and joyful concentration in any enterprise arises from the conviction of its viability. In the normal cases it is not necessary to 'go cosmic'; faith can be re-charged from inside the enterprise. It is the more difficult cases which drive us to religion. But both alike spring from a *natural resilience* transmitted by the creator to the creature for continuing the work of creation. It is pre-eminently displayed in the learning process of a well-balanced child of fifteen months – going from one uncelebrated triumph to another without haste or fuss – before he encounters his early crises at the hands of unskilled parents and makeshift schools. It is this complete freedom from fear and self-consciousness that Jesus no doubt had in mind when he said to a complicated and self-righteous generation, 'Except ye become as a little child . . .'.

5. Faith has nothing to do with resignation to the inevitable. Those who counsel resignation have stood the Christian religion upside down. Faith, as we have studied it, is a denial of the inevitable; if, on one front, it is opposed to fear, on another it is opposed to fate. This is where technology comes in on the side of faith. Limitations taken for granted for the whole of human experience are being removed every day. Those who identify God with the pre-technological dispositions of nature are disturbed; and so they ought to be. Removing mountains by faith sounds ridiculous; but only to those who expect the thing to be done over their heads and not through the subordinate initiatives of human beings. The instruments of faith in this instance are engineers.

6. From all the above considerations, it is clear that faith

arises in the first instance in the context of action. All the classical instances relate to something being *done*. This is the foundation on which the more sophisticated elaborations are created and which, in expounding them, we must never be tempted to forget. Faith as a whole relates to life as a whole, and life as a whole is a doing – even if the particular kind of doing is, in a few selected cases, thinking. For this reason, it will be denied that faith is a kind of perception: it *employs* perception, the more delicate the better, but it is itself an attitude of confidence and trust, in which we dispose of our little problems happily and speedily, and meet our big ones with courage and mastery.[5] We think of Abraham, whose faith took him into a far country, knowing not whither he went – a pioneer with a practical edge to his dreaming: and of those persecuted for conscience' sake, from the list in the Epistle to the Hebrews to the victims of the Nazi-Communist concentration camps. In the light of these momentous exhibitions, adherence to propositions is an anticlimax. But in any case, at the level of 'first faith', though they may be implied, they are not entertained. The theologian resembles the philosopher in Hegel's famous parallel: like the owl of Athena, he comes out after the sun has set.[6]

With what I hope are pardonable digressions, we have set forth the simple faith which is continuous with the vitality

[5] This is not the Thomist emphasis, but I quote with admiration St Thomas's magnificent epigram, 'Faith is the courage of the spirit'.

[6] At this point we must set out a general principle of interpretation. Believing, having faith, is not seeing (the principal biblical contrast), and still less surveying; it is being involved. (This makes it difficult for artists, who are involved only by way of imagination, and especially for thinkers, who are supposed not to be involved at all.) Consequently, any attempt to represent faith as a report from a superior point of view must be mistaken. First faith, which does not reflect on itself, qualifies as authentic without trouble. It is something people have, or have not, or have enough of to see they need more: it is not, it cannot be, something they *think* they have. But 'faith in' is not only exhibited, but also reflected upon. This is an advance in culture and sophistication; but it provides, like all such advances, an opportunity for that spurious substitution of the thought for the deed which crystallizes in philosophical Idealism. 'Believing in', often extolled for being more inward than 'believing that', has its own hypocrisies, and they are directly consequent on its inwardness. It is possible, for example, to *believe* in God, and to worship him, in all sincerity, and still to do nothing about it: 'Why call ye me, Lord, Lord, and *do* not the things which I say?'

and elasticity of nature on the one hand, and is the first movement towards God on the other. We now have to trace its development into its more complete manifestations. We shall follow this general rule of interpretation: its developments may be circuitous and unexpected, and they will certainly sharpen the distinction between the faith of nature and the faith of religion; but the superstructure must not be allowed to crush the foundations. The complexities of a more sophisticated faith may outsoar, but they cannot displace, the simplicities of 'first faith'.

2. *'First Faith' and Faith in God*

The development from first faith to 'faith in' seems at first sight quite simple. First faith is, at the very least, an alignment of oneself with the course of the world. Fear and pride break that alignment. The sick, the sinful, the self-sufficient, the self-righteous are all in their several ways 'out of touch'. They are in the grip of a disabling past. Those who have become as little children have the whole future before them. The persistent *future* reference of faith brings before us the picture of a world which is full of accidents, and we are some of them, but is essentially right-side-up. When we have faith, we are behaving as if, and in an inexpressive way testify that, the run of things is with us. This does not mean in the least that the things we dread will not happen to us. As John Macmurray pointed out, that is the expectation of false religion.[7] True religion says: 'Of course it will happen to us – so what?' To be in any way exempted from the run of the world would be to be excluded from it – any plea for exemption is therefore faithless. What faith implies – even at its simplest – is that no matter what happens to us, all is well. And this is getting very close indeed to believing in God.

But 'faith in' may be approached from another angle. 'Faith in' a friend or a spouse is a specification of 'first faith' to a particular person. It not merely radiates hope and accomplishment but is also a 'tutoiement' – so lamentably lost in the unaffectionate English language. But, right from the beginning,

[7] *Freedom in the Modern World*, 1932, p. 59.

let us insist that in specifying it does not displace any of the characters of 'first faith', and least of all the element of risk. As applied to other people, it sometimes is a risk; friends and spouses may be disloyal. As applied to God, it often looks like a risk; the world is full of suffering, disappointment and hard-heartedness, and it is not always easy to see it as a field of divine opportunity. In both cases it may be our own fault, and it is never wholly not our fault; but to have faith in people, and in God, is worth the risk, for it makes possible achievement which would otherwise have wilted in despair or burnt itself up in defiance. Loyalty is not something to be emotionally hoarded; it is the prerequisite for common action: and it is two-sided; it means not only that we can rely on another, but that another can rely upon us.

Where God is concerned, it has become a habit to think of faith as one-sided; we have (if we have) faith in God, but God does not similarly have faith in us. This is wholly out of line with the biblical tradition, which speaks of a 'covenant', and wholly out of line with experience, which shows that God still has faith in some very bad risks indeed. The mutuality of 'faith in' is evidenced from both ends, and any 'faith in' which is merely ours is fruitless, however honourable. The word 'encounter' may have been overworked in recent theology, but the essence of faith is in it. Similarly, we may be tired of hearing that 'God' can be pronounced only in the vocative (not in the nominative, and still less in the accusative), but at least it brings out what the Neo-Platonist and Aristotelian loan-concepts in Christianity obscure, that faith works from both ends, because God is a creator, not a focal point for the longings of philosophers. By keeping in mind the first stirrings of 'first faith', in which response is primary and recognition incidental, we can avoid one-way interpretations of 'faith in', such as allow of a gap between faith and action.

It was doubtless for some such reason that Martin Buber, in *Two Types of Faith*, distinguished between absolute faith and faith in an object, and argued that direction to an object was sometimes a limitation of faith itself.[8]

---

[8] *Two Types of Faith*, tr. N. P. Goldhawk, 1951, p. 23.

'He who believes', believes absolutely: the fact that nothing is added to what the man of faith believes has a strong meaning and reason. It is not by any means an abbreviated terminus, arising from the permissible omission of 'in God'. Indeed, the addition of this takes from the idea its essential character, or at least weakens it. The absolute construction . . . conveys the absoluteness of what is meant.

Belief, I take him to mean, is no belief unless it is perpetually enacted and re-enacted. It is not an idea to be entertained, idly, imaginatively, or with an agonizing sense of powerlessness. The men of the Bible 'found eternity, not in the super-temporal spirit, but in the depth of the actual moment';[9] Abraham, for example, 'believes because he trusts, not the other way round'.

A first impression is that Buber is setting up a contrast when he ought to be seeking an accommodation: how should it strengthen faith to leave 'in God' out? The footnote on Abraham provides the clue. What Buber complains of is that in this matter of faith we have found God in the wrong place: properly speaking, he is not an *object* of faith, but its *author*. In a way, it weakens the case to add 'in God', because God is in *it*. It is not only or mainly when we face God that we exhibit faith; it is when we face the world, with his assurance behind us. As Buber superbly states it, 'the man who believes acts in God's tempo'; and this is something he might do without officially 'believing in' God at all.

The conclusion is sufficiently important to warrant a parenthesis. It means that acts may be directed *by* God without being directed *to* him. This is important, because it breaks down the distinction between the religious and the non-religious.[10] If, as we have indicated, we find the makings of religion wherever activities are conducted disinterestedly, then unbelievers can be instruments of divine purpose. True, they can be used only on limited sectors, and not over the whole front; but that may be what God's tempo requires. An occasional one-eyed preoccupation with natural science may be necessary to

[9] *Op. cit.*, p. 34.
[10] This, I venture to think, is what is important in Bonhoeffer and Bishop Robinson; but Buber stated it as part of the Jewish tradition, and not as a Christian deviation for the sake of up-to-dateness. It sounds more attractive that way.

shake priests, politicians and philosophers when they start settling down and digging in. Atheists have considerably helped theologians by pointing out difficulties and forcing them to reconstruct. But the scientists, and the conscientious atheists (not the cynical ones) are, in their way, men of faith: they are deeply and disinterestedly concerned for the truth. What they are doing is religiously important: they are displaying, on their own sector, the freedom from self-preference which is the very heart of religion. All this we can consistently say, provided we begin our study of faith from the side of action, and not otherwise. As it seems important to be able to say it, our procedure is thus far vindicated.

But, to return, is there not an ambiguity about 'believing in'? It may mean 'trust' and it may mean 'accept as being'.[11] Buber appears to identify it with 'accept as being', and to assign to a pre-conscious phase the religious phenomenon of 'trust'. But, where God is concerned, 'believing in' is not an alternative to trusting; it is a consequence. It is an expanding into consciousness of the basic trust, a meditative awareness of what is implicit in the act of trusting. There is every reason to approve this transposition, provided it is a supplement to faith in action, and not a substitute for it. It is just as much part of our vocation to call a halt and review what we are doing, as it is to keep on doing it; the fundamental religious interest may settle now on the theoretical activity, and now on the practical.

There is thus no conflict between acting in God's tempo and acknowledging its source, except when acknowledgement is a substitute for action. This is not in the nature of the case, in fact it is a deformation. For one effect of the acknowledgement is to provide rational support for the God-authorized actions and so to maintain them in the face of obstacles. In many particular hard cases, in which such actions seem impossible, it is necessary to go beyond them to the ultimate congruence in which they take their natural place: it breaks upon those who cannot carry them through that 'with God all things are

---

[11] On a point of usage, 'he believes in devils' does not mean, 'he trusts devils'; that is why devil-worship is irreligious. It does mean, however, 'he responds to devils as a factor to be reckoned with in practice'; it describes a vivid and alarming experience far removed from the mere conviction that 'devils exist'.

possible' (though we should always add, with Buber, 'in his own tempo'). But this cannot happen unless they become conscious of the God to whom their actions testify, and 'believe in' him.

Thus, 'first faith' tends to develop into 'faith in God'; what was implicit in it from the first has now been brought out into the open. This is something which Buber, I am sure, would not wish to deny. For God cannot be the promoter of actions without being there to be believed in; even though (unfortunately) he can be there, and be believed in, without being the promoter of actions. But it is time to pause and make distinctions.

1. It does not mean that faith in God is logically irrefragable. That it should be based on first faith makes it much more reasonable. Any insight which sustains familiar experiences, giving them root and depth, has to be taken seriously. When it joins hands with the first principles of a broadly conceived empirical philosophy, it has to be taken so seriously as to be treated for *practical* purposes as indubitable. As we shall see, it is in practice that it is finally tested. But in the meantime, neither empirical philosophy nor faith, nor faith crowning empirical philosophy, can engender *logical* necessity. Nothing we have said in the last few pages should be so interpreted.

2. It will be asked: Why should 'first faith' develop into 'faith in God', rather than in anything else? 'Faith in' is a common human experience, attached to diverse and often dubious objects. Othello had 'faith in' Iago, and Caesar in Brutus. But these are human analogies: what about 'faith in' other deities? What about faith in Aphrodite, or Moloch, or the vengeful deities of the Aztecs, or, for that matter, the declamatory Jehovah of the early books of the Old Testament? We are inclined to say that it falls short; but why? The answer is that it denies the first faith which at the same time it continues to exhibit. They were all believed in, most devoutly and sacrificially, but the link binding them to the worshipper was fear, or, at the best, a sense of inevitability. They were not at all concerned with an expanded future; only with averting a present evil. But that is not a continuation of first faith; it is a violent reversal of it. It takes away the abundance of life

and keeps the worshipper in just those shackles which Jesus gave his life to remove. 'Faith' in the simple sense grows naturally into a Christian pattern, but collides inevitably with these repressive substitutes. This is not merely because Christianity inherits from Judaism its doubling of faith and hope. It is because the situation represented by Christianity and Judaism is the real situation. Fear is a contraction of life as well as the foe of faith, and for the same reason. It limits the range and possibility of human action to what at the moment seems feasible. It is true that we have usually to go one step at a time, but it is also true that each of these steps reveals undisclosed possibilities, to which we have to keep ourselves open. *This is the way things work*; and if the Judaic-Christian tradition insists on it, it is right, not as authoritatively delivered to Jews and Christians, but on the facts of the case.

3. 'Faith in' is frequently attached to a person because he is felt to have this liberating quality. This was manifestly the case with Jesus, and it is instructive to note how he dealt with it. There is a danger to which psychiatrists properly draw attention: that the person who liberates may find himself the object of an oppressive devotion. When this happens, the cure is only half completed; the patient is still tied to his fears, through dependence on his deliverer. Now Jesus did everything possible to check this side-effect; he played down his miracles, swore the patient to secrecy, and told him to stand now and henceforward on his own feet. Faith in him was switched back onto God and his world, exhibited by renewed capacity to take part in it. He was, and always regarded himself as, an instrument of self-dependence. He did not want faith to result in any kind of fixation, even on him. And if 'he that hath seen me hath seen the Father', God also will repudiate fixations. The man of faith is recognized by his ability to cope with varied situations on his own initiative. To require the stage to be set for him by another is dependence, not faith: the two are antithetical.

4. But is faith in God a liberating faith? So much faith, even religious faith, one might even say, especially religious faith, is not liberating. It has two central virtues: it is not self-centred, and it is whole-hearted; that is what makes it religious.

But, devoted to what is unworthy of it, it is not liberating, but tragic. God can easily be experienced as restriction, limitation, command from without; or again, as all-powerful inevitability which crushes everything in its path. Faith in God is a liberating faith on two conditions. First, there must be no concession either way on the concurrence of his power and his goodness. To see out of the corner of one's eye that the thing is not worth doing, or cannot be more than half done, is to fix faith on what is felt to be impossible, and that is to deny it. Second, there must be a continuity between God and the world to facilitate the adjustment of detail. A faith in a God who is unapproachable or (to come nearer home) 'wholly other', however good and powerful, will fail in relevance to the occasion – which is the great problem of organized religion at any time.[12] These are conditions which are hard to fulfil, because we are all disposed to swing from one extreme to another, and the circumstances which have to be provided for are constantly changing. Any attempt to pin God down to finite absolutes is bound to be self-frustrating. Yet how else can God be available for the intricate and unceasing remodelling of our lives? Only if a particular channel of his power and grace is at the same time universal; only if from its single centre no cultural variation is formally excluded; only if there is a sure sense of direction linked with a sensitive adaptability to special cases; and Christians believe that this extravagant list of conditions is wholly fulfilled in Jesus Christ.

5. The reason why faith has to consolidate round a sufficient object is that it is confronted with discouragements. The point has already been made in passing, but it has to be re-emphasized. Faith cannot triumph until it has faced up to sin and death. The evidence for faith is the evidence against it. Sin and death are the great failures, spiritual and physical; they are reasons for not believing in God, and, until we know that God has their measure, they are valid reasons. If first faith encounters them without being fixed on a God who has their measure, first faith will fail. For it is not possible not to think

[12] It is no worse today, when the irrelevance has been exposed and exaggerated, than it was in the high noon of the nineteenth century when the irrelevance was so fashionable as to pass unnoticed.

about them, and even a God-authorized faith which is un-
prepared for their challenge will be distressed and diverted.
But if faith is directed to a God who has fought and beaten
them, there is no end to it: the wages of sin is death, but death
is swallowed up in victory. That is why, in that tremendous
chapter, I Corinthians 15, so much emphasis falls on the
Resurrection.[13] 'If Christ be not risen, then is our preaching
vain, and your faith is also vain' (v. 14). 'If Christ be not
raised, your faith is vain; ye are yet in your sins' (v. 17). Any
kind of faith which consoles itself by fastening on what is
pleasant and harmonious and justifies the run of things on the
whole, leaving the counter-evidence unexplored, is vain in every
sense of the word: it is both complacent, and no use. Faith is
directed precisely to the apparent disasters of the world: *real*
disasters, if faith cannot mend them. That is the whole point
of it; philosophy can look after the rest.

3. *'Faith In' and 'Faith That'*

So far nothing has been said about faith as the holding of
propositions, or of the acceptance of dogma. To many this will
seem to be a sheer perversion of usage. It is usual, for example,
to talk about 'revealed truth', by which is meant truth accessible
to faith but not to understanding unaided by faith. What, for
example, of the doctrine of the Holy Trinity? It is not possible
to appropriate it by the methods of philosophy, because it rests
not only on cosmic considerations but also and principally on
unique historical events. It certainly requires high intellectual
refinement to state it consistently, and congruently with average
Christian experience, but no amount of thinking could supply
the premises; they are a matter of revelation, but at the same
time they are claimed to be *true*. As a matter of fact, Christian
dogma provided a solution to some of the perplexities of later

---

[13] The contention here, and in I Corinthians, has nothing to do with
matter-of-fact reports about an empty grave, which, indeed, St Paul does
not even mention. He does mention Christ's appearance to various disciples,
and once to a body of five hundred of them (I Cor. 15.6). These were
verifications for those who, at the time, were disoriented and dismayed, and
did not in the least expect them. They did not occur within the circle of
faith, they created it.

Greek philosophy.[14] It could not serve this purpose unless it is advanced as truth: perhaps not truth as philosophers understand it, but in a sense which includes and transmutes philosophy. Thus St Thomas speaks of 'divine faith, exceeding the human intellect',[15] and he formally defines faith as a 'sure and solid assent', differing from opinion, which does not express assurance, but like it in the respect that it is 'concerned with things that are not clear to the understanding'.[16] The central word is 'assent' (*assensus*), which means without question assent to propositions. It is not simply *fiducia* or *fidelitas*, though it arises from it.[17] Assent, then, is to propositions, on the authority of someone whom there is reason to trust: as, for example, God speaking in Scripture or through the interpretations of a church. The term 'Articles of Faith' expresses such a view: especially when it is said that some 'items that are known by some people . . . are presented as articles of faith to others'.[18]

The tradition thus established is not baseless. In the elaboration which it undergoes in the life of a church, and in communication with secular cultures, faith is far from simple, and we have already argued that it must include an intellectual component. There is room both for *assensus* and for *fiducia*. The issue before us concerns the relation between them. The view here put forward is that the 'articles of faith' are empirically elaborated from the structure of faith itself, and that faith itself is not a matter of assenting to articles. The traditional view is that they are delivered to us as articles, or at any rate as a system of articles, by an authority which we absolutely trust. The intellectual component, in the first case, is a corrigible transcript of faith; in the second, it is an infallible dictate of

---

[14] Especially to Neo-Platonist difficulties about form and matter: cf. the splendidly devised discussion between Hypatia and Raphael in Charles Kingsley's *Hypatia*, ch. xxvii, and the sustained contention of Werner Jaeger that Christianity was the completion of Greek *paideia*.

[15] *Summa Contra Gentiles*, Book IV, ch. I.

[16] 'Exposition of Boethius on the Trinity, III, I', tr. Vernon J. Bourke, in *The Pocket Aquinas*, 1960, p. 287. The words 'sure and firm' and the contrasts between faith and opinion are echoed in Calvin's *Institutes of the Christian Religion*, Book III, ch. II, § 15. The view of St Thomas may therefore be taken as representative of orthodoxy, both Catholic and Reformed.

[17] In the next paragraph of the *Exposition*, St Thomas observes that 'faith is necessary in the intercourse of men, that trust whereby one man believes what another man says'. [18] *Op. cit.*, p. 290.

faith. In the first case, the problem is to find an appropriate set of conceptual symbols for a total response. In the second case, the problem is how a conceptual assent shall (as Calvin put it) 'penetrate to the heart, so as to have a fixed seat there'.[19] The distinction is crucial for those exploring the empirical approach to religion.

Paradoxically, it was the father of British empiricism, John Locke, who most unequivocally identified faith with assent to propositions. His definition, which has become classic, is: 'Faith is the assent to any proposition, not made out by the deductions of reason, but upon the credit of the proposer, as coming from God in some extraordinary way of communication.'[20] As the whole context shows, his sole concern is to distinguish one kind of proposition from another; the vast hinterland of unacademic trust and loyalty is outside the scope of his discussion. That does not mean that he is not very respectful to revelation, or that the respect is not wholly sincere. But it does mean that revelation takes, for him, a purely propositional form, and that faith is a peculiar kind of knowing. If we were studying Locke in detail, we should have to note that he claims to be able to demonstrate the existence of God, very much in the Cartesian manner; that he places a remarkable reliance on miracles, as the source of credit for such propositions as reason cannot compass; that in any case of conflict, reason must prevail; but that there ought not to be conflict if we properly delineate the boundary. Many consequences in the philosophy of religion follow from this chapter: on the one side the passage into deism and, after Darwin, into atheism; on the other, Cardinal Newman. But we are concerned with the doctrine of assent in itself, which, in our view, is not any kind of faith, but only one of its possible consequences. We shall try to pursue it further.

We have seen how Calvin tried to distinguish *mere* assent from assent which has made its way to the heart. In stressing this point, he recovers, though back to front, the full patrimony of faith, and, perhaps unfairly, puts the blame on Schoolmen. 'Here the Schoolmen go completely astray, dwelling entirely,

[19] *Institutes*, Book III, ch. II, § 10.
[20] *Essay on the Human Understanding*, Book IV, ch. XVIII, § 2.

in their consideration of faith, on the bare simple assent of the understanding, and altogether overlooking confidence and security of heart.'[21] Of this Locke shows no sign. His doctrine of assent is rationalism with a spice of miracle. But it lingered long enough to serve as the basis for Newman's *Grammar of Assent,* which is by far the richest and most rewarding statement of the standard doctrine. For Newman was aware that 'the firmest hold of theological truths is gained by habits of personal religion';[22] he distinguished between 'notional assent', which is purely intellectual, and concerned with the relations of things, and 'real assent', which is the assent of the whole being and is directed to existing things;[23] he gives us the story of Mother Hallahan, who 'might not be able to separate the heresy by analysis, but she saw, and felt, and suffered from its presence';[24] and lastly, he gives us the doctrine of the Illative Sense, by which he means 'right judgment in ratiocination'.[25] Newman's insistence on judgment, as opposed to 'argumentative compulsion', as the proper channel for certitude in all concrete questions, like the similar contentions of Anglo-Hegelian logicians (we are now far enough from the scene to discern the likeness which neither would have admitted) means 'the *active* recognition of propositions as true'[26] – a kind of personal appropriation with overtones almost existentialist.[27] Given his initial assumption that faith is a kind of assent, he does everything possible to extend it to cover the whole religious horizon. Yet, when it comes to a showdown, Newman is more unyielding than either St Thomas or Calvin, and in his intellectual interpretation of faith more like Locke than either of them. 'Theology

[21] *Institutes,* Book III, ch. II, § 33. It is not fair to St Thomas, who quoted Isaiah 'Unless you have believed, you shall not understand' (Vulgate, ch. VII, v. 9), and who affirmed that 'faith is the courage of the spirit'. But St Thomas is not Calvin's usual target. When he gives a name to generalities about Schoolmen, it is most often the more primitive Peter Lombard (d. c. 1160) – the writer of *The Sentences,* a textbook which lasted for generations. It should be added that though Calvin is right to insist on the emotional overtones, he has read them wrong; faith has nothing to do with security; security is what we are driven back to when faith is lacking.
[22] New impression, 1906, p. 117.   [23] *Op. cit.,* Part I, ch. 4.
[24] *Op. cit.,* p. 335.   [25] *Op. cit.,* p. 342, and Part II, ch. 9.
[26] *Op. cit.,* p. 345.
[27] Cf. p. 83: 'Real assents are of a personal character, each individual having his own, and being known by them.'

may stand as a substantive science, though it be without the life of religion; but religion cannot maintain its ground at all without theology.'[28] The propositions are central; the rest is, very percipiently, ranged round them.

This view about faith is in conflict with that which we have tried to put forward. At the same time, and especially as set out by Newman, it contains elements which it would be helpful to appropriate. In what follows, we shall take both of these points into consideration.

4. *Assent*

As a preliminary, we propose to look more closely into the notion of 'assent'. It is not, and in the case of Newman explicitly not, men's intellectual acceptance, or even recognition. It is an activity, an appropriation, a decision. It is saying Yes with everything that is in one. To assent to articles of faith is already to have faith. But, if that is so, having faith cannot spring from, though it may be reinforced by, the decision to adopt the articles. Any but the most passive interpretation of assent takes us back to our own position. It is not without significance, though it is curious in one who protested that he was no Pelagian,[29] that Descartes should have written: 'The faith we have in things revealed, as is the case with everything else that is obscure, is an act, not of intellect, but of will.'[30] In assent there is definitely an element of will: not that it is arbitrary, but simply that in the presence of constraining fact or authority it converts contemplation into decision. We shall have more to say about this when we come to consider the relation of faith to practice; in the meantime, we note that it illustrates on the cognitive side the devotion of the whole person to God which is the essence of faith.

So far so good: our analysis of 'assent' has turned a liability into an asset. But the 'faith that' so far under review refers to the propositions of revealed theology. Now, according to our

---

[28] *Op. cit.*, p. 121.
[29] To Mersenne, Adam and Tannery, I. 366 and III. 544.
[30] *Regulae*, Adam and Tannery, X. 370: for further development see my *Philosophy of Descartes*, p. 288.

account of the matter, 'faith that' is also a proper attitude to the propositions of natural theology.[31] Speaking of fringes and prolongations, we express a reasonable expectation, but not a certainty. Such a conclusion became inevitable when 'proofs' were reduced to 'good reasons', and indeed from the moment it was decided to approach God from the side of experience. At the stage of philosophical preparation, God is not available without faith – in the first instance a natural faith, but, as the difficulties crowd in, a faith based on the particularities of the Christian evidence. Unlike the Thomists, we have not been able to demonstrate even those features of divine existence which are said to be independent of Christian evidence. Our procedure has saved us from the will-o'-the-wisp of a philosophers' God; but it brings the problem of faith back from the propositions of theology to the heart of philosophy itself. This apparently unmanageable extension may prove to be a blessing in disguise; but for the moment it is a complication, to be taken into account as we now attempt to formalize our findings.

We are driven to the conclusion that, 'faith in' being anchored to an object, 'faith that' is already implicit in it. Therefore, to retreat from the intellectual complexities of 'that' to the religious simplicities of 'in' is a mistake, both religious and philosophical. It is a religious mistake because all retreating is a religious mistake; it displays a failure of original faith. It is a philosophical mistake, because what is denied reappears in what is affirmed. What has rendered it plausible is that 'faith that' may exist without 'faith in'; there may be a sincere belief concerning matters recognized to be important which nevertheless has no power to move. The belief *that* God exists does not necessarily carry a belief *in* him. As H. H. Price pointed out,[32] it is possible to be a theist and to dislike the God one believes to exist, like the devils referred to in the Epistle of St James, who 'also believe but tremble'.[33] All this is true enough:

[31] That is why F. R. Tennant was right to dispute the common identification of 'natural' and 'rational' theology. See *Philosophical Theology*, Vol. II, p. 79.
[32] In the essay 'Faith and Belief', in *Faith and the Philosophers*, ed. John Hick, p. 9.
[33] How much contemporary atheism might better be described as antitheism (i.e. disbelief in God, rather than affirmation of his non-existence)

but it does not entitle us to draw a sharp distinction between 'faith that' and 'faith in'; for although there may be 'faith that' without 'faith in', 'faith in' always presupposes 'faith that'. The presupposition is not explicit: at the high moments of 'faith in', 'faith that' is not even contemplated; but it is taken for granted, as may be seen when the worshipper comes down from the heights and asks himself what he has been doing.

It may be urged that in explicating the moment of 'faith in' we have turned from religion to philosophy, and are no longer engaging in worship; we are viewing what we felt from the inside, or subjectively, from the outside, and objectively: in thinking about the experience we have lost touch with the experience itself. This, as we have noted, is the core of Kierkegaard's objection to philosophy in respect of religion; and it has been tirelessly and tiresomely repeated in the recent literature. As an observation it is true enough; but it does not constitute an objection. In the first place, as we have said in discussing Kierkegaard, objectivity is an intrinsic element in religion; it is the makeweight for an unceasing drift to self-centredness, which in interiorized subjective religion is purified certainly, but also magnified. In the second place, in the working life of a believer, there are slack moments when the intensity of belief flags and it is helpful to have objective translations, both liturgical and theological, to hang on to. In the third place, religion does not exclude, but comprehends, intelligence, including the intelligence which sorts out the data of religion. When Hegel replied to the landlady who urged him to go to church, 'My work is my worship', he was unduly restrictive in his view of worship, but he was right as far as he went. But, finally, the objection to 'faith that' as prejudicial to 'faith in' stems from a view about thinking which would be misleading in contexts other than of religion; and this is an opportunity for considering it in general terms.

The view is that the thinker, in shaping concepts and working out their mutual relations, is somehow deforming the data of human experience. He is justified (it continues) in formal logic, and perhaps in the natural sciences – anywhere, in fact,

---

would be an interesting study. In Antony Flew's *God and Philosophy*, 1966, anti-theism is the better half of the atheist profession of unfaith.

where there is no experience to deform. But in human affairs conceptualization sets 'out there' what belongs 'in here'; it takes away the feel of the situation and reduces it to a graph. Some may say that this is the right manner and approach. That is to aver that feeling is irrelevant. It is as a protest against these over-simplifications that intelligence has been warned off the inner preserves of the spirit. But both the mistake and its correction rest on the same mistaken premisses. In thinking about our experiencing, we do not eliminate the experience: we find for it proper symbolic forms which communicate it to others and make it available for them. If there were no trace of feeling in the transcript, it would indeed be mutilation; but there is as much trace of, e.g., the experience of believing in the delineation of its objects as there is of the painter's vision on the canvas before him. The concept is first and foremost a symbol; it is other things as well (what it symbolizes is general as well as particular), but it is a symbol first, and as such it reflects the passion of the original. That is why those who lack sympathy and empathy are well advised to avoid literary criticism and history and all but the most statistical branches of psychology, and also the study of religion. In these fields the concept retains the warmth of what it stands for, while at the same time transcending its particularities. Herein lies the peculiar value of Newman's distinction between notional and real assent.[34]

For these several reasons, we deny that 'faith that', which retrieves the implications, is false to 'faith in', which exhibits but does not explore them. But it remains true that 'faith that' disengages them and does not justify them. Faith does not need to be justified by anything other than practice, or, if

[34] It may be said: 'faith in' is the faith of each person for himself – 'my faith', 'thy faith', and (descriptively) 'his faith'. 'Faith that' claims to be everyone's faith; rightly or wrongly is not here in question. 'Encounter' with God can occur only to individuals, even when they need public worship and ceremony to sustain it. Or, to use another favourite locution, the vocative case is more typical of religion than the nominative or accusative: it is a question of I and Thou; a relation which cannot be replaced by third-personal description or argument. All this is true; but if thinking is capable of making the distinction, it does not eliminate encounter and invocation: on the contrary, it explains to all and sundry the difference between them on the one hand and description and argument on the other. What remains true is that the third-personal statement does not *replace* the first-personal.

practice already embodies it, it does not need to be justified
at all.[35] The same problem arises when a search is made for
the 'basis' of faith: 'basis', in this context, is in fact a *kind* of
justification, and an inapposite kind at that. The Tübingen
theologian, Gerhard Ebeling, in *The Nature of Faith*, pertinently
asks: 'What does "the basis of faith" mean?', and he very
properly replies: 'Certainly not support which relieves us in
part of the need for faith. Rather, the basis of faith is that
which lets faith be faith, which keeps it being faith.'[36] And the
only thing that can keep faith faith is 'God existing'. So with
'revealed' theology: 'Christian faith is not directed to the
trinitarian dogma, but to God in threefold form.'[37] Perhaps
that is what St Paul meant (Rom. 3.28) when he affirmed for
his community: 'We hold that a man is justified by faith.'
The justification of faith is that a man is justified by it.

This having been freely admitted, there is everything to be
said for disengaging the presuppositions and setting them out
in order. That is theology, in the narrower sense of the word,
and the activity of correlating our profoundest experiences
(including their concealed intellectual content) with each other
and with the secular world, with the aid of a conceptual
apparatus not wholly distinct from that employed elsewhere,
but adapted to the particular concerns of believers, is one
without which both philosophy and religion would be the
poorer. To serve its purpose, however, it will have to conform
to requirements which may be considered unorthodox, but
follow inevitably from our description of faith.

The first is that it is a rendering of a particular kind of
experience, one that is particularly difficult to pin down, and
may therefore be expected to vary with the degree of faith, and
with the secular assumptions and the personal idiosyncrasies
of those who evince it. Take a comparatively simple case, that
in which there is a central core common to the experiences of
many people: faith in and devotion to Christ. The interpretations of that experience will be as subtly variable as the lives

[35] The justification of faith here resembles in both respects the justification
of induction.
[36] Translation by Ronald Gregor Smith, 1961, pp. 70f.
[37] *Op. cit.*, p. 107.

of those who carry it. Even within the bounds of a rigid orthodoxy there are stresses and slurrings of one or another of permissible expressions or aspects of it. That they do not cause more stir than they do is due to ecclesiastical discipline or self-censorship based on the need for a united front. There is, then, a tendency for renderings even of a common and unforgettable experience to diverge. It is in accordance with mutual respect and intellectual honour to let the process continue unimpeded. The limit will be reached when the experience, instead of giving rise to fruitfully divergent interpretations, is itself called in question. To go back on Peter's exclamation, 'Thou art the Christ', in the course of trying to account for it, would be a case in point. Even so, it is a matter for doubt whether Arianism did or did not have that effect; my conviction would be that it did, but it is debatable and it was right that it should have been debated. If, for the sake of order, it is decided to follow one course rather than another in a collective declaration of faith, that again is proper if it is recognized as a progress report and not as a final statement. The principle is stated by St Paul, I Cor. 14.29: 'Let the prophets speak two or three, and let the other judge', and v. 31: 'Ye may all prophesy one by one, that all may learn, and all may be comforted.' If he had been followed, theology would have been from the first empirical and experimental openly, and not merely surreptitiously, as has happened almost up to our own day.

In thus following the Independent tradition, I raise the second question, that of 'revealed truth'. The simple interpretation of these words is that some authority, church or council or congregation, is recognized as infallible – infallible, and not merely entitled to close down on disputes for the time being for the sake of peace. But once infallible, always infallible; what was infallibly declared to be the case cannot later be called mistaken. That the emphasis does shift after all (too slowly for comfort) shows that the authority can learn, and it is a pity that it should be so loath to admit it. But the worst effect of this pretension is the curtailment of faith. Instead of finding new paths, faith is fastened to the old ones: when its genius is to create, it is constrained to follow. No one denies that there is

value in a tradition; what has to be added is that there is value
in developing it. The conception of 'revealed truth', as commonly understood, is once for all. But perhaps it can be
differently interpreted: 'The Lord hath yet more truth and light
yet to break forth out of his holy word.'[38] A *continuous* revelation
finds room, as a fixed revelation does not, for the exploratory
genius of faith.

If this analysis is accepted, there must be a reappraisal of
'revealed truth'. 'Revealed truth' is not presented to us in
slabs, but quarried by us out of the total revelation. It is not a
super-philosophy; it springs from the self-examination of a faith
which crowns philosophy. This view of the matter is in fact
confirmed by the form of the creeds: 'I *believe* in God the Father
Almighty', not 'there is an omnipotent God'.[39] The propositions of faith filter through the experience and express a
determination to understand it: an enterprise in which some
succeed better than others, but, just because it is so marvellous,
they can never grasp the whole of it. Strictly speaking, it is
not the truth that is revealed; it is the being of God; and our
propositions hobble along after him.[40]

Here we encounter our third problem, the relation of 'faith
that' to general philosophy. Both are concerned with statement; and, on our account, neither is concerned with incorrigible statement. Both are exhibitions of empirical reasoning
and neither can lay claim to necessity. Moreover, they move in
the same area: they deal with the general characters of things;

[38] Pastor Robinson's farewell sermon to the Pilgrim Fathers as they set
out for the New World.

[39] The point was well taken by R. G. Collingwood, *Metaphysics*, 1940, p.
187. We are not obliged to follow him in denying ontological reference to the
belief (cf. his gibe about *un nommé Dieu*, p. 189), or to interpret profession of
belief as a statement of presuppositions. Collingwood holds that presuppositions cannot be true or false. No Christian, or any other believer, will say
that his beliefs cannot be true or false.

[40] If it should be said that 'revealed truth' rests on authority, it none the
less rests on faith, differently located. The truth is believed because the
authority is believed *in*. I believe in the theory of relativity in just this way;
I do not understand the arguments by which it is established, but I trust
Einstein and the honour of scientists. Many people feel the same way about
God, and their faith depends in no small degree on the quality of the
Christians they have known. They believe *that* as a consequence of believ-
ing *in*.

and both are concerned with problems about God.[41] But they are directed to them at different levels of a spiritual dialectic. Philosophy deals with the most general features of the universe as pointers to a faith in God which follows philosophy but outruns it. 'Faith that' results from an exploration of the faith, in the light of secular experience, and with reference to the all-importance of certain actual events. Without philosophy faith would lack rational antecedents. Without theology it would lack rational formulation. It will be shown that its rational formulations may supply an answer to the counter-evidence which our philosophical inquiry was unable to accommodate. We shall find ourselves nearer to the Thomist model than at first appeared: the distinction between natural and revealed theology will be retained, together with the hierarchical relation between them. But faith will not be identified with any assent to propositions, however supernatural; it is the initial and sustaining activity which carries the propositions on its shoulders.[42]

5. *Faith and Belief*

It follows that a sharp distinction has to be made between 'faith' and 'belief'.

[41] The last statement will be denied as respects philosophy, not so much by atheists, who think of God all the time with a minus sign in front of him, but by positivists and anti-metaphysicians who, though they sometimes let God into their lives, keep him out of their discourse. It is in fact lack of interest about God that makes them what they are. Bradley was right (*Appearance and Reality*, pp. 5f.) when he said that 'with certain persons, the intellectual effort to understand the universe is a principal way of experiencing Deity'. And Ryle is right when he says in his introduction to *The Revolution in Philosophy* (1956): 'In Bradley's youth ... the burning theoretical issues were between theologians and theologians, or else between theologians and anti-theologians. Beneath and behind the more philosophical divisions of opinion there commonly lay the division between faith and doubt. By the 1920's all this had gone' (p. 2). Being an obstinate survivor with a dominating interest in religion, on both these showings I can be expected to prefer Bradley's conception of philosophy to that of his juniors, and as for being up-to-date, only an up-to-date vulgarism can describe my sentiments: I couldn't care less. My business is not to be topical, but to seek the truth.

[42] Gabriel Marcel, in the second volume of his Gifford Lectures, aptly distinguishes 'between belief taken in its full or comprehensive reality and a particular belief which may always lie open to the attack of primary reflection' (*The Mystery of Being*, Vol. II: *Faith and Reality*, 1951, p. 80).

In English, it is difficult, because, for the two nouns, there is only one verb: 'to believe'. The ambiguity spreads to derivative nouns when those who have faith are called 'believers', a term which in general usage denotes those who accept dogma. If challenged, those who use it would not deny it denotes also a living faith in God; but its general effect is to obliterate the difference. Faith and belief, if not positively identical, are two sides of the same thing. On our showing, belief, in its most exalted sense, is the articulation of faith, but not faith itself, and without faith evaporates for lack of matter.

The confusion goes back a long way, for in New Testament Greek there is the same trouble as there is in English. As in English, there is only one verb for two meanings, πιστεύειν (*pisteuein*); but Greek is even worse placed than English in that there is only one noun, πίστις (*pistis*). The result is an elevation of πίστις far beyond its range in Greek philosophy, where frequently (as in Plato) it means surmising as opposed to knowing. It is still a falling short: it is what is available in this life in the absence of sight. Moreover, it is still a *cognitive* falling short; in faith, we do not know even as we are known. The promotion of πίστις by early Christianity shows most clearly in its specification to God; as applied to doctrine, it belongs to a later and more Hellenistic phase of Christian history.[43] But the cognitive implications survive, and indeed multiply; πίστις is knowledge, though inferior knowledge, gaining ground because it is never formally dissociated from 'trust' – the usual sense, in classical Greek, outside the philosophers. What is not captured at any time by the word πίστις, and can be represented by the word 'faith', if not by a corresponding verb, is the whole-hearted unambiguous trust, including, but only incidentally, a reference to the truth of propositions about what is trusted, which appears (I rely here on the scholarship of colleagues) to be conveyed by the Hebrew word *emūnah*. This is what we have taken to be the full sense of 'faith', and it is clear that 'belief' will not encompass it.

[43] There is a linguistic preparation for it in New Testament (as opposed to Attic) Greek: in the latter the construction is πιστεύω τινί, in the dative; in the New Testament, it is πιστεύω εἰς, or even ἐπί: e.g. at random, John 14.1; Acts 9.42. The prepositional construction is less tied to a person and more easily transferable to 'faith that'.

For faith is not knowledge, even intuitive knowledge. Above all, it is not inferior knowledge: but it is not superior knowledge either. It arises from knowledge of the world, which is fallible, and strives to express itself in knowledge of God, which is even more fallible. If that is what is meant by belief, then faith is related both ways to belief, and it even entails belief, but itself, as the total confidence of the human being, body and spirit, in the presence of God, in including belief, it transcends it.[44]

It follows that belief, unlike faith, is not wholly a good thing. The flagging of faith is a misfortune for which every activity will be the poorer. A decent modicum of disbelief is a spiritual asset, and in no way interferes with, indeed, may spring from, the initiative of faith.[45] To have faith is to be sure of better things, and it is sometimes necessary to question the old good things that stand in the way. What is damaging is disbelief as a final attitude; but faith may need it as an engine of reconstruction.[46]

It follows also that the belief in believing, i.e. believing not from faith, but from the lack of it, has, at the best, the dubious merit of good intention, and at the worst is what might be called a paralogism of the practical reason. Charles Kingsley, in *Yeast*,[47] describes its practitioners as follows: 'They are sinking out of real living belief into that dead self-deceiving belief-in-believing, which has always been heretofore, and is becoming in England now, the parent of the most blind, dishonest and pitiless bigotry' (Collins ed., p. 4). Naturally, a failure of faith in those who do not have it but believe in having it makes them harsh with those who display its lack too openly. It is not only from personal experience but from expert

---

[44] That is not to deny it: it means merely, that in man as in God, being is not simply knowing.

[45] Cf. René Le Senne, *La découverte de Dieu*, 1955, p. 15: 'Il y a deux consciences qui ne doutent pas: Dieu, et le fou.'

[46] 'Unbelief' is an ambiguous term. It may be used to denote scepticism concerning propositions; if so, it is not so evil because thinkers in the appropriate field (including theologians) can always formulate propositions better. It may also be used to mean that total disbelief which is the intellectual aspect of a failure of faith. As applied to adherents of other religions, it cannot be used in the latter sense, and is a needlessly offensive way of challenging comparisons.

[47] Not by any means the best of his novels, but very revealing about average religious discourse and attitudes in 1850.

observations on this great church-going period (by Kingsley, Kierkegaard, and, of course, Samuel Butler) that one is driven to find a correlation between intolerance on the one hand and, on the other, religion practised from a sense of duty or respectability. The error could never have occured if faith had not been confused with believing. Faith-in-faith would be too obvious a contradiction in terms.

Whether what is known and what one has faith in can be one and the same thing, is a question more difficult to answer.

1. Supposing there were to be knowledge of God, as there is not now, but, we are promised, there will be hereafter for those who love him, would there be an end of faith? A familiar hymn tells us that 'faith will vanish into sight';[48] but surely the more we know of God, the more we shall trust him; in this case, at least, knowledge would consolidate faith, and increase it. On its own assumptions, the hymn must be wrong, as hymns so often are. The reason for the mistake is that faith is envisaged as an inferior form of knowing: a view rejected in respect of our present situation, but affirmed in respect of heaven, where everything is still supposed to stand still in the best Neo-Platonist tradition. It is guesswork anyway, but the alternative suggestion could be offered that the better one knew God, the continuous creator, the less one could be sure what he would do next. In that case, faith would still be the absolute anticipatory trust that it is now. The notion that it is a stop-gap is bound up with the view that it is an inferior kind of certainty.

2. Returning to the other end, it may be objected that in tracing the passage from philosophy to faith we allowed no premonitory gleams of faith to the activity of philosophizing. If that were so, it would indeed be a mistake; but it can be removed by reflecting in general on the empirical approach to God. The prolongations of God into the world, as we have insisted, cannot be grasped as such without premonitions; if we had no incipient faith, we should take the facts as we find them without the sense of something missing which leads us to look beyond them. Faith, then, is not something which supervenes on philosophy in difficulties, but something which has inspired

[48] In this case it follows a Thomist formula, *fides non potest esse de scitis.*

the enterprise from the beginning. The empirical approach to God relies on faith and calls for faith and can only be completed in faith: and (as we shall see) its verification is in action.

3. It could be objected again that our account of the matter places faith indeed at the far end of knowledge, but in necessary relation to knowledge. That would exclude from faith the most typical instances of it, which is far from our intention. Catholic theologians have made much of the *vetula*, the happy uneducated old woman, 'la bonne vieille' in French, and picturesquely Englished as Newman's 'chaste and ignorant charwoman'. She is, of course, philosophically innocent, but no less faithful for that; indeed, more reliably faithful, for faith comes much harder to intellectuals. Any account of faith which excluded her would be drawing a line in the wrong place. In our account we have introduced faith at the point where philosophy is going as well as finite enterprises can go, but needs to be supplemented. It has to be made clear that we were trying to find out how far reason could go, and not how far faith could go. Of course faith can try short cuts, provided it appeals to intuition or authority. It is just the burden laid on the philosopher that he has to reason it out, in the interests of those who will believe it anyway, but do not experience God as a promoter of questions. He is justified because the questions have to be answered, both for atheists, and for himself. But he ceases to be justified as soon as he gives himself airs in the presence of *vetulae*, who, being spared his temptations, may be expected to enter the Kingdom of Heaven before him. Here, at least, we agree with St Thomas who wrote (*Contra Gentiles* I, 4): 'The divine clemency has made this salutary commandment, that even some things which reason is able to investigate must be held by faith.'

To conclude this discussion: if there is knowledge of God, then, seeing that there is also faith in God, what can be known and what there is faith in are identical; and even when (as with us) knowledge of God falls short, but faith completes it, by virtue of the continuity they are still identical. It was therefore inappropriate that Pascal should deprecate 'the philosophers' God' and distinguish him from the 'God of Abraham, Isaac and Jacob'. The philosophers are not setting up a God of their own; they are scanning the world as they know it for evidences of what is not only completed in faith, but prefigured in the world itself.

6. *Faith, Freedom and the Counter-evidence*

It has been hinted more than once that the approximations of philosophy are fulfilled in the Christian faith. The time has come to be more explicit.

We have contended that a faith in God is the natural culmination of what is to be observed in the world, under the headings of order and creativity. But God, so understood, is a climax for the good in the world, and not a cancellation of its evils; and it is those evils which are the main part of the counter-evidence. Now we have also noted that faith in God may be particularized, and that the particularization may be intellectually translated into a confessional theology. Thus if it is true, as has been suggested, that theology is the completion of our wisdom, it will be in virtue of its particularity. It will be argued that the difficulties of philosophers about 'evils', i.e. suffering and wickedness, are in fact met by the theology of redemption, and can be met in no other way.

In chapter IV, 5, we have noted some of the traditional defences and have seen that they are not good enough. 'It will come right in the end'; yes, but what about the meantime? Suffering is something we ought to put up with; yes, but why is it there, and what about other people? Or, 'Cheer up, it isn't as bad as it looks': but it is; many things since 1914 are too bad to have been imagined. These are the defences of popular theology, and they need to be repudiated more firmly than is usually thought proper; at any rate, they are alternatives to the Christian view, and if the Christian view is accepted, they cannot stand. On the other hand, natural theology cannot be wholly discontinuous with the faith to which it gives rise; the particularist elaborations of theology depend on the evidence which they transform. The connecting link is the concept of creativity.

Referring back once again to chapter IV, 5, we note that 'our sin is the price we pay for our freedom'. The conclusion follows from our revised account of omnipotence, and our declared view that God is a 'creator of creators'. If creativity is passed on to us as the mark of our divine origin, *we* are responsible for the use we make of it. Dorothy Sayers, in *The Mind of the Maker*, points out how a novelist's characters tend to develop a life of their own, and, in a sense, once they have been launched, take charge of the story. If these attenuated forms of existence can accomplish their own destinies, surely the human creature, *a fortiori*, can do the same. If so, then God cannot be blamed for all that we do. If he could, it would be the end of our responsibility, and would annihilate our role as the bearers of creativity.

Freedom, then, is a conclusion concealed in our various premisses. Some will hold that our premisses are shown thereby to be mistaken. Unfortunately, it is impossible in passing to stage a full-dress debate on freedom. I hope those who object will forgive me for handling a huge subject almost incidentally, in relation to a specific purpose. The reason why freedom, the human expression of creativity, is important for us is that it provides for centres of decision other than God, so that God cannot directly at least be held responsible when things go wrong. It is with this end in view that the following cursory observations are advanced.

1. Freedom, as we understand it, is first of all a theological concept, and its antithesis, in the first instance, is not determinism, but fate. It is a protest against the view that God (or History, or Destiny, or *Moira*) settles everything. In fact, the evolution of the idea of God is at the same time a protest against fixity. Nowhere does fate play a smaller part than among the Hebrews; and the reason is that they resisted more firmly than any other civilization the assimilation of God to nature. Even the arbitrariness of their God had its compensations.

2. Owing to a mistaken view of what constitutes omnipotence, the place of Fate was taken by the monopolistic agency of the Wholly Other. It happened just at the time when the Christian humanism of Erasmus and More might have spread throughout a united Christendom; and the wrecking of these hopes by the Reformation and the Counter-Reformation

between them set the whole prospect back for four hundred years. Freedom, i.e. initiative, effort, causal efficacy and the open decision, were treated not as instruments of grace, but as its rivals. The natural result is that freedom should become the slogan of atheists, and this is in fact what has happened in the works of Jean-Paul Sartre: freedom is poised against *Le Néant* (let us say, not-being), and the attributes of God devolve upon man, who is termed the creator not only of his values, but of himself.

3. That this development was so long delayed, and is infrequent even now, was due to the rise of natural science, against a Calvinist background, in the seventeenth century. Natural law took the place of fate and omnipotence, and freedom was declared to have died from natural causes. By an odd flick of the wheel, it was associated by the new materialists with the theism against which they were in revolt: both freedom and theism, presumably, were metaphysical survivals and therefore unworthy of their attention. But, in fact, natural law is the secular descendant of unreformed omnipotence. Both are suspicious of free will because it is a threat to dogmatic simplification.

4. The subtlety so obviously lacking in the earlier versions of scientific determinism has more recently been supplied by the psychologists. They have carried natural law into the very citadel of freedom, and have finally forced us to decide whether natural science tells the whole truth about anything. It was a bad day for philosophy when Descartes failed to distinguish between the new physics and the philosophy of nature, and, to establish the one, drove the other out of business. It led to, and was indeed based upon, the assumption that the scientific account is the whole account of the matter in question. The error did not come home to him, because he was at the same time elaborating his personalist metaphysics; but when his dualism was found unworkable and the range of the sciences extended, his own precedent favoured the extension of his account of matter to things in general. The alternative suggested by his own technological ambitions, that scientific knowledge derives its certainty from being directed to a convenient extract of things and not to things in themselves, did not occur to him.

However this may be, the consequences for morals are

revolutionary. If men are only complex machines, they may, it is true, help each other – machines can repair machines – but they may equally well *not* help each other, and they cannot decide whether they will help each other or not. A decision is mainly the clicking together of two mechanisms which will run thenceforward on a single path. The notion of responsibility disappears – we must insist that it *has* to disappear, for attempts have been made to keep it alive when by all the rules it should be dead.[49] What keeps it alive is the non-mechanical activity of trying; and that is what the modern full-dress attack on the notion of responsibility attempts to suppress. It appeals to psycho-analysis to show that people are unable to try, or try without the slightest possibility of succeeding, like a bird in a cage. It should be admitted that we have sometimes ascribed responsibility unfairly; but in so doing we assume that in other cases it can be ascribed fairly. Moreover, the psycho-analyst as a practitioner is attempting to produce the freedom which the psycho-analyst as a theorist declares impossible; and in this, as in other matters, what matters is the good the man does, even if it makes nonsense of his explanations. But on both counts we meet the unyielding answer; if a man is able to try, if he can help other people to learn to try, he deserves no credit: 'he is lucky'.[50] The answer surely is that if he *can* try, no matter why, he *can* make the sort of difference to his conduct which is the essence of free will. It may be bad luck that some people can't try, and it is unfair to be too hard on them, but it does not follow that trying is meaningless. If the result of my conditioning is that I *can* try, i.e. if I am determined so as to be free, I *am* free.[51]

[49] There is a sort of surrogate responsibility arising from the duties of one's status – a responsibility to social order, which holds merely because one is part of it and is compatible with a total incapacity to fulfil it. An Indian friend suggests the (imaginary) case of a district officer, good enough for ordinary times, whose territory lay right in the line of the Chinese invasion of 1963. He is unable to cope with the complications and he has to be replaced, even though he has done his best; he is not incapable of trying, he is just inadequate. See my treatment of this case in an article 'On Imputing Responsibility', *Dr S. Radhakrishnan Souvenir Volume*, 1964, pp. 126–31.

[50] John Hospers in the collection *Free Will and Determinism*, ed. B. Berofsky, 1966, p. 39.

[51] Professor P. H. Nowell-Smith tries to disqualify trying by charging that if it (or more precisely, making an effort: this equivalence we need not deny)

The point of this digression is to prepare the philosophical foundation for a particular act of faith. Naturally, the act of faith can proceed without it; but, without it, it cannot be defended against criticism. If we wish to avoid the either-or of faith and reason and to display as far as possible their continuity, we must be able to give a rational account of human freedom. For, if there is no such thing, then God, if there is a God, is responsible for everything, including the wickedness of human beings, and the dilemma of Carneades has us by the throat. If, on the other hand, we are created creators, i.e. creators, but finite, we shall expect to make mistakes, some of them serious, and God, having made us creators, cannot be saddled with the blame for them. He cannot even be blamed for making us finite creators; anything that shares his nature must be creative, and anything he makes must be finite.

But the defence of freedom, though necessary, is not sufficient to refute what we have called the 'counter-evidence'. If the misuse of freedom goes on unchecked, a whole sector of creation can be devastated, and, for a God who creates, the most companionable sector at that. Yet he cannot stop it without shackling creation, i.e. denying part of his own nature. So it just goes on, till non-intervention begins to look like helplessness or connivance. True, the misuse of freedom is in many cases self-correcting, and this in itself is an indication that things are, as we put it, right side up. But even this semi-automatic rectification has to be carried out by individuals, and in the meantime there has been much suffering and wickedness which the proper use of freedom could have averted. Ivan Karamazov, it may be remembered, was ready to believe that suffering would be healed, but he was not ready to accept the universe in which it occurred. (His horrible examples of cruelty to children were real; they were clipped by Dostoevsky from Russian newspapers during 1876.) Happy endings to such episodes are not to the point. If God has no way to stop them happening, should we not, like Ivan, 'hand back our entrance

---

'is to be relevant to responsibility, it must be thought of as something which a man can choose to do or not to do' (*Ethics*, pp. 285f.). In that case, it is subject to a vicious regress: 'I try to try to try . . .' But whether or not I choose to try, I do try, and this is very relevant to responsibility.

ticket'? And should we not prefer the security offered by the Grand Inquisitor to the 'terrible gift' of freedom?

7. *Freedom and Identification*

Freedom, then, needs to be supplemented. But, in general terms, it cannot be supplemented. There cannot be something added to freedom which would determine it; for then it would not be freedom.[52] Freedom cannot be guaranteed against itself. The only way of setting freedom right is that it should be infiltrated by the source of all freedom; that a new man should emerge from the old, with his will intact and directed to purposes no longer self-destructive. But this is a particular operation requiring the collaboration of God and man – or rather, *each* man, for man is an abstraction which (not who) can collaborate with nobody.[53] The transaction, being in time, must take the form of a historical intervention. There is no other way for it to happen; if the intervention is not historical, it cannot happen at all. It must be specific, for the misuses of freedom are specific and cannot be rectified by generalities: they may be dispelled in various ways but not by an appeal to God-in-general. And it must be efficacious in dispelling the counter-evidence; for, as we have seen (p. 105), the reasoning of empirical metaphysics can do no more than amass the evidence and question contrary assumptions: enough to make the venture of faith plausible, but not enough to see it through. The counter-evidence is challenged by the venture of faith itself (unfaith may in fact be described as being bogged down in the counter-evidence), but it can be finally dislodged only if it is actually incorporated in the process which dislodges it.[54]

[52] Cf. as above, p. 180, Gerhard Ebeling's argument that no guarantee should be sought for faith which would make it less faith. Like faith, of which it is a support, and an ingredient, it cannot accept supports which would make it less itself.

[53] Unless the term is used collectively to denote organized mankind, which would be concrete, but has not yet happened, and is not what is meant by 'man' in theological discourse.

[54] As I pointed out in an article, 'Empirical Evidence and Religious Faith', *Journal of Religion*, Vol. XXXVI, No. 1, January 1956, it is a mark of religious faith that it snaps its fingers at evidence which would cause a scientist to withdraw his hypothesis for reconstruction: 'the kind of assurance which stands out against the evidence cannot be produced by the evidence

The counter-evidence, it will be recalled, consisted of suffering and wickedness. As they stand, they are asymmetrical, both in themselves and in their relation to what dislodges them. It is far too simple, on the basis of the hangover, or because it antagonizes, to say that wickedness explains suffering. It is equally too simple, on the basis of case-histories concerning 'rejection' and 'alienation', to say that suffering explains wickedness. The relations between them are devious and complex; some wicked men do not suffer, some who suffer were not wicked, some are wicked and suffer, some, by the grace of God, neither are wicked nor suffer, and others, by the still greater grace of God, suffer and are not wicked. And suffering and wickedness themselve admit of degrees, inter-mixtures, specifications, intermissions, desperations, reticences, bouts of pain and shouts of triumph. It is part of their disorientation that they fall apart. But the one thing which suffering and wickedness do not suggest by the light of nature is that the one can be used against the other. This is what is presented to us against all our expectations in the life and death of Jesus Christ.

That, however, is to anticipate. We have still to justify the canalizing of faith in God in a single channel. Let us say at once that the specification is not absolute. There are fringes, borrowings, similarities between the great religions of the world, and all must be treated with the deep respect due to any revelation with roots in the soil. If distinctions are made, it is not on the basis of the empirical approaches, which are available to all, but because some kinds of faith are better able than others to deal with the counter-evidence. To make the point it is first necessary to distinguish and to grade the elements of the counter-evidence,

---

alone' (*op. cit.*, p. 25). Is this not a most unempirical proceeding? The answer is that, for faith, evidence is not something that stays put; it is always being transformed by the operation of faith itself. 'Faith confronts the evidence dynamically – not contemplating it as it is (which will always induce despair), but rising to greet it and to be gathered up into the sovereign charity which has power to change it. If faith persists in the face of evidence, it is because it will not count as evidence what is being continually rebuilt into the living substance of what it is evidence against' (*op. cit.*, p. 27).

If I have not made it clear in the text that the behaviour of the man of faith in the presence of counter-evidence is different from the scientist's and in fact the distinctive mark of religious behaviour, I allow myself to quote in this footnote from earlier writing by which I still stand.

because considerations applying to suffering do not necessarily apply to wickedness, and vice versa.

In the light of what has been said about freedom, the case of wickedness is the less embarrassing. It can be unloaded on human decision; this is in fact the story of the Fall, demythologized. Yet, as we have seen, this alibi for God becomes less and less convincing the further we go from the source and the more widely wickedness extends. By the time human decisions have multiplied and grown upon each other, even if they are not infected by a 'radical evil', but simply jostle each other, good and bad indifferently, they will have wandered from the divine intention, if not as far as Sodom, at least as far as Laodicea. They may be unable to establish the Kingdom of Darkness, because darkness cannot make a kingdom, but they may well shed only so much light as is needed to avert catastrophe. Moreover, some of the more execrable displays of wickedness issue not from the misuse of freedom, but from the lack of it. We are apt to think in post-Puritan terms of those cases where wickedness is the result of failing to realize the good that we know. But the Puritans were a moral aristocracy; much of what is worst in our civilization comes from those who have not the faintest idea what the good is, or whether there is one. In the absence of any point of reference, they are ridden by their impulses, the source of which is buried in a subconscious obscurity. Aristotle, in the Seventh Book of the *Nicomachean Ethics*, distinguished between *akrasia*, in which the will is weak, and *akolasia*, in which it is corrupted at the root; not having read Freud, he regarded the latter (though not the former) as irreclaimable. He saw that in the *akolastos* the whole frame of reference is twisted, and that those so afflicted are unable to make the proper responses. This is not a misuse of freedom: it is a deprivation of freedom: and if it were not that the psycho-analysts provide a means of redemption, it is almost enough to make one a Calvinist. In these cases the defence of freedom is not enough. No doubt men were meant to be free, and the psycho-analyst, as a practitioner, helps them to be free: but such crimes as result from the corruption of the whole frame of reference cannot be attributed to the freedom which in them is inoperative.

Even so, the case of wickedness is less difficult for the theist than the case of suffering. In the first place, there are plenty of people who run into trouble through not trying hard enough; and plenty more who, obviously discerning their weaknesses, learn to live with them and to circumnavigate them and even to use them. If they fail, they can fairly be blamed. But, in the second place, to the extent that wickedness is not blameworthy, it is the product of suffering. The case-histories show that neglect or rejection at an early age gives rise to a suffering all the more intense for not being understood, from which spring the various fixations so inimical to growth in freedom. And for this suffering the agent concerned cannot be held responsible. Suffering is beginning to emerge as the centre of the problem; if it were only perversity, the solution would be so much easier.[55]

In this predicament, it is a help to recede from the moral plane to the religious. The conception of sin, as presented in the New Testament, is much wider than that of immorality; indeed, the conception of immorality is a moralistic limitation of the conception of sin. Sin means being cut off from God in any mode whatever: in the bodily mode, by sickness; in the subconscious mode, by repressed complexes (it does no harm to call them devils); in the moral mode, by leaving undone the things we ought to have done, as well as by doing the things we ought not to have done; including wrapping ourselves up in our own virtue and thanking God that we are not as other men. The word 'sin' encompasses all these things at once: and its elimination from the current vocabulary, or its debased use as an equivalent for sexual deviation, is a serious loss to the language, and therefore to thinking about religion. Now it is part of the Christian faith that Jesus Christ came into the world to save sinners. If that is true, then the need for God to step in to save us from the misuse of freedom expands into the need for him to step in to restore freedom.

Let us consider how this could be done. Not merely by

---

[55] In all this there is no intention to deny freedom or responsibility or to deny that much of the trouble in the world is due to avoidable thoughtlessness, over-precipitancy, and sloth. We are merely reminding ourselves that there are evils to which freedom cannot serve as a defence.

preaching, lay or clerical; preaching may show us up to ourselves and make us think; it may draw attention to facts about
the world, and to ways of looking at it, which we had not
thought of: in general, it can remove blinkers; but it cannot
create sight. Consequently it can pave the way for faith and
confirm or recover faith, but it cannot create faith. Let us be
grateful for what it can do, and pass on.

Still less can it be done by laying down laws. If these are
civic laws, they can only protect conditions. If they are moral
laws, they will be judicious and helpful extracts from experience, but their function being to prescribe, they can do no
more than maintain a minimum level of conduct among those
who can understand them, and for the alienated and resentful
they can do nothing at all. Once again, let us be grateful for
their mapping of the moral world, and pass on. Maps instruct;
they do not save.

Nearer to the mark, but still not sufficient, is doing things
to help people. Much of the jeering about 'do-gooders' is
unfair: their sincerity and their sacrifice are unquestionable;
their techniques are constantly improving; they act, often
enough, not merely from duty but from fellow feeling; and at
least some of the prejudice against them stems from the malice
of sinister interests which would suffer if they succeeded. But
the do-gooder traffic is a one-way traffic; some devoted people
do things and the rest have things done for them. We could
not get on without them, but they are incitements to ingratitude.
Unless they are careful, they will feel bigger after the event and
their beneficiaries will feel smaller.

As a matter of fact, the Christian way of life embodies all
these activities, and in their places they are indispensable. But
something else is needed to make them work – something which
will remove suspicion, respect hurt pride, establish mutuality,
and promote freedom. There is only one way, and that is the
way of identification. If those who have the good news about
the world built into them can identify themselves with those
who are standing out against it, so that they can approach them
without privilege and without condescension, and can work as
one of them, taking over the intolerable burdens of fear and
pride which have kept them aloof, and sharing the actualities

of their suffering. It is a heroic and impossible undertaking, for it has to be completely objective in its feeling for facts, alive to the dangers of deception (which is why social workers are warned against over-identification), and yet compassionate in the literal Latin sense of the word ('feeling with', not 'being sorry for'), and powerful enough to make the dislodging of a psychical obstruction a genuinely co-operative effort. We feel, perhaps, that it can't be done, but it has been done; in Galilee, in the tetrarchy of Philip, in Samaria and in Jerusalem about AD 30–33.

Now this is the reinforcement that natural theology requires. We noted that its impressive cosmic evidence was confronted with counter-evidence which would tend to induce disbelief, if in the buoyancy of faith we were not convinced that somewhere, somehow, it could be countered in its turn. But we were unable to particularize; and indeed, as long as we remain in the context of contemplation, it cannot be done. One can think about the possibility of dissipating evil, but while we think, it goes on: we cannot think it away, and if we think we can think it away, we deceive ourselves. Now, for the first time, but in the context of a particular revelation, we see how the promise of faith might be fulfilled. If God is what Christ is, it *will* be fulfilled.[56]

1. If God is what Christ is, his concern about evil is primary. He demonstrates it, in the first place, by healing the sick, and especially the mentally sick. No one can read through the earliest gospel story, Mark's, at a single sitting, without being impressed by the predominance of straight psychiatry. Moreover, Jesus did not ask the moralistic question, Is the man's condition due to a bad way of life?, but the medical question, How can we cure him?[57] The usual picture is of a God sitting

[56] It will be said that under a good and omnipotent God there should not have been any evil to clear up. We have argued that under a *creative* God – an aspect slurred by the traditional dilemma – the handing down of freedom is as necessary to God's being as the founding of order has always been recognized to be: God cannot do the inherently impossible, and freedom without the possibility of mistakes *is* inherently impossible. If our earlier comments on omnipotence (see pp. 90–93) have not made this clear, we shall have the opportunity of revisiting this area of discourse in chapter IX. In the meantime, we proceed.

[57] See especially John 9.3.

aloft, indifferent to what happens among men; but this Aunt Sally of a God is not Christian. He is a relic of eighteenth-century Deism. Let us be clear, then: there *is* physical evil, and God is *doing* something about it.

But he is also concerned about moral evil. He is doing something about that too, and something so unorthodox that psychiatrists, when they try to do much the same thing, fancy themselves as irreligious. He got among the disoriented and made friends with them. No accusation against him was more persistent than that he moved in bad company – *God* moved in bad company. He attacked not the sinner but the sin; all he wanted for the sinner was to save him – and so he got to know him and discovered his troubles and took them upon himself and set him free. He was much more in earnest about evil than were the righteous, who glared at it from behind their defences and did nothing about it.

2. In pursuing this mission, he found himself at odds with the priesthood and the politicians, and he was condemned to death precisely for being God. He was put on a moral level with slaves and thieves – how, after that, should slaves and thieves be morally set apart? But, above all, he suffered, and by standing firm on his mission to the disinherited, he consecrated suffering for all time. This is a point of logical interest. It is not possible to consecrate wickedness, but it is possible to consecrate suffering and so to avert wickedness. If everyone took his suffering sacrificially, spinning radiance out of it – and many have been known to do it – it would at least serve as a beacon to other sufferers, and if the impact were strong enough it might take them out of their suffering altogether. So much suffering is self-induced and could disappear, in the appropriate action. You are 'rejected': all right, don't snivel about it, see what use your rejection can be turned to. God was rejected, and he did just that. His suffering saved the world.[58]

3. If God is what Christ is, he carried identification with men so far that he actually went through the process of dying.

---

[58] It will be said that God the Father does not suffer, only God the Son, and that we have been 'confounding the Persons'. I reply that those who say so are 'dividing the Substance'. If the doings of each Person do not resound through the whole Divine Being, we have not Trinitarianism, but Tritheism.

Death is not an evil in the same sense as suffering and wicked-ness; it is simply a limitation. But that God should put himself under a limitation from which he could have kept himself exempt, shows how much he feels with the imperfections of his creatures, and how far he is committed to them. And in this case, he promises that those who have committed themselves to him may come out, as he did, on the other side.

4. It will be said that in 'redeeming his people', God has not eradicated the evil in the world: it goes on as before, just as vigorously, if with less justification. That is inevitable, unless we are to be saved over our heads; a view which atheists rightly consider demoralizing. But we have been shown in a human career (so human that Kierkegaard could speak of the divine *incognito*) that the hold of pride and fear has been shaken once for all: 'Be of good cheer, I have overcome the world' (John 16.33). All that is now needed is enough Christians to do the job. What is expected of them is recorded in John 14.12: 'He that believeth on me, the works that I do shall he do also; and greater works than these shall he do' – a summons so staggering that I wonder there are not more sermons about it. But in carrying the succession forward we shall 'have tribulation': we shall be called upon to harness our suffering to the service of God and man.

5. If God is what Christ is, the so-called 'problem of evil' thus loses its sharpness. That is because it is transposed from the sphere of reflection to the sphere of action. A non-involved God is exposed to the full force of Carneades' dilemma. But it was (and remains) a Greek dilemma, reflecting an agreed account of God as standing outside the process. But Christianity brings God inside the process, working without pause or limit to save people from their mistakes without curtailing their freedom. To expect this effort to achieve finality is to ask God to contradict himself. But the plan has been laid down and the methods tested – there is no way but that of identification and sacrifice. This is dogma, no doubt, but in no *a priori* sense; the hold which it has as dogma depends on the experience of pride and fear in oneself and in others. It tells us that God is actively engaged in the only way possible to remove the obstacles he is alleged to connive at. And if it be asked, 'Why are they there at

all?', we refer back to our section on creation and freedom (p. 192). It is, we repeat, the price we pay for not being perfected robots.

6. Thus, if God is what Christ is, the counter-evidence is accounted for; the anticipations of natural theology and the expectations of faith are fulfilled. What are we waiting for? Only the 'if'. In any ordinary instance, a supposition which and which alone makes sense of the assembled facts would be accepted with gratitude. In this instance it is frequently rejected, even though it is recognized as thus making sense, partly because it appears to be in itself incredible, partly because the terms used have lost their meaning outside the immediate circle of faith. There has been a failure of understanding and communication for which both Christians and their critics are responsible.

The doctrine of Incarnation is represented as a piece of theological expertise in which no vital issues are involved. That they *are* involved should be evident to anyone who is not, on the side of religion, totally uneducated. The doctrine of Incarnation changes the whole face of the problem of evil. But the failure to press the point home lies with those of its exponents who do not actualize it in psychological terms, who do not relate it to the human dealings of Jesus Christ. To reverse the normal order: he did not do what he did because he was God: he was God because he did what he did. It is useful to over-simplify in this sense, because it brings out a fundamental ambiguity. If it is part of the definition of God to be up-there and *not* down-here, then of course Incarnation is impossible, *a priori*. But that definition of God, like all definitions, has to run the gauntlet of experience, and the time came when it wore out. That was when people found out that God was amongst them and could not make God real to themselves in any other way: those 'who through him do believe in God, who raised him up from the dead and gave him glory' (I Peter 1.21). The concept of God, at that moment, turned a sharp corner. And once it was turned, it was realized that what had been revealed had always been there. 'Before Abraham was, I am.'

What makes sense of the counter-evidence, then, is also part of the nature of God, and the power of the counter-evidence came (and comes) from a restriction of the concept of God to pre-Christian dimensions. This is too good for a coincidence. If everything fits together as well as that, it seems perverse to resist further. To deny the conclusion it will be necessary to deny at least one of the supporting premisses. Either there is something wrong with the empirical metaphysics of order and creation; or there is incomprehension of the phenomenon of faith; or the drift from the faith of nature to the faith of religion is misdescribed; or the argument that a particular specification of faith can absorb the empirical counter-evidence is at fault; or, enslaved by the mood of the times, people have decided that good news must be false. We have tried to argue the first four points. With the fifth, which may be suspected to be the drive behind the others, one cannot argue: one can only exchange experiences over an emotional barrier. For what it is worth, we put it on record that the experience of joy in the world outlasts and cancels the misery. We might even subscribe to the notable utterance of René le Senne: 'For me, the principal proof of the existence of God is the joy I feel at thinking that God exists.'[59]

8. *The Consecration of Suffering*

We have spoken of faith as if its function were to break down a theoretical objection. So it is, amongst others: but faith is not primarily a theoretical activity. It is, in the widest sense of the word, a practical activity: in the sense, that is, in which practice includes theory but surpasses it. 'First faith' is a total attitude of mind spreading over every kind of activity. Faith in God is, incidentally, faith in his existence, but primarily the circulation of his presence through everything we do – he is, to use Buber's contrast, the author of faith first and the object of faith afterwards. The specification of faith in God on Jesus Christ not merely delivers us from metaphysical distress, but does so because it shows us God in action against the counter-evidence and the continuation of that action in the lives of those who love him (which means more than 'acknowledge him as Lord'). All through, the reference is to a practice which outruns theory.

With this is combined a demand for verification. The trouble

[59] *La découverte de Dieu*, p. 18.

about the so-called verification principle, like the trouble about empiricism in general, lies in its limitation to the area of sense-perception. In itself, it is not only unobjectionable, but, as a sequel to empirical philosophy and religious faith, indispensable. It is in the moment of practice that the philosophy is vindicated and the faith receives embodiment. The whole venture has been a risk. At the level of philosophical discussion there was counter-evidence, and the faith in which it is submerged, while it may imaginatively anticipate, can be evinced and tested only in action. It is, in fact, part of the faith itself that this should be so. What is now required of us is a re-interpretation of the verification principle which its usual exponents would energetically repudiate. This will appear in detail in chapter VIII. In the meantime, there are a few subsidiary clarifications.

1. It needs to be repeated that faith is a completion of philosophy and not a reversal. The completion is necessary because suffering and wickedness cannot be talked out of existence; they have to be worked out of the system of things by assimilation and sacrifice. As Butler observed, 'No revelation would have been given, had the light of nature been given in such a sense, as to render one not wanting or useless.'[60] But there is a continuity; as Butler says again, strikingly enough, 'Christianity is a republication of natural religion.'[61] Christian discourse coheres throughout with the empirical observations of philosophy. What happens is that it gathers them together and clinches them and removes a considerable source of disquiet. It is certainly not the case that philosophical reflection *cannot* formulate the essentials of the Christian answer: all one can say is that it normally does not, and that formulation is in any case not enough.

2. Faith as the Christian conceives it is not the only way of dealing with the counter-evidence. It can equally well be argued that suffering being the root of all evil, and being itself the product of self-affirming desire, evil can be extinguished by the discipline by which the self-affirming desire is extinguished. This is the Buddhist alternative. It has a strong appeal, because the 'problem' of evil does not arise; Nirvana may be more positive than the old-fashioned Christian picture of it, but it is

[60] *Analogy of Religion*, ed. W. E. Gladstone, 1896 p. 153.   [61] *Op. cit.*, p. 156.

certainly not creative, and so far from being analogous to a person, it is that in which all personal distinctness is dissolved. Thus suffering is extinguished only by the submergence of individuality: the disease ceases to be a disease when the patient dies of it. In the interval, there is much to be done by way of reducing it, and the resultant ethic is strongly humanitarian; but there is no gathering up of it, no infiltration into it of the grace which makes it an instrument of redemption. Those who wish to affirm existence, suffering and all, cannot respond to it. It is a question of valuation. Granted that if there were no affirming desire there would be no suffering, do we prefer to have both, or neither? We say, both; and, having taken our stand, point to the part that suffering can play in the affirmation. That, and the wider range of an affirmative religion, are reasons for valuing as we do.

It has to be admitted, however, that what we have been shown is the *possibility* of consecrating one's suffering. Many people still respond by despair, anger, and blaming others – parents, the social order, or God, anyone but themselves. If the possibility has never been presented to them, such responses are only too natural. The divine break-through has to be followed up. It is precisely on these terms that we are, unbelievably, fellow-workers with God and joint-heirs with Christ. And if it be objected that it is not in our power to consecrate our suffering, the answer lies in the lives and acts of those who have done it. They grew to the stature of their dedication with the help of God. So can we.

And yet, asking perhaps too much, we are not satisfied. We are still haunted by the spectre of Ivan Karamazov, that creation of a believer in God who grew to such dimensions that he nearly wrecked his creator's story. Ivan concentrates on the sufferings of children. The adults have 'eaten the apple and know good and evil, and they have become "like gods". They go on eating it still. But the children haven't eaten anything and are so far innocent.'[62] The children can neither convert nor have they desired suffering; they do not even know what is happening to them. Yes, the balance may be rectified afterwards; but how? All right; shall we become embittered

[62] *The Brothers Karamazov*, tr. C. Garnett, Everyman's Library, Vol. I, p. 242.

about it or do what we can to make up for it? The godless look backwards and harp on rights; those who love God look forward and offer themselves as instruments of his continuing redemption. It is no accident, and would have loomed even larger in the sequel to the story, that there is so much otherwise irrelevant writing in *The Brothers Karamazov* concerning the Snegiryovs and Kolya Krassotkin: they contribute nothing to the main plot, but a great deal to Alyosha's recovery of faith. He had to go to the children and live their lives with them as an 'equal'[63] to break down the challenge of Ivan's terrifying case-histories. In the attention given to the murder story and the philosophical debate (which, by the way, remains in the air: Ivan is never formally answered), it has not been noticed that the climax of the novel is the boy Ilusha's funeral – a harrowing occasion if ever there was one, but one turned to a source of strength by his school-fellows under Alyosha's guidance. 'Such sorrow and then pancakes after it, it all seems so unnatural in our religion', observes the precociously percipient Kolya.[64] But what with intimations of immortality and a consciousness of an unforgettable common experience, the sorrow and the pancakes mix, in the penultimate sentence of the story;[65] something is at work in them all, converting the sorrow, without the slightest diminution of its sharpness, into an occasion of joy. Alyosha, who started it all, and Alyosha's creator, knew where it came from.

But this kind of justification applies, not to a God who stands aloof but to one who actively intervenes. Only that kind of a God *can* be justified: one whose power is shown in doing things, in the rush of time, and against the stress of interruptions: one who works through those who love him; in fact, the Christian God, the author of faith where the evidence of nature falls tantalizingly short. But such a God cannot be pushed back into the traditional dilemma, for the God who is trapped by that dilemma does nothing. The First Person is incomplete without the Second or the Third. Put that abstraction to the test, and no wonder something goes wrong.

3. As stated, our description of the varieties of faith may seem not to do justice to the role of theology. But no one, least of all

[63] *Op. cit.*, II, p. 187.   [64] *Op. cit.*, II, p. 437.   [65] *Op. cit.*, II, p. 440.

the theologians, wishes it to be coterminous with philosophy; and despite some intellectualist overstatements, no one wishes it to be coterminous with faith. For this reason M. J. Combès, in a recent illuminating article,[66] distinguishes between the 'verbe sur Dieu' and the 'verbe de Dieu', and warns us: 'Le courage de la théologie consiste à faire rentrer son discours dans ses propres limites.' Its limits, we have suggested, are that it serves as an interpretation of faith, and not as truth in the full metaphysical sense of the word. But as metaphysical truth is never complete, and as the faith which springs from it also completes it, the limitation is not a hard one. The limited role of articulating the content of faith is specialized and exacting, and there is only confusion if it is extended to elaborate the metaphysical substructures on the one hand, or to serve as an equivalent for faith itself on the other. Yet it is influenced by the methods of the one and depends entirely on the data of the other.[67]

4. Finally, we may be reminded that for the whole of this chapter we have been elaborating faith, and we have not shown that the conclusions arising from it, even if adequately described, are rationally acceptable. There is some justice in this claim. We have denied ourselves the easy escape: equating the philosophy of religion with its clarification. On that basis, we could reject the challenge as being outside our terms of reference. By insisting on doing metaphysics, we have laid ourselves open to it, and are confronted again with the problem of faith and reason. And here, after the event, we have to repeat what we said in anticipation (p. 106), that empirical methods in metaphysics have to be supplemented by faith. After the event, however, the position can be rationally defended.

(*a*) In elaborating the procedures of metaphysics, we noted that the structural characters of the world (including the human world) pointed persistently beyond themselves. At the same time there were features of the world, perhaps not structural, but alarmingly efficacious, which, if they pointed at all, pointed to disorder or uncreativeness, or both.

[66] 'Philosophie, Théologie, Religion', *Revue de Métaphysique et de Morale*, 1965, p. 347.

[67] Cf. Combès, *op. cit.*, p. 346: 'Le contenu de foi reçoit une forme qui, déjà reliée à quelque logique *ex parte rationis*, se relie à ce contenu *ex parte fidei*, mais sans le lier à elle-même.'

(*b*) We then pointed to the phenomenon of faith, which in practice disowns the counter-evidence, though it admits and insists upon it as a factor in the situation. We argued that this is not arbitrary: it is the 'courage of the spirit' which gets things done. Practice without faith is dead – as St Paul, in his own dialect, truly testified. It was only when 'faith' was equated with 'beliefs' that this simple and satisfying doctrine became corrupted.

(*c*) In its full development, i.e. its development according to the law of its own character, 'faith' is shown at work in a death-grapple (literally, a death-grapple) with fear and pride (the main expressions, in men, of disorder and uncreativeness respectively), in such a way that the frontiers are rolled back and the counter-evidence is appropriated as the field of operations for the testing of the evidence.

(*d*) At the very least, this is something which should be taken into account. What lies at the root of practice cannot be without significance for theory, even if theory can never quite catch up with it. A final review would have to align the requirements of practice with the drift to self-transcendence of the structures of the world as disclosed by empirical metaphysics.

(*e*) Neither the one nor the other nor both together constitute demonstration; they provide a high degree of probability. If demonstration is required, they are not enough. We have tried to show that it is not required, and we shall proceed to show that practical reason belongs to a different order of discourse.

(*f*) In any case, faith is to be given verification. Without it works are dead, with it, works are unimaginably possible. And they are its only real test. It is so easy to 'have faith' and do nothing; to let the clue to history run away into high-minded imagination. How such verification is possible, and what are the implications, we shall see later. All we are concerned here to establish is that our proceedings so far are for anyone but a rationalist, entirely reasonable.

VIII

FAITH AND PRACTICE

1. *What is Action?*

ANY FAITH of any consequence carries with it a distinctive pattern of action; and any action of any consequence illustrates a distinctive pattern of faith. Faith unenacted is incomplete; action without faith is uncompletable.[1] The intellectual premisses of faith may be acceptable; it may be imaginatively entertained with great devotion; but unless it breaks out into action it is only a blue-print or a heart-warming. It started out to be faith, but it did not last the distance.

So much will be generally admitted, with various degrees of discomfort.[2] But faith, unenacted, though incomplete, is a fact; as is activity without faith, however erratic and undependable. Practice and faith do not always go together, though they belong together. We have already attempted an analysis of faith, in which both these points, it is hoped, have been sufficiently elaborated. We have now to attempt a similar analysis of action.[3]

1. 'Action' is not merely 'event'. It has to do with the bringing about of events. No doubt the bringing about of events *is* an event, but, among the multitude of events, it is a rarity. It expresses the capacity of human beings to lift themselves out of the flat succession of events to survey and rearrange

[1] The connecting of 'faith and practice' by means of a conjunction, as if they were different things, even though the phrase occurs in some ordination vows, reveals an over-intellectualized conception of faith.

[2] If anyone feels no discomfort, he should read the dialogue between Faithful and Talkative in *Pilgrim's Progress*.

[3] In presenting it, we must bear in mind the following dilemma: if faith is taken to include practice, it cannot be tested in practice, because that would be to test it by itself; and if faith is not taken to include practice, the practice which it fails to include will not serve as a criterion.

them.[4] The effect of this move is to upgrade, some might say
indefensibly, the concept of action. So long as we are clear
what is happening and do not exploit the ambiguity, that should
not matter, and it is certainly convenient. It will at least prevent
passive responses from laying claim to full human status. That
they enter into it, guided and suffused, is of course not disputed.

2. Action, like other events, not only takes place *in* time, as
thinking does, but is directed *to* time, as much thinking is not,
and, what is more, is directed to the particular moment of its
accomplishment. Here the trend of action is distinct and apart
from the trend of theory, which is to group temporal events in
respect of their similarities, or in terms of repeated sequences,
or with reference to 'eternal objects' – in all cases directing
attention away from their temporality. In preparation for a
discussion of faith and action, it should be said at once that if
faith culminates in action, it completes itself, through however
roundabout a circuit, in the things of time.

3. Action is exercised by people with bodies. So, for that
matter, is thinking; but thinking may conjure up the immaterial
and dwell there; action not only starts from a material base,
but is directed back to it. The issue is of some importance to the
philosophy of religion. Religion is sometimes described, and
even commended, as moving away from the world of nature.
That is to confuse a phase of the circuit with its terminus. It is
particularly important for a religion centred on Incarnation,
with which any sort of philosophical immaterialism, from
Plotinus through Berkeley, is incompatible. Some thirty years
ago (I quote from memory) the late Archbishop Temple
described Christianity as 'the most materialist of all the great
religions'. That is not only not a paradox, but greatly to its
credit.[5]

4. It may be noted that what, on this account, marks out

---

[4] E. D'Arcy, *Human Acts*, 1963, p. 4, notes that the word 'action' is used
of the heart, salivary glands, etc. – processes which certainly do not conform
to the above description – and therefore prefers the term 'act'. But etymologically an act is a thing done, as opposed to the doing of it: and on the
balance I prefer the more ambiguous 'action', in the permissible transitive
sense of 'acting'.

[5] For some disturbing but inevitable metaphysical implications, see
chapter IX, 3.

action from other events is precisely those qualities which, in our metaphysical preamble, caused us to look beyond their human exemplifications: viz. order and creativity. The element of order is exhibited in dispositional constancy and the habit of planning: the element of creativity in the imaginative construction which changes dispositions and renders planning possible. When writers (e.g. John Macmurray, *The Self as Agent*, p. 84) speak of the 'primacy of the practical', they are justified only if they take 'practice' in this expanded sense. If they meant that intellect should serve the predetermined ends of a 'practice' not responsive to it, or that the wings of the visionary should be clipped by efficient operators chanting 'business as usual', they would be undermining practice itself. Whatever may be said of the lesser sort of pragmatist, Macmurray has no such intention; indeed, his account of the differentia of action closely resembles our own.[6]

5. In all action can be discerned the stirrings of 'first faith'. It includes the assumption, made sometimes too easily, but sometimes also with too much fear and trembling, that there is some congruity between the enterprise and the possible. We are so accustomed to presuming on it that we hardly notice it, and still less do we consider it a cause for gratitude. Usually we just complain that there ought to be more. But, if there were, there would be no need for good sense and planning, and we should be literally shorter by a head. In fact, we should be doubly grateful, both for the coincidence and for the gap. In the ordinary run of things, the capacity is matched with the occasion, and the occasion elicits the capacity. This is perhaps our first intimation that the run of things is with us rather than against us.

This being what we mean by action, what do we mean when we say that faith is completed in it? Do we mean that faith is to be verified by some standard other than its own – e.g. the good interpreted as utility, or the greatest good of the greatest number, or the spiritual power it confers, or its contribution to the formal fulfilment of duty? If so, we must face it: believing in God is in the long run a means to an end. Some pragmatic

---

[6] 'Action without thought is a self-contradictory conception', *The Self as Agent*, 1957, p. 87.

defences of faith amount to just that. They stress the good it *does*, not the good it *is*. They praise God for ministering to the moral devices of men. Such defences we must disown, if only for the reason that a faith serving an end is tied to that end, and no end as we conceive ends can carry the whole weight of faith in God.

But, if that is so, the role of practice must be within the scheme of faith, and it may be asked how in that case faith can be verified in practice. The answer is that the verification of faith is also a completion. The experience is in fact not as peculiar as the austerities of science might suggest. Faith in another human being is verified in the network of mutual responses which make up, e.g., friendship, or marriage, but in the process it becomes more itself, as well as raising practice to a higher power. So, with deference to the distinction between finite and infinite, the faith in God which spills over into action reveals itself more profoundly as faith in God. It is present, so to speak, in its own verification.

2. *Extending 'Verification'*

The word 'verification', we should note, has slipped in sideways. It is a loaded word, with hard-boiled associations; and it may be asked why it should be used in connexion with faith. It would be part of an answer that men of faith habitually so use it when they contrast faith with sight: 'Now we see through a glass darkly, but then face to face.' But this kind of verification makes no impression on convinced verificationists, for they admit only the evidence of sense-perception. We have seen in chapter I that the term 'empiricism' should not be so limited, and what goes for 'empiricism' goes also for 'verification'. But some men of faith take the verificationists at their own valuation and say that verification is not necessary for faith, or is even inconsistent with it. As a riposte *ad hominem* their intransigence is understandable: but it raises difficulties the moment we reflect on the ebb and flow of faith, and still more on the cases where its loss is more permanent. D. M. MacKinnon, reported in *The Listener*, November 10, 1966, spoke of the 'vulnerability' of faith, and added, significantly: 'Those who are working in the sort of field I'm working in are not altogether inhabiting a different world from that inhabited by the scientist, who stresses the vulnerability of his hypotheses to refutation' (pp. 688f.). As we have pointed out (see p. 106 above), God is metaphysically only probable, and it is faith which lifts him into a practical certainty. The point at which faith might break down is the point at which it carries the weight: the overcoming of suffering and wickedness. If faith cannot overcome them in practice, it is not only vulnerable but already wounded. The wound shows itself precisely in the inability to express in action conviction of intellect and integrity of feeling.

To speak of faith as being verified (or falsified) in action is therefore not wholly inappropriate. Indeed, if we take up MacKinnon's analogy with the sciences, there are several points in common. A hypothesis, though well supported by reasons, is still a venture till the crucial experiment has verified it, and even then there is no last word. Similarly, action, though guided, at its best, by all the available knowledge, is still, and particularly at its best, a venture; and every venture requires a verification, if only for the sake of the next venture. If anything, the venture of action is more exposed than the venture of science. In a crucial experiment complicating factors are carefully excluded; if things happen as predicted, the hypothesis can be regarded as established; if they do not, it will be abandoned or sent back for modification, as the case may be. In practice, it is not only more difficult to exclude the complicating factors; it is positively undesirable, for action demands that we keep our eyes open to the whole complex of our surroundings. Moreover, it is impossible to send an action back for modification. In both respects, the agent is more exposed than the scientist; he is both more liable to error in the first instance, and he has to commit *himself* with his experiment, and can escape from it only by a circuitous round of compensations. The risks being so much greater, verification is not less, but more, indispensable.

Yet action has been indicated as the field for the testing of faith. How can faith be verified amidst such complexity and imprecision?

Here we come to the principal distinctions between verification in science and verification in practice. In the first place, science tests specific hypotheses, while practice tests an approach to an infinitely variable range of situations. In the second place, what science is concerned with is the truth of propositions; what practice is concerned with is the adequacy of a way of life. Both these differences throw light on the peculiar and inward linkage between faith and action.

Let us recall that faith is not intellectual certainty, but rather a personal confidence in the run of things in the absence of that certainty. Consequently faith does not demand, and cannot receive, the kind of verification which is proper to science. Verification can only take the form of a gradually widening conviction, spread over the years from the hopes of youth to the meditations of age, and over situations swinging between crisis and routine, that the way of faith is the sufficient way, and one which in each of its phases promotes its own perpetuation. The verification of faith is not, like the verifications[7] of science, particular verification, though it is shown forth in particulars, even in 'minute particulars', but an overall verification, broadening as it goes along, starting as an unforgettable firing of the imagination, and validating itself in every actual situation, both through its own successes and through the manifest failure of the recognized alternatives. This does not make it any the less a verification. It means that verification in science, which is often taken as a universal model, is only one kind of verification.

The second differentia is already before us. Faith includes, but does not stop with, the affirmation of propositions.[8] Its vindication has to be over the whole field of experience. That includes propositions, as we shall see in a moment; but one difficulty at a time. But how can we vindicate a whole way of life? Not merely by being convinced about it (though that counts), but principally by living it. Does it provide both for everyday dealings and the removal of obstacles? Does it go the whole distance, or at some point contradict itself?

[7] The switch from the singular to the plural is significant.

[8] What is here said holds of religious faith in general. It is as true of Buddhism as of Christianity; it is even true of atheistic cults like Comtian positivism or Marxian Communism. What distinguishes Christianity is not that it is a faith, but the kind of faith it is.

The principal concern of all religions is how to get rid of evil.[9] There are three main policies: to diminish evil along with oneself; to contain evil by effort; to turn evil to good. The first policy is one of compassionate self-elimination. It solves the problem, but at the cost of all positive affirmation. The second affirms endlessly, but it does not solve the problem; it only shelves it. This is the policy of so-called 'realists'; that is to say, of most serious-minded people for most of the time. It is therefore appropriate to point out that it is conspicuously inefficient. The most that the suppression of evil can do is to postpone the issue; and that is a help only if we are preparing to change the policy. 'Evil', after all, is an abstraction: what it points to is the existence of bad men. But bad men can be changed only from the inside: 'containing' them may prevent contagion (we admit this, though it is doubtful), but it only hardens them, just as it hardens the otherwise good men who conduct the exercise. The world is divided (by the sheep) into sheep and goats: and how very sheeplike the sheep are. Quarantine and non-involvement are the weapons of those who, being faithless, play for a draw. The only active policy, which both affirms the agent and gets rid of the evil, is the way of identification and sacrifice, with the consequent acceptance and consecration of suffering, and of course of unpopularity; it gives the moral down-and-outer the human consideration which the good man feels he alone has deserved. So the sequence proceeds: acceptance of the rejected, their ambivalent response (they may be grateful, or, if they are especially hard-boiled, angry and contemptuous); the mounting hostility of men of good-will threatened with the loss of their moral privilege. This is a true story; it is also the story of the Atonement.

Now, if faith is to be vindicated or verified, this is the region in which it must happen. As has been noted, it is the central feature of faith not to be daunted by the counter-evidence, but to go out and appropriate it. If a faith and nothing else can succeed in the enterprise, there is verification in the most literal sense of the word: a making-true. It is triumphantly affirmative: it does not contradict itself; and it goes the whole distance. What more can we ask?

[9] This is what makes it so odd that they should be accused of slurring evil.

3. *Thought into Action*

Nevertheless, there will be protest. Faith, as we have described it, has an intellectual base and an intellectual component. How can propositions be verified in practice? Do not practice and propositions run on different tracks, which only occasionally coincide, and then at haphazard? Yet we have affirmed, and we must repeat, that the propositions, in their context, must be shown to be true, or at least, have as much truth as the context allows. The 'veri-' in 'verification' has to be taken seriously. To play its part as a constituent element of faith, intellect must retain its integrity. To deny this is to hold by implication that what men have faith *about* makes no difference. But, for example, Communists, in their way, are men of faith; they believe with terrifying intensity that the world is on their side – and from this point of view it does not matter that they deny God and talk instead about History or Dialectic: in fact, the capital letters give them away. Moreover, they are more than usually concerned for the unity of thought and action.[10] There is in fact no difference on this subject between Christians and Communists; yet there is a deep divergence about what is true and what ought to be done. The verification through a living faith of thought in action is indeed a necessary, but by no means a sufficient, vindication of its truth-component.

The first approach to an answer (or rather, a supplement, for the indictment is wholly true) is to inquire into the passage from thought to action. There is certainly nothing like an entailment, but that mode of vindication is not required of empirical scientists, and should not be required of us, either.[11] We are on surer ground if we note the 'drift' from thought to action, 'necessarily tending' to its appropriate fulfilment.[12] Restricting ourselves for the moment to thought about action, it may be said that in it action is already incipient. At any

[10] E.g. Marx, Eleventh Thesis on Feuerbach: 'Philosophers have only *interpreted* the world differently: the task, however, is to change it.'
[11] That it sometimes is required of us is partly our fault: theologians have sometimes tried to *derive* the criteria for action *a priori* from their understanding of God.
[12] Cf. J. N. Findlay, *Values and Intentions*, p. 212, and reference above, p. 67.

stage there may be interruption: what 'necessarily tends' may
never arrive. But the interruption cuts across what would
otherwise be a natural ripening and development. If I believe,
for example, that the only way of transforming a hardened
disposition is to go along with it and get inside it and infect it
with what William James called 'the expulsive power of a new
affection', it is only too likely that from sloth or lack of technique
or moral inadequacy I shall do nothing about it; but then I am
harbouring impulses not to realize which produces in me a
state of what may be called 'practical contradiction'. It is not a
logical contradiction, for in fact it happens; but it *is* a contradiction, because my belief, if given scope, would issue in a
course of action incompatible with that to which I actually
resort – for example, just applying a rule and hoping for the
best. There is a *natural* carry-forward from a conviction about
practice to the practice itself. The mere entertainment of the
conviction is an incitement to action, other things being equal.
It operates, fulfilled or unfulfilled: in the latter case in the form
of 'bad conscience', a phenomenon peculiarly apt to bring
home the incongruity of the interruption.

In the case quoted, the belief in question is a belief about
practice. The objection might then be raised: Yes, there is a
carry-over from such a belief into practice, but the totality of
religious apprehension embraces also propositions in empirical
metaphysics and dogmatic theology. The question then takes
the form: is there a carry-over to practice from beliefs, not about
practice, but about the state of the case? If there is not, then a
faith which is realized in practice is cut loose from its intellectual
moorings, and there is every reason to put philosophy and
theology on one side, after the manner of Dr van Buren;
indeed, for all the effect it has on practice, the intellectual
commitment could be discarded and make way for the non-
theistic agapaics of Professor Braithwaite.

But to reach this conclusion, there must be a total dis-
connexion between practice and the state of the case; whereas,
as a matter of fact, knowledge of the state of the case must
include knowledge of practice. Long ago[13] W. R. Sorley began
his series of Gifford Lectures by insisting on this point. 'Morality

[13] *Moral Values and the Idea of God*, 1918.

is a factor in experience; ethical ideas have a place in consciousness. Our theory of reality as a whole must take account of these things.'[14] A theory of the world, let alone of God, in which practice does not figure at all, is a truncated theory, a point to which we shall return in the next paragraph. But, in that case, there must be a link, both ways, between the knowledge of what is and the knowledge of practice, and hence, indirectly, with practice itself – a conclusion empirically reinforced by a study of the great religions, in all of which views about God and views about conduct are interlocked.[15] If this holds from the very nature of both philosophy and religion, it holds particularly of Christianity; for the Christian God *engages* in practice, even human practice; the Christian apperception of God includes (uniquely) an apperception of perfect man. Not only is there no state of the case which is not linked with activity; there is no state of the case which *is* not an activity. Thus the carry-over from thought about practice to practice itself holds also of thought about God. To think of God and do nothing about it is as much of a practical contradiction as to think of one's neighbour and do nothing about it; the interruption of the sequence produces a similar sense of conflict. That people are often worse, and sometimes better, than their ideas about practice, or about the world, is of course not disputed. But, when this happens, there is, at least, an incongruity.

4. *Thought and Abstraction*

The case for a linkage between affirmations about the world and certain modes of practice has so far been conducted in terms of ethical and general philosophical concepts. But ought we not, in a general review, to take into account affirmations about the state of the case which give rise to *no* practical consequences? By way of drawing a contrast, even at a certain risk of digression, it is important to examine these affirmations, and to note why they do not resound in practice. It is this lack of resonance, not its opposite, that needs explaining.

[14] *Op. cit.*, p. 22.
[15] For that matter, the same is true of atheists; cf. R. Robinson, *An Atheist's Values*, 1964.

1. One feature which distinguishes them is that they are not concerned with the future. This covers two important classes: statements concerning the past, and statements to which time is irrelevant. Both kinds may be put to use by those who for other reasons are concerned about the future: but by themselves they do not refer to it, even by implication.

Historical statements in their chronicle form refer merely to the past. The battle of Hastings took place in 1066, and that is that. It is true that a speculative historian reflecting on the Norman Conquest may ask what effects it has had (i.e. he surveys what was then the future from the standpoint of 1066); he may generalize about people whose culture is at odds with their racial stock, and argue that the disparity is (or is not) favourable to the growth of a new culture on the new ground. But this is to use the past (wisely or recklessly) as a guide to the future, and exceeds the limits of thinking about the past. In the same way, the natural sciences may instigate technology; but that is not their primary object *as sciences*, though it may be the object of their government subsidies.[16] They are also interested in the passage of time, but in general terms ('what follows what', not 'this follows that'); and if their discoveries apply to events which will occur in the future, they are not focused on the future like deliberation in morals, and religion in its prophetic mode.[17]

2. As the exclusion of the future is a form of withdrawal, statements which do not instigate practice are the result of contracted attention. It is sometimes convenient to disconnect types of events from their context for closer examination. The emphasis then falls on the type and not on the event; the event is considered as a 'what' and not as a 'that'. There is everything to be said for this de-temporalizing of temporal events or sequences of events, as a means of discovering uniformities; it is of immense assistance to practice. But, because it does not itself point forward to practice, it should be recognized for the abstraction that it is. It is the business of philosophy

[16] It was also a driving force in the early history of modern science; it figured largely in the encomia of Bacon and Descartes; and it is the working frame of reference among medicals and engineers.

[17] The popular misuse of the word 'prophetic' is not wholly misleading, because what a prophet 'speaks forth' about is what has to be *done*.

to restore the context, and of faith to live in the context as restored.

On both these grounds, then, we reaffirm our conclusion that statements which do not instigate practice are truncated statements: truncated because they are disconnected from the future, and from each other. Their failure to carry over into practice is an intellectualist specialization which adds powerfully to our understanding, and should not be deprecated, but also should not be taken as standard. Normal thinking occurs in a running context of action; it is an incitement to do, if only to think more or think again. In ordinary life, as in the total context of religion, a check or blockage between the thought and the act produces a deep sense of dissociation – and why not call it a sense of sin while we are about it?

5. *Verification and Faith*

It thus appears that the verification of faith in practice – over its whole extent, including its intellectual component – is not impossible or unreasonable. But the word 'verification' has of late been used in such a specialized philosophical sense that its unsophisticated employment (as here) is certain to be mis-understood. To verify something, in ordinary parlance, is to verify it in existence, not to verify it out of existence. In the famous sentence, 'The meaning of a proposition is the method of its verification', such an extreme position may not have been intended. At the beginning of the controversy, J. R. Weinberg said, roundly:[18] 'it is not to be interpreted as signifying that the meaning of a proposition *is* its verification'. As he rightly points out, on that interpretation we should have to say that 'a proposition could not have sense until it was verified'; whereas, unless it makes sense first, it could not be verified at all. If Wittgenstein's adage, 'Look for the use and not for the mean-ing', calls for the positive substitution of the one for the other, it is subject, retrospectively, to Weinberg's criticism. If it does not, verification resumes its unprofessional significance, and to speak of faith as being verified is perfectly meaningful.

What conceals this truth is the false dissociation of faith from

[18] *An Examination of Logical Positivism*, 1936, p. 178.

action. Action supplies the experimental test which the general theory of verification requires. A. J. Ayer holds propositions in theology to be nonsensical. Yet his own criterion is one to which they quite easily conform:

> We say that a sentence is factually significant to any given person if, and only if, he knows how to verify the proposition which it purports to express – that is, if he knows what observations would lead him, under certain conditions, to accept the proposition as being true, or reject it as being false.[19]

We know perfectly well what would verify the Christian faith: its success in disposing of what we have called the 'counter-evidence'. We also know what would falsify it: its inability, in practice, to handle the counter-evidence. What is up for testing is not 'consistent with any assumption whatsoever'.[20] We may therefore speak, without compunction, of faith being verified even if we do not go so far as to say that what faith means is what verifies it.

There are, it is true, complications, to which we have already alluded. The verification of faith is not simply the verification of propositions: there has also to be verified a whole manner of feeling and acting. But, as we have shown, the propositions are fused with it and diluted in it, and without them the verification is incomplete. Precisely for this reason, it has to come by way of a whole life and cannot be pinned down to a controlled experiment. Also, it has to come as all religious intimations come: individual by individual. It can be spread by example and preaching: it cannot be fixed by generalization. It is therefore never final, but, in those in whom it has taken place, a sure source of encouragement to the rest of us.

With these reservations, then, the verification of faith in practice is something we should openly acknowledge. Only if we do so can we decline the amendment that the faith *is* the practice. What nourishes this deviation is the suspicion that practice is one thing and faith another; and this in turn derives from the description of faith as holding propositions to be true on the authority of church, or scripture, without the quickening of personal experience. Once admit that theology and meta-

[19] *Language, Truth and Logic*, 1936, pp. 19f.
[20] The alternative as stated by Ayer, *op. cit.*, p. 20; cf. Antony Flew in *New Essays in Philosophical Theology*, 1955, p. 106.

physics can flourish without ethics, and the conclusion will
naturally be drawn that ethics (even Christian ethics) can
proceed without metaphysics or theology. Hence the pious and
high-minded elimination of the intellectual component in
religion, from the elder Pliny's *Deus est mortali adiuvari mortalem*
to Braithwaite's subtler formula: 'A religious belief is an intention to behave in a certain way' (agapaistic, like Pliny's)
'together with the entertainment of certain stories in the mind
of the believer.'[21] In allowing and trying to explain the verification of faith in practice, we forestall the attempt to dissolve it in
practice.

Before drawing the consequences, we have to recall that faith
is a living complex of which the provisional metaphysics of
order and creativity are detailed articulations. They are the
intellectual supports which faith needs; they point to One who
orders by creating, or creates by ordering; and even though
they do not establish him, because they do not account for the
counter-evidence, they are strong enough to make us believe
that the counter-evidence can itself be countered. In the final
practical reappraisal, it may be expected that these supports
of faith will be vindicated, together with faith itself.

6. *Verification and Ethics*

The principle that there is a carry-over from God to practice
does not settle the matter, for there are many ideas of God and
many more or less consequential kinds of practice. Admitting
that faith in God completes itself in practice, which God, and
what practice?

We have met this problem already, and have noted that
some ideas of God are disqualified by the kind of faith or practice
which they require. Apotropaic religion in general is in this
class: so is religion restricted to a single community. Both set
limits to the range of practice, and the former, at least, invokes,
along with faith, its incompatible, fear. The principle we invoke when we decide against them is: (1) that there must be no

---

[21] 'An Empiricist's View of the Nature of Religious Belief', p. 71 in the
reprint in *Christian Ethics and Contemporary Philosophy*, ed. Ian T. Ramsey,
1966.

collision between religion and other excellences and (2) that there must be no limit to the field in which religion operates. The first of these requirements is fulfilled by a wide range of alternatives. In Buddhism, for example, there is an admirable continuity between the Four Noble Truths and the Eightfold Path. In Christianity, intellect and the arts have sometimes seemed to be submerged in Puritanism or mysticism, but they return enhanced: it is part of the genius of that religion that it operates rhythmically, even dialectically. On this issue there is nothing to choose, unless it be regarded as a merit that Buddhism is more straightforward and less surprising.

The second requirement is similarly unselective. To confine the religious community to tribe, class, nation or culture is manifestly a limitation; but again, all the great religions have stressed the point, and it provides no way of choosing between them. Alternatively, though they all *aim* at universality, they are all particularist either in their origins or in their current presentation; so much so, that it is tempting to say that each faith is the right faith for its own culture-group; and again there is no way of choosing between them.

The obvious tactic at this point is to consider the truth-components of various religions in respect of truth; i.e. to compare their philosophical assumptions or implications. There is merit in this proposal, for faith takes off from philosophical probabilities. If a religion were systematically to downgrade order or creativity, it would fail to connect with the best we know, and it would seriously limit its field of operations. An outside opinion is that formal or cyclic religions are defective on the side of creativity. But Judaism and Islam as well as Christianity comply with the prerequisite, if it is one. Proper philosophical preparation is necessary but not sufficient.

Thus we are driven back to the structure of faith itself, and in particular to its ethical implications. For example, Islam has always insisted on definiteness and codification. Huston Smith remarks: 'The distinctive thing about Islam is not its ideal but the detailed proposals it sets forth for achieving it';[22] and he quotes a Moslem authority as saying: 'The work of Jesus was left unfinished. It was reserved for another Teacher

[22] *The Religions of Man*, 1964, p. 223.

to systematize the laws of morality.'[23] This is much safer than 'The wind bloweth where it listeth, so is every one that is born of the Spirit', or 'Love, and do what you like'; but in attempting to provide answers in advance to all possible questions, it is to that extent lacking in faith. It is true that the anticipations of casuistry may be subtle and acute and not by any means tied down to the letter of the law; it is also true (as we shall see later, for it is a standard accusation against Christian morality) that the extreme open-endedness of the Christian injunction ('Thou shalt love the Lord thy God, and thy neighbour as thyself') lends itself all too easily to the higher hypocrisy – that of accepting grace and turning it into law. Nevertheless, the attempt to circumscribe the future does scant justice to the 'unforgiving minute'. It purchases safety at the expense of opportunity. It pigeon-holes the infinite mobility of God. It assimilates faith not to adventure, but to obedience – and in this it could claim a powerful but misguided Christian support – misguided, because faith faces open alternatives which obedience closes. And perhaps it is not unconnected with the extreme pre-destinarianism with which, theologically, it is associated. The Christian ethic requires an open future and continual inventiveness: that is why it is so difficult and unenforceable, but it is also why it is equal to all possibilities.

Mutatis mutandis, this is the type of argument which should be used to sort out the claims of the various major religions. It is in a sense an appeal to their ethical potential, but it is primarily an appeal from fixity to faith. It is in respect of faith that the more flexible and dynamic ethic is to be preferred. In respect of formulae and definition it is provisional and inexact, because it knows that formulae have to be revised and that definitions, even if conceived in the same spirit, conflict with each other.

We have spoken of faith and hope; but the greatest of these is charity. The way our minds work when we genuinely care or have a concern for people is far more like faith than definition. We do not, of course, deny that they have rights; but the edges of their rights are blurred by our affections: we owe them what we should have wanted to give them anyway, and we certainly

[23] Ameer Ali, *The Spirit of Islam*, 1891, p. 274.

do not find ourselves disconcerted by their lack of deserts; it is part of our concern that the discrepancy between what is due to them and what we have for them should be blurred, if only because we know how little is due to us and what, in a right relation, they have to give us in return. In charity the attitude is absolute and the means of expression as varied as the situations. It is as continually inventive as faith itself; how else could it respond to the intricate delicacies of an ever-changing mood and environment? If God is love, the flexible way is the best way.

7. *Practice to Concept?*

With *détours* and halts to clear up difficulties, we have argued that there is a carry-over from the concept of God to practice, such that differences in the concept may be tested by the quality and range of the practice. But, as we have already noted, the problem exists also in reverse. Is there a carry-back from the practice to the concept? Assuming that the concept is significant, it would not be difficult, starting from the end of practice, to show certain affinities such that it could be said: if the one, then the other. An outgoing and expansive ethic suggests an outgoing and expansive God, if indeed there is a God. But does the mere fact of a practice to which an outgoing God would correspond suggest that there is one? Just now, when an improved statement of the Christian ethic is allied with serious doubts about Christian theology and the supporting metaphysics, this is a highly pertinent question. We have alluded to it above (p. 74); those who are utterly convinced that only agapaistic ethics work – what need have they to call in a God to make them work? Historically, it may be that those who first took agapaistic ethics seriously derived them from an original and (by existing standards) heretical conception of God; but that was because they believed in God anyhow. Now that moral practices do not have to be referred to God, why should 'the secular meaning of the Gospel' not stand on its own feet, without theological and/or metaphysical assurances? Particularly as these assurances (we are reminded) are precarious and, what is especially damaging to our thesis, 'unempirical'? Or, if we are not willing to lose the special religious aura attaching to the ethics of charity, why should it not be merged or identified with the practice? In looking for verification in practice, have we not established practice as independent of, or, alternatively, as identical with, what it is proposed to verify? And, in either of these cases, how is the verification to proceed?

The answer must relate particularly to the claim that *agapaistic* ethics can be self-sufficient. It is not enough to say (as is said quite often, and, in the proper context, quite relevantly) that the good atheist may be a man of principle, but cannot rise to the agapaistic level. That could have been true of the period when Christians were confronted with Pharisees or Stoics, but it is not true of the post-Christian societies which retain the agapaistic tradition and have lost touch with religion. It is necessary to show of the agapaistic tradition *specifically* that it requires a divine context.

From this point of view, most of the classical ethical arguments for the existence of God, most of the time, are beside the point. For instance: God is necessary because the moral law needs an author. But charity is not a law. Or: God is necessary because the conception of a *Summum bonum* requires a reference to happiness which must be excluded from the moral motive; hence it cannot be elaborated under the head of morality alone, and God must be invoked to bring the recalcitrant elements together. But in charity happiness and goodness are not separated and do not need to be brought together. Or (if law seems too strong a word): if there were no God, there could not be 'moral objectivity'. But, as H. D. Lewis has pointed out,[24] the objective interpretation of morality has in our time been most conspicuously advocated by G. E. Moore and C. D. Broad, men not conspicuously interested in religion, and by Sir David Ross and A. C. Ewing, who are in fact religious, but whose religion one would not deduce from their manner of defending moral objectivity. Is there anything about agapaistic ethics to exempt it from this common predicament?

Two things can be said, not conclusively, but, it is hoped, persuasively:

1. 'Law' and 'objectivity' (even when hitched to a mysterious

[24] *The Philosophy of Religion*, p. 260.

summum bonum) are safety concepts. The arguments which employ them proceed direct from morality to God as from a suppliant for certainty to a source of certainty. In so doing they telescope the intermediate phase of faith, and subject religion to ratiocination. Now the agapaistic ethic, more than any other, is a matter of faith, that is to say, risk. It has precedents to guide it, and a wealth of possibilities which in favoured cases may be provisionally sorted out beforehand; but the act expressing it does not conform to law (on the contrary, the law hobbles after the act); and though it is 'objective' in respect of the constancy of what it expresses, it cannot be pinned down to any discernible external signs. But the very characterizations which make the traditional arguments inapplicable suggest an alliance between agapaistic ethics and religious faith. 'Faith', not metaphysics, even empirical metaphysics, for the metaphysical endeavour, even at its most modest, is an instrument of order, whereas agapaistic ethics, while not rejecting order, is creative and 'situational'.[25] It ventures with the unknown and devises its own expedients. But if it is open at the far end, it is open at the near end also. It does not expend a calculable motive-power. It receives the strength that it hands on. From other people? Certainly, but the proportion is again incalculable, and an effective practitioner, not being limited to a scale of rights and duties, puts in more than he takes out. Unless he had faith, unless he rejoiced in the world and its limitless possibilities, unless he were convinced that the enterprise is one with the scheme of things, unless he drew strength from prayer and contemplation, he simply could not do it. And at this point we can substitute for 'the scheme of things' its author, and also its exponent, God. For the enterprise is continuous and exacting; there is no corner of experience which does not call for it; in fact, it is so exacting those who attempt it frequently and flagrantly fall back on the law, which is both the line of least resistance and a second line of defence. It is an enterprise for saints; and on the one occasion

---

[25] There is so much to be said for Joseph Fletcher's 'situational ethics' that I hesitate to hint at criticism; but to say that what is required of the Christian is love 'and nothing else' is to ignore the element of technique. If you cannot swim, you cannot effectively save your drowning 'neighbour'.

on which it was flawlessly carried through those who saw it at close quarters called the practitioner, God. The morals of charity being unlimited, they are purposely presented as a revelation – precisely because they know no bounds and are driven by an unstinted love. Any honest well-intentioned agent will recognize that this is more than he or the whole company of his fellows can rise to. Yet it has happened. It must come from God.

8. *The Viability of the Christian Ethic*

Let us be clear what has and has not been shown.

1. The 'carry-back' is not a demonstration, any more than the 'proofs' from the structure of the cosmos. It is an inescapable venture of faith.

2. It is an argument from practice, and practice can justify a venture, but cannot verify a theory. What is vindicated, if anything is, is the faith which crowns a theory.

3. It has been assumed that the morals of charity really do work. The first two points have been elaborated several times over, and we cannot be called upon to repeat ourselves. The third requires some amplification.

It is a frequent criticism of Christian ethics, not only among unreligious Westerners, but also and particularly among adherents of other faiths, that they enjoin the impossible. If it is in practice that faith finds its fulfilment, the charge is indeed damaging. And there are not wanting awkward indications to make it stick. They all concern a discrepancy between insight and achievement. To take an example: Moslems allow the right of retaliation, and if the case is a good one they exercise it with a clear conscience. Christians also exercise it, but as they are enjoined to turn the other cheek, they do it, if they are serious Christians, with a bad conscience, and, consequently, not quite so effectively. Or, alternatively, they do not exercise it, and the tensions mount up inside them. Such an ethic, it is said, is not in accord with the way things work, and it does not help to vindicate the faith from which it issues.

The difficulty has been noted by theologians, and variously answered.

1. The perfectionism of charity was propounded as an

'interim ethic', a stop-gap, to cover the short period before the Second Coming.

2. It was meant for a priestly or saintly *élite*, and not as a general rule of life.

3. It is directed to a particular set of virtues and vices held (not always relevantly) to be central: e.g. Catholics on divorce, Quakers on war (and cf. Moslems on alcohol); more elastic standards being employed in other contexts.

4. Most of all, and most generally, it is formally acknowledged, and it is explained that it cannot be expected to have much effect on current practice, though we should be duly grateful for the little it has. That is called 'Christian civilization'.

None of these answers is satisfactory. They allow the critic to ask the question in his own way. What they tell us about the difficulty of integrally Christian conduct is well known to us; so is the hard fact that so little Christian conduct is integral. What they do not tell us of is the peril of any possible alternative. The most perilous of all 'interim ethics' is that which extracts (in Bentham's words) 'golden conduct out of leaden motives'. It can last only for the duration of a fortunate coincidence. Only less perilous is the weight of the moral law, which imposes burdens where the ethics of charity at least call for positive action. Or, to take the example cited on the previous page: where do we get with the healthy-minded and all too possible ethic of retaliation? Where does the grim cycle of justice end? Worldly wisdom is not as wise as it looks; its special genius is to make the best of a bad job, and if the general level were higher its particular kind of cleverness would rust unused. It is just as unwilling as any other professional skill to do itself out of employment.

At first sight, this conclusion is depressing; for it undermines our faith in human devices without explaining how the morality of perfection is possible. It silences the critic with a *tu quoque*, but it does not show that his criticism is misplaced. As a matter of fact, much of it is quite in order. But the failure to state the alternative puts it out of focus. The question is whether we are to prefer the hundredth chance or the certainty of a deadlock. There are many situations in which only the deadlock is possible; though the fact that there are such situations is often due to taking the deadlock for granted. Retaliation, if not on one's own behalf, then on behalf of others who cannot help themselves, though it only postpones the reckoning, at least gains time for anyone who is minded to use it: and, as St Thomas drily remarked, 'It is no part of Christian charity to endure with equanimity the troubles of another.' But there is all the difference between accepting the deadlock *faute de mieux* and accepting it in the spirit of a so-called realism as a permanent feature of the landscape. In fact, provided it is *faute de mieux*, the *mieux* is already on the horizon.

It does not follow that perfection is at hand. What does follow is that the quest for perfection will make a difference to our choices between the greater and the lesser evil. As Reinhold Niebuhr says – and he has done so much to clarify this region – 'the relativity of all moral ideals cannot absolve us of the necessity and duty of choosing between relative values'.[26] And this, in itself, is a matter of no small importance. Even if the Christian ethic were as literally impossible as Niebuhr believes, if it, and it alone, can facilitate the best possible, that is a strong case for preferring it, and a part-of-the-way vindication of the faith it springs from. But in fact, every now and again, it proves not to be impossible for an unpredictable *élite*. Niebuhr has what a Protestant may not unfairly call a Protestant suspicion of religious aristocracies. Once they begin to formalize they are in danger of acting up to his anticipations, and that is why I write 'unpredictable'. But there are people with a genius in these matters, and in them the pretension all but becomes the truth. On one occasion, it was the truth without reservation.

To this we may add that in limited personal contexts it is not impossible even for the ordinary believer to practise the ideal. The network of circumstance may be slight enough for individuals, and especially dedicated groups, to disentangle. Either way, by its small-scale triumphs and by the large-scale catastrophes that attend its absence, the ethic of charity,

[26] *An Interpretation of Christian Ethics*, 1936, p. 142. That is the point of his paradoxically entitled fourth chapter, 'The Relevance of an Impossible Ethical Ideal'.

always on the offensive and concerned, not with blamelessness
but with redemption, shows itself the only exit from the
cynicism and defensiveness of current practice. It is the only
kind of practice that can win. Any other will only ease the
burden by shifting it somewhere else.

And so, if it is asked whether a practice admittedly sporadic,
and therefore fitful in its sociological consequences, can serve
as a verification for faith, the answer is that, given the grim
alternatives, it can. But the faith to be justified in its constituent[27] practice is a religious faith, involving the assertion of
a God who, on the empirical evidence, is only highly probable.
From this point of view, the difficulty of the ethic of charity is a
positive recommendation. The alternative is that the ethic of
charity is self-generated in human experience. It certainly
finds a response in human experience, but it needs a great deal
of sustaining, and it is noteworthy that Braithwaite finds it
necessary to keep nourishing the imagination with ritual and
stories. Would ritual and stories serve the purpose if the ritual
were merely an artistic performance and the stories merely
untrue? If, as Braithwaite suggests, a Christian can be nourished
by *Pilgrim's Progress* or *The Brothers Karamazov*, that is because
they are held, and rightly held, to present in fictional guise
truths about the world which, because they have to be received
personally and existentially, are better presented in fiction
than by professional philosophers. The more difficult it is to be
a Christian, then, seeing what is at stake and that some people
succeed, the more necessary it is to invoke assistance; and God
can provide it better than 'stories' – unless he is already
incapsulated in the stories.

9. *The Moral Argument for God*

There remains to be considered the relation of a practice to its
theoretical supports. The authority here is Kant, from whose
Critique of Practical Reason all fruitful speculation on the subject
descends. As is well known, he was arguing within his own
conception of ethics, which is based on the authority of the
moral law as the highest expression of human reason. We do

---

[27] N.B. not its consequential.

not share this view, and Kant thought it inseparable from his general view about theory and practice; but he could have been right in his primary intention and wrong in his application, as he certainly was when he particularized his moral law into moral laws. In the hope of further enlightenment, we shall conclude this chapter by examining what he explicitly calls 'the Primacy of Pure Practical Reason in its Union with Speculative Reason'.[28]

The argument runs roughly as follows.[29] Speculative reason necessarily leaves the higher questions of metaphysics open. Now, if practice were simply applied theory and could offer no insight of its own, speculative reason with its unsolved metaphysical problems would have the primacy. But practical philosophy gives a positive answer to one of the open questions, namely, freedom: not in theoretical terms, but as a prerequisite for the government of action according to law; and, deriving from it, similarly as practical postulates, immortality and God. We shall postpone consideration of Kant's moral theology; here we are concerned, in general terms, with 'the primacy of practical reason'. *Why* should the postulates of practice have priority? *Prima facie*, what we take for granted when we act is less thoroughly considered than what we conclude theoretically at our leisure. But Kant has in mind a special kind of action, namely action according to the moral law, which imposes the canons of reason not on appearances, as in the investigations of science, but on things in themselves, thus revealing structures which theoretical reason as metaphysics struggles after but cannot attain. This, after all, is what is to be expected. 'All interest is ultimately practical, and even that of speculative reason is conditional, and it is only in the practical employment of reason that it is complete.'[30]

The conclusion is carefully hedged with conditions.

1. The primacy of practical reason holds only on the supposition that the question is theoretically open: if practical reason were to go back on speculative reason, there would be conflict and contradiction.[31]

[28] *Critique of Practical Reason*, tr. T. K. Abbott, 6th ed., 1909, p. 216: headline for Book II, ch. II, section 3.
[29] *Op. cit.*, pp. 216–18.   [30] *Op. cit.*, p. 218.
[31] That, incidentally, is why Kant will not allow them to be 'co-ordinate';

2. The *postulates* of practical reason can never be more than *hypotheses* of speculative reason, and unverifiable hypotheses at that[32] – 'conceptions which speculative reason might indeed present as problems, but could never solve'.[33]

3. 'The assumption is as necessary as the moral law, in connexion with which alone it is valid':[34] it is the majesty and indubitability of that law which establishes the postulates and they should never be treated as straight indicatives rather than as the postulates that they are.

4. If the requirements of practical reason were based on inclination, they would carry no weight whatever; and under this heading Kant includes not only 'Mohammed's paradise' (no doubt unfairly construed as sherbet and odalisques[35]), but also 'the absorption into deity of theosophists and mystics'[36] – no one had less sympathy than Kant with those who claim special access to God. It is only because practical reason pronounces absolutely and *a priori* that its claims have to be considered by speculative reason even as possibilities.

Nevertheless, as there is such a thing as practical reason, and reason in both aspects is 'one and the same', though reason in its speculative capacity is 'incompetent to establish certain propositions positively', yet as soon as they are '*inseparably* attached to *the practical interest* of pure reason then it must accept them'.[37] They are not, it is true, 'additions to its insight', but they are 'extensions of its employment in another, namely, a practical aspect'.[38] In that sense practical reason is more intimately reason than is speculative reason, which, in its metaphysical modes, busies itself with the same problems to no purpose. Now, if anything like this is true, our programme of

---

if they were, speculative reason could close its boundaries and refuse to admit the evidence of moral experience; and practical reason could claim to determine theoretical issues as well as its own (that, at least, is how I interpret the tangled German original and the exasperatingly faithful translation); and reason would be, absurdly, divided against itself.

[32] *Op. cit.*, p. 240.   [33] *Op. cit.*, p. 230.
[34] *Op. cit.*, p. 242, note.
[35] He makes amends in *Religion within the Bounds of Pure Reason.*
[36] *Op. cit.*, p. 217.
[37] *Op. cit.*, p. 217: italics Kant's.
[38] *Op. cit.*, p. 218.

verification through practice is more than justified: practical reason is reason at its highest pinnacle of rationality.

On the other hand, unless something like this is true, our programme will fail, for the same reason. If the postulates of practice are to be subjected to the tests for indicatives, the result, as Kant says, will be problematical. We recognize, it is true, the intervening phase of faith, in which the probabilities are welded into certainties, but this is only in virtue of its practical component: it is in *action* that the counter-evidence against God is rebutted. To take the Atonement in any but an active sense – to take it, for example, as accomplished not through us, but over our heads – is to ask for the moralistic attacks so often directed against it. It is also true that, in opposition to the Kant of the First Critique, we do not find irresoluble antinomies in metaphysics, because we do not demand of metaphysics that its conclusions should be necessary; and we have already noted that the antinomical predicament results from necessitarian ambitions. But we do consider that its conclusions are probable, and that they have an overwhelming claim on us if the counter-evidence can be disposed of. Less urgently than Kant, but in the long run as dependently, we look to the practical component of faith for confirmation.[39]

The question must then be raised: was Kant right in thinking that moral rectitude is a higher expression of reason than theoretical insight? He was certainly right in thinking that thinking is not the only rational activity. It certainly makes sense to speak of emotions as rational (not merely as being controlled by reason) and similarly to speak of rational conduct (not merely of conduct under rational supervision).

---

[39] Kant does in fact introduce the concept of faith: it is the attitude directed to what, as a principle of explanation, would be called a hypothesis, considered as a requirement of moral practice. So considered, it is a 'pure rational faith', 'since pure reason (both in its theoretical and its practical use) is the sole source from which it springs' (*op. cit.*, p. 223). The only use of a historical faith is as a spur to moral excellence (cf. the detailed exposition of this point in *Religion Within the Bounds of Pure Reason*, Part III, sect. I, chs. 6–7); but it is interesting to note that 'pure reason in its theoretical use' contributes to 'pure rational Faith'. This is to give the positive theses of the antinomies a priority over the negative, as being supported by the requirements of pure practical reason: and it is closer to our own position than to the *Critique of Pure Reason*.

Rationality is expressed in the form and contour of these activities, and in fact being too intellectual about them sometimes spoils the style. But that is compatible with the theory of co-ordinate reasons which Kant has rejected. He insists, and we need to insist, on the *primacy* of the practical.

The heart of the matter is that in moral conduct we embody reason, and in thinking we merely exercise it. Suppose we start with a disinterested inquiry not forced on us by circumstances – I take this case so as not to introduce the practical connexion at the wrong end. We reach a certain conclusion. The question then arises whether anything shall be done with it. The answer may, for various reasons, be in the negative. It may be in principle inapplicable; e.g. the interpretation of a doubtful reading in a Greek manuscript. It may have results only incidentally, e.g. the discovery of a law of language, such as Grimm's, which gives a non-practical regularity account of vowel-changes, but nevertheless could be used to discourage or to develop the Australian variation of English in which it is still operating. It may be a technological innovation which needs to be thoroughly tested before it goes through to the assembly line. But, unless and until it is embodied, reason is stalled at the stage of planning – if indeed planning is ever intended. In that case, it stops short. It does not go as far as reason which carries over into practice.

This is true even when the ascent from theory to practice is possible, or deliberately proposed. But not all rational action is applied theory; much ordinary behaviour, if not rational in the pretentious sense of the word, is extremely reasonable, and probably all the more so for the absence of undigested theory. Moral action is taken by Kant to be the only case, and it is certainly a significant case. For here we have intelligence circulating in the organization of things, and expressing itself among them in the form of standards or decisions. It may be that morality in future may be more and more like technology and depend less and less on an inbuilt sense of balance; but even if, instead of controlling ourselves, we take pills to resolve our tensions, we still have to decide to take them: decision is still not deduction. In any case, directly or indirectly, reason is asserting itself in the behaviour of things and not merely in the sequences of our sense-data: and that is precisely the point Kant was seeking to maintain.

There are two reservations which, in conclusion, we have to make to consolidate our own position. Kant's ethics are based on the moral law, with a side-reference to the *summum bonum*. They are explicitly not agapaistic. The 'holy will' is not a human will. We have challenged this dichotomy, and we expect to find the finest moral conduct not in the affirmation of law *a priori*, but in the handling of intricate and perplexing detail.[40] This very considerable difference in ethical theory does not, however, affect the issue now before us. Indeed, the case for the primacy of practice comes out even more strongly. The operation of reason among things as Kant views it stops with the universal. It does not have to proceed to the particular case. As Hegel pointed out, this is to leave the universal in the realm of abstraction, and, as I cannot help adding, it misses the essential point about duty itself: that it can be categorical only in particular cases: *a priori*, it can only be hypothetical. The reason which Kant properly recognized in moral action reaches its terminal point only when it reaches the farthest limit of particularity.

The second reservation concerns Kant's reasons for believing in God. He is properly clear in his own mind that God is a postulate of morality and not an object of contemplation. It is therefore against his intention that anyone should speak of his argument as an 'ethical proof'. But it is partly his fault, because he proceeds not from morality to its presupposition, but from the need for harmony between the moral law and the highest good.[41] The reason for this indirection may be left to the scholars; a strong contributory factor is Kant's fear lest God should enter as an object into the consideration of the agent, and so infringe the purity of the moral law. As we have argued, this fear is misplaced: God's method is to reinforce autonomy and not to replace it. But in any case the highest good is a complication. It is a compound of two factors, virtue and

[40] For an argued statement of this point of view, I may perhaps refer to my article, 'Reason in Practice', in the *Australasian Journal of Philosophy*, Vol. 45, No. 1, May 1967.

[41] *Das höchste Gut* in German; oddly Englished by Abbott into *Summum bonum*.

happiness, which by themselves 'restrict and check one an-other',[42] and are 'specifically distinct'.[43] The adjustment being morally necessary (i.e. morality, though disinterested, demands the adjustment), and the resources for the adjustment not being present in morality itself, the highest good 'is possible in the world only on the supposition of a Supreme Being',[44] 'having a causality corresponding to moral character'. That is to say, the highest good is (a) evidence that duty is not in vain (but should such evidence be asked for?) and (b) something which requires a God to adjust it to duty, and even, to produce it: 'the postulate of the possibility of the *highest derived good* (the best world) is likewise the postulate of a highest original good, that is to say, of the existence of God'.[45] The conception of a postulate is thus developed into a proof of one postulate from another; a proof which closely resembles the cosmological proof, but lacks both its subtlety and its deliberation.

All through the discussion there are typical illuminations bearing on his all-important practicalist theme; and for the originality of his enterprise he has never received the praise due to him. The very obscurity of its presentation is what we should expect from a man working unaided through uncharted territory. But we can admire and learn while avoiding the complications. We have been attempting to verify faith by reference to its practical component. Without accepting in some sense Kant's doctrine of the 'primacy of the practical', we should have no warrant for so proceeding. But, because we have accepted provisionally metaphysical theses which Kant thought inadmissible, and have been verifying faith rather than erecting postulates, we can appeal directly to practice for our sanction, instead of finding, indirectly, a sanction for our practice. That the ethics of charity work, and work triumphantly, when every other device stalls at some point of the journey, is all the verification we need. But unless we had adopted the stance of practice it might not convince us. It is because we are thinking practically that we are not dismayed

[42] *Op. cit.*, p. 208.
[43] *Op. cit.*, p. 209.
[44] *Op. cit.*, p. 222.
[45] *Ibid.*

about there being evils. It is because so many thinkers, before and after Kant, have been stuck in the theoretical standpoint, that evils have ridden them so hard. From the standpoint of practice, if we know how to get rid of them, following a faith which shows how God can get rid of them, that should satisfy us both about the faith, and about the condition of mankind.

IX

RETURN TO METAPHYSICS

1. *Metaphysics after Faith*

WE BEGAN this work by pleading for a wider interpretation of 'empiricism' than is normally current in the writings either of its denigrators or of its sponsors; one which would extend it from sense-experience to experience of any kind. We then argued that experience recognizes two organizing concepts, creativity and order, asymmetrically related, capable of expansion beyond the limits of experience altogether. We noted that, taken together, they coincide over a wide extent with traditional attributes of God, and that their open-endedness points over the frontier to a God overlapping with the world. We noted, however, that recognizably in human behaviour, and conjecturally in the universe at large, there are counter-tendencies which, as they stand and in the eye of the beholder, are evidence against God in the same way that creativity and order are evidence for him. We then allowed ourselves to diverge into a study of faith, observing that faith is at the very root of it a confrontation of the counter-evidence, and in its full Christian florescence faces and overcomes it. To express things thus, however, is to admit that it is there; and in this context we contrasted the theoretical attitude, for which its mere existence is disquieting, with the practical, which goes about the business of getting rid of it with compassionate assurance: in the case of the Christian practicalist, the assurance that God in his infinite compassion has already met the brunt of it blazed the track for the followers-up.

At this point, we can resume our interrupted metaphysical inquiry. Assuming that a faith verified in practice can take care of the counter-evidence, how can we now elaborate the concept of God?

Two preliminary precautions: we must not elaborate it too much.

1. There can be no more than a penultimate approach to an ultimate mystery. The most we can do, but it is something, is, to quote Maurice Blondel, 'préciser les contours d'un abîme mystérieux que nul regard ne saurait sonder en lui-même'.[1] With this chastened purpose, we shall examine the conception of God which emerges from the consecutive phases of our argument.

2. Having reached the summit, it is tempting to say: now all is clear, and we may read our assurance back onto the tentative recognitions of empirical metaphysics. But consider what that would mean. It would mean that through faith the empirical metaphysics of the upward journey would be gathered up into a completed system in which faith would find itself supplanted. That is a conclusion at all costs to be avoided: it would turn religion into a prelude to philosophy. In the renewal of metaphysics, faith must remain faith; otherwise, there would be no renewal of metaphysics; and metaphysics must remain empirical, otherwise there would be no room for faith.

Does faith, then, add *nothing* to intellectual assurance? Far from it, for two reasons. In the first place, it shows a new dimension of God: he is no longer merely prolonged in the excellences of the world, but at grips with its disasters. In the second place, it refers philosophy back to practice: to real practice, not merely to practice considered as an object of contemplation. In this extension of our view we are that much the wiser. In this chapter it will be our task to record it in detail.

2. *Ens Necessarium*

First of all, God as necessary being. We have noted already that there is nothing particularly divine about necessity; we have only to refer to scientific determinism. But, in any case,

[1] *Exigences Philosophiques du Christianisme*, 1950, p. 22. I have quoted the passage beforei n an article, 'Religion minus Intelligence', *Hibbert Journal*, LVII, October 1958, pp. 31–8. With an eye to 'empirical' metaphysics, and I hope in harmony with the author's intentions, I here add his reference (*op. cit.*, p. 28) to 'une coincidence entre les données empiriques et les enseignements transcendants'.

the God who is the author, and, reflexively, the object of faith neither necessitates, nor is necessitated. He is just overwhelmingly there. The evidence of faith powerfully confirms this impression, which in any case is foreshadowed in the programme of empirical metaphysics. What we have is good reasons converted in faith into *practical* certainties, which in turn are tested in the exigencies of action. Even if there were necessary being, we should never be in a position to know it as such; and the radiance which at the best and rarest moments descends on us does not raise the question of necessity at all.

The latter point is important, because the classical contrary of 'necessary' is 'contingent', and it would misinterpret the mind of the believer to suppose that God just *happens*. It is more appropriate to observe that the application to God of 'necessary' and 'contingent' is a category mistake.[2] These are words which belong in the world and to the world, and they do not register in respect of a relation one factor in which is not restricted to the world. We may recall for our profit the argument used by Kant against all forms of natural theology: that God cannot be represented as the end point of a series. The very evidences of his engagement in the series point beyond the series. And in that perspective the conceptual distinction between fact and necessity no longer holds. We do not have to choose between 'necessary' and 'contingent'. God appears to us as continuous event and as compassing all events. He supremely happens and he could not not-happen; which is subtly different from saying that he could not happen. It is also incompatible with intellectual unavoidability, but that is more proper to mathematics than to religion, where QED is considerably out of place.[3] Of course, if 'necessary being' is

[2] Fr H. Paissac, in a luminous exposé, *Le Dieu de Sartre* (1950): 'L'acte même d'être, s'il apparaît d'abord comme contingent à titre d'existence singulière, se dévoile enfin dans sa pureté comme la nécessité la plus forte.' That is as may be: 'nécessité' is preserved by being interpreted as 'pureté'. But then: '*ou plutôt sont dépassées à son niveau les catégories du nécessaire et du contingent.* Les mots: absurde, nécessaire, absolu, contingent, sont autant de vocables destinés à exprimer tant bien que mal l'affirmation de l'identité parfaite, caractère transcendant, impossible à representer, de l'acte pur' (p. 61). The context is admittedly not ours: but the comment is just exactly right.

[3] The mathematical model for natural theology belongs to a quasi-

taken to *mean* 'the most being kind of being',[4] being *in excelsis*,
as would appear from certain standard expositions, no objection
can be taken, except to the use of the word 'necessary' to
convey the meaning. For that which is supremely just *is*,
whether it has to be or not.

It will be urged that it is not possible to imagine any moment
of time in which God is not, and that it is impossible therefore
to imagine him as other than necessary being. Otherwise,
the God who is for us here and now has no anchorage, and
depends on local and temporary conditions for his being – not
merely for the shapes of him that appear to us; and that would
be incompatible with the attitude of worship. All that is true,
but what emerges is not that God is exempt from occasions,
but that he is the master of all occasions. That is a conviction
which can only establish itself by first going beyond the
evidence. It is a shared personal certainty expanding under
experience sufficiently to be imputed to all persons. It is not a
preliminary certainty applying to a fixed state of affairs. The
master of all occasions is also the servant of all occasions; he
rules by an infinite responsiveness. He is unique by being at
everyone's disposal.[5] That is not the kind of thing of which
one can be sure in advance; at every moment, he is a discovery.[6]

But, if God is the master of *all* occasions, how could he on
any occasion not *be*? And in that case, is he not necessary
being? 'All occasions' means presumably 'all possible occasions'.
And if it is not possible that something should not be, it is
necessary. But we must distinguish. 'What is not possible' may
be understood absolutely or contextually. What we have
asserted is: 'if occasions, then God'.[7] But in strict logic there

---

philosophical modernist revival of Greek paganism; it is suitable in that
context, and not in the very different context of Christianity.
[4] As in the accompanying quotation from Paissac.
[5] Gabriel Marcel's 'disponibilité': cf. his essay 'On the Ontological
Mystery', in *The Philosophy of Existence*, tr. Manya Harari, 1948, p. 25.
[6] As a venture, the stress laid on necessity is due to the emphasis of
philosophers, both scholastic and deist, on the *ordering* function of deity, at
the expense of the creative.
[7] We may refer back here to the quotation from Kemp Smith: 'we
experience the Divine solely through and in connexion with what is other
than the Divine'.

might be no occasions and no God: and this is contrary to the formal requirement of necessity. But if we then appeal to the fuller dispensation of faith, there is by hypothesis no necessity, or faith would be displaced by knowledge.

Taking this discussion together with our detailed treatment of the 'proofs' in chapter VI, we conclude that necessity has no stranglehold on things, and least of all on God.[8] It is a mathematical category not conversant with individual cases. If the evidence for God in the world were only from the side of order, God could be, indeed would be, describable in terms of necessity; and as *some* of the evidence *is* from the side of order, the element of necessity cannot be wholly lacking in him. But as our most pressing evidence comes from the side of creativity, what in God *must* be has to be regarded as subordinate. There *are* immutable (not merely unchanged) structures in the world, and they are genuinely prolongations of God; but they are the skeletal fixed points round which the infinite mobility of the creation moulds its rich variety of kaleidoscopically changing detail. Taken by themselves, they are necessary elements of any possible combination; that is how they are exhibited in the natural sciences. But they are only extracts of divinity, imperfect in their own kind, and embedded in a context of creativity, human and divine.

By way of a footnote, this is perhaps the place to recapitulate what has already been said about God and time. As we have seen, the timeless apperception of God is the product of a one-sided approach (originally Pythagorean) through mathematics and mysticism. As no approach is barred, this one is permissible, and contributive; but, as we have presented the picture, only as a stage on the journey. We have to press on to divine creation, and to the activity which is the imperfect human counterpart. God, then, is not timeless. He is coeval with all possible time[9] and he is expressed in the world in some structures admitted to be changeless. But changelessness is not timelessness: it could just as well be indefinite continuance. And as the changeless structures of the world reappear in different contexts in different individual cases, being integral

[8] God is above all things not Fate.
[9] In the sense of the word *possible* outlined above, p. 127.

elements in the most variable situations, this would appear to be the more appropriate form of expression. God, then, as shown by his prolongations, has his continuances and his mobilities; in our picture, the latter predominate, and even the former do not suggest timelessness. That conception is bound up with that of necessity, and the considerations which tell against the one tell against the other also.

3. *God and Body*

The Christian tradition, summed up in the first of the Thirty-Nine Articles, is that God has 'no body, parts or passions'. We shall not concern ourselves here with 'parts'; if 'passions' means 'capability of being affected', the absence of passions in God is decidedly unbiblical, but that has already been noticed;[10] and we pass on to 'body'.

There have always been dissenters on this issue. One was Tertullian, who took his scripture neat and had no use for Platonic immaterialism. Another was Henry More, who regarded space as a divine attribute and considered extension in God to follow from his omnipresence.[11] The problem has been complicated by several confusions. In the first place, as a matter of history, the notion that God has a body was for a long time associated with Spinoza, who wrote *Deus sive natura*; he did not distinguish God from nature. That is a possible but by no means a necessary consequence: we have tried to protect ourselves by insisting on the 'not-quiteness' of the natural and the human scene. In the second place, one of the results of mind-body dualism is a materialist view of body; i.e. the view that it is wholly passive and incapable of sharing in the divine initiative. Spinoza knew better: he did after all distinguish *natura naturans* from *natura naturata*. If body were nothing but 'matter', as understood from the seventeenth-century documents, to say that God has a body would be to cut off one part of his being from another. But there is no compulsion to think in these terms. On the contrary, we have seen reason to hold that

[10] See above, p. 199, n. 58.
[11] As More considerably influenced Newton, the move was not without importance in the history of British thought.

'matter' since the seventeenth century is an abstraction, and what it abstracts from is the presence of God. Thirdly, as the result of an earlier dualism, the contrast between body and spirit was equated with the contrast of good and evil. But it takes spirit to be really evil, as is suggested by the account of the devil as a fallen angel. These misunderstandings have stood in the way of the only coherent interpretation of God and his dealings with the world. Once they are removed, it will be seen: that to be totally immaterial is to be totally ineffective; that any totally immaterial God can act upon men only by being contemplated, or at the best, with Aristotle, by being loved; that the creation of the material, including the human body, is under such conditions inconceivable; that every analogy supports the view that a creator has a body – even the creator of mathematical systems or musical compositions, whose *creations* are as nearly as possible out of nothing, but who, as *creators*, have to push their brains through an agony of parturition, and in the process become nearly as hungry as wharf labourers, and more emotionally exhausted; that in general a mind-body dualism is irreconcilable with feeling and action; that in the case of God even the heroic expedient of occasionalism is of no avail, for though God might intervene as a third party to raise my arm when I wish to move it, he cannot intervene as a third party in respect of his own activities, e.g. of plan and execution; and that if God has no body, there is an unbreakable dilemma between universal Idealism and universal materialism, under both of which dispensations God disappears.[12] All this follows without any reference to the specific features of Christian revelation; but as the latter raise certain general problems of interpretation, we shall have to digress before we return.

The Christian view of God is that he is incarnate and continues incarnate in the structure of the church and/or the intentions and behaviour-patterns of those who love him. That in this sense God has a body there can be no doubt: he inhabited a human body, nay, he *was* a human body, and the

---

[12] Idealism as well as materialism has this effect, for God as Idea is only the idea of God, and hence not God: see the usual versions of the ontological proof.

Spirit works in the bodies of his followers. The questions of method are these:

1. Is the Christian revelation a reversal of God's nature – did he, so to speak, acquire bodily standing for the first time in Jesus Christ? 2. When we speak of his body, are we referring to the whole of nature, or to certain specific features? We shall take these problems in order.

1. The first question raises within the Christian faith all the problems outside the Christian faith which it should dispel. How can what is wholly immaterial become body *at any time*? The philosophical dogma renders incarnation logically impossible – as Unitarians, for example, have quite properly noted. But suppose this difficulty overcome: suppose, for example, in defiance of Thomas Aquinas, that God can do what is intrinsically impossible: that his will can in case of conflict override his intellect. If you prefer, wipe out philosophy altogether: how will revelation fare under the immaterialist formula? Very strangely. The God of the Old Testament, in all his evolving phases, is the first casualty: the only thing to do with him is to reduce his magnificently concrete activism to the pallid purity of self-contemplation. So philosophy, precluded from interfering on behalf of revelation, intervenes to neutralize it. Then again: is there *no* presence of God at all among non-Christian peoples? Has he *no* body in their midst? We may think they misunderstand him; in many cases they may think they have got rid of him; but though religion is a comely and appropriate response to God, God does not depend on responses. Bonhoeffer may press the point too hard when he writes of 'God without religion',[13] but what he envisages is a bleak possibility and not a contradiction in terms.[14] Surely in the physical foundations of the world which are common to all of us, and not least in the universally accessible beauty of nature, there is his presence: as there most certainly is in mosques and Buddhist temples. It is not to pure spirits that God is a presence; spirits are forms, outgrowths, precipitations

[13] *Letters and Papers from Prison*, Fontana edition, 1959, p. 92.
[14] He is greatly to be preferred to those who reverse his option and declare for 'religion without God', particularly when they do not seem to notice the difference.

of body through which the Presence is available to the person as a whole. For all these reasons, it is better to say that incarnation is perpetual, and what is unique about the Incarnation of God in Christ is its definitive form and direction: it perfects a long-standing process, and provides for its perpetuation in the perfected form.

2. That leads us to our second question. The embodiment of God is not something that either is or isn't. It is partial, scattered, here hardly discernible, here operative nearly one hundred per cent; traceable wherever and to the extent that material things exhibit order or creativity; and always at odds with the chaos and torpor which obstruct design and initiative. It does not coincide with everything that happens. On the other hand, it does not coincide with spirit. Some spirits are evil, and no spirit is exempt from material stresses; if it were, it could not participate in the course of events.[15] It could be, since here we are speculating, that the body of God is material in Aristotle's sense rather than the modern, and is composed of the spiritual existences of men; but Alexander, who advances the suggestion,[16] admits minds into the concourse of things as emergent qualities on a secure material foundation. However this may be, neither mind nor body nor both together embodies completely the purposes of God, for both are subject to evils and dissolutions which in God are excluded. A complete embodiment would require the exclusion of the exclusions; one which takes the sting out of sin and death. That, on a stupendous occasion, was just what happened. But it was the crown of nature and not its overthrow. And perhaps that is the underlying truth of the orthodox contention that the Son is consubstantial with the Father, and of the dramatic exclamation ascribed to Christ himself: 'Before Abraham was, I am.' The divine body pre-dates the Incarnation, though it is only in the Incarnation that it achieved perfection and was backed into a point of time.

Thus, on the one hand, if God is by nature, or definition, immaterial, the whole notion of Incarnation crumbles; or, to

---

[15] One could go further and say that no spirit is immaterial; but the point is not here relevant. If one did, it might complicate the ensuing argument.
[16] *Space, Time and Deity*, Vol. II, p. 349.

put it the other way round, the doctrine of Incarnation conceals the philosophical assumption that immaterialism is false.
In that sense, to repeat Butler's epigram, 'Christianity is a
republication of natural religion.' On the other hand, that the
Incarnation should have taken the historical form it did is not a
matter of philosophy. It may be, and in our view it is, just what
is wanted to fill the gap which philosophers find between the
empirical pointers and the conviction of faith, and in that
sense it might well be the fulfilment of their dreams; when it
has happened all sorts of things are clearer; but that it has
happened is a datum (in the most literal sense: a gift) rather
than a conclusion.

That being so, we return to the general problem; particularly to the objection that God is wholly himself and
therefore not divisible. As body in general is divisible, it might
appear that God cannot have or be associated with a body.
This point was taken up in the seventeenth century by Henry
More, whose way of expressing it was to say that God has
extension but not body. Body, he tells us, is 'impenetrable but
discerpible' – in opposition to spirit, which is 'penetrable but
indiscerpible'. Now God must not be 'discerpible'; but need
we accept the tradition that body has that quaint differentia?
More himself admits that spirit is 'extended' – as it must be
unless it is to be nowhere. That is why he can insist 'that there
is no purely mechanical phenomenon in the whole universe'.[17]
This is a matter of terminology; it would be just as easy, and
nearer to the case in hand, to say that what distinguishes the
body of God is precisely its 'indiscerpibility'. In fact, Spinoza
made use of precisely this distinction: 'No corporeal substance,
in so far as it is substance, can be divided into parts' (*Ethics*,
Part I, prop. 12). It is in fact possible to take extended substance infinitely or finitely: as an attribute of God, it is infinite,
and therefore not divisible (*Ethics*, Part I, prop. 15, note).
These hints from an excommunicated Jew should be helpful
to Christian theologians in trouble.

If, then, body is, as an attribute of God, not divisible,
the main traditional objection collapses, and we can sustain

[17] *Divine Dialogues* (1668) p. x; quoted by W. R. Sorley, *History of English
Philosophy to 1900*, 1920, p. 80.

without deviating from philosophical procedures what must be maintained if Incarnation is not to be rationally incredible. That does not alter the conviction that, rationally speaking, it eclipses all possible expectations.

4. *Transcendence*

The prolongation of God into the material world raises acutely the problem of divine transcendence. It is clear that, so prolonged, he cannot be 'wholly other'. The point has already been argued, and need not be repeated. The danger is rather the other way: lest God himself be absorbed in his prolongations. We have tried to guard against it by arguing that the prolongations cannot stand alone, and are so described on that account. From the side of natural theology, there is no risk of pantheism. Nor, as I understand the position, is there any risk of that much more illuminating deviation, panentheism.[18] The reason is that in an empirical philosophy there is no 'pan' of any sort. There are a number of pointers and a sense of direction. But then it may be asked: is there any transcendent either? Yes, by anticipation: the pointers are encouraging, if only we could account for suffering and evil. If these can be accounted for – the way we have suggested is not contemplative but pragmatic, the using of the one to defeat the other – the picture we shall have of God will be in an important sense transcendent; the God who is in the process will be *over against* some factors in the world, and even though he is victorious they remain to be reconquered by those who love him. If to be transcendent means to be out of reach, of course God is not transcendent; if it means that he is not wholly immersed in the process which he redeems, then he is certainly transcendent. So far it is simply a matter of semantics.

The problem, however, comes up from a different angle as the result of a widespread revolt, spearheaded by Bishop Robinson in *Honest to God*, against 'the God out there'. 'It is precisely the identification of Christianity – and transcendence

---

[18] In *Philosophers Speak of God*, ed. Professors Charles Hartshorne and William L. Reese, 1953, p. 22, panentheism is the view that though all things are not God, all things are in God.

– with this conception of theism that I believe we must be prepared to question' (*op. cit.*, p. 41). How far, in our defence of theism, are we committed to 'this conception'?[19]

In the first place, if 'the God out there' meant 'the God up there', we are not implicated at all. But Robinson himself makes this distinction (*op. cit.*, p. 13) and argues that 'out there' is only one stage more sophisticated than 'up there', and subject to the same objections. What is at stake is the existence of a 'supreme and separate being'. Here again we must distinguish: no Christian, if he takes Incarnation as seriously as he is supposed to do, will accept 'separate'; we have just argued that body *cannot* be 'separate'. There is an existential line of communication between God and the world. But Robinson then argues that no lines of communication are needed, because God is *here* and not *there*. He might almost be taken to mean what he just stops short of saying, that Christ is not an aspect of the God we worship, but the whole of him. He develops Tillich's metaphor of 'depth' and prefers it to 'height', for the reason that God is the 'ground' of our being rather than its cause. But he continues to speak of transcendence: the confrontation takes place, though with the God within.

I am reminded of Huston Smith's exposition of Hinduism: 'The infinite is down in the darkest, profoundest vault of our being, in the forgotten well-house, the deep cistern',[20] and if I were an orthodox Hindu I should feel that an eminent conversion was near at hand. But that is not the point. What we have to consider is whether our 'kind of theism', which certainly requires transcendence, can be satisfied with transcendence so understood. And, far more than the traditional theist who argues from effect to cause, we are exposed to the imputation. For we have insisted that God can be known only through and with his fringes, and these include the kind of inward infinity indicated by the depth metaphor and identified by Robinson with the presence of Christ. But it should be noted: (i) that the fringes are also prolongations, i.e. there is something which is prolonged, though recognizable in the activities of man and creation; (ii) that our exposition affords no encouragement to

[19] Robinson is careful not to say '*the* conception'.
[20] *The Religions of Man*, p. 39.

those who find God in humanity *only*; we have found prolongations through the whole scheme of nature; (iii) that the
prolongations do in a sense transcend their neighbourhood in
the world (so far we seem to be in agreement with Robinson),
but do so in virtue of characters which are not limited to the
world; (iv) the evidence of valuation is that even when it is
most spontaneous it is responsive to the structures of the world,
including its spontaneities. Thus, indirectly, the transcendence
with which we are confronted is not a deeper layer of ourselves;
it is an other with which we are in overlap. In terms of the
controversy started by Bishop Robinson, this is a compromise
position: but it was not devised as such, and develops directly
from our own primary assumptions. It would be fortunate
if it could serve to mediate between the Bishop and his
critics.

But, it will be said, empirically speaking the whole notion of
transcendence, in either mode, is at fault; what is found to be
there is just found to be there, and is not to be overshadowed
by the spectre of completion. To that there are two things to be
said:

1. Very different kinds of things are found to be there. Some
are obviously evanescent; others are so constant that the
imagination construes them as necessary. The latter serve as
structures or rallying points; this is a matter of experience, not
presumed as a condition of experience. The togetherness of the
given is as much given as the elements themselves. Progress in
togetherness-insight (as the Germans would say) is as much
discovery as turning up new factors. The move towards an
(uncompleted) transcendence is a major part of what happens.
What 'merely happens' is an abstract from experience, and the
only reason for appealing to it is to show that something *really*
happens. It is not the whole story: it is an exaggeration dialectically incited by too much talk of necessity.

2. That is the verdict of empirical philosophy; but what
about faith? Faith, it will be remembered, is both the companion of empirical philosophy (they are mutually inter-
dependent) and its completion (it submerges its theoretical
tentativeness in a practical certainty). As its completion, it
introduces a transcendence far in advance of the progressive

transcendences of empirical philosophy. True; but wait. (*a*) Faith has nothing to do with certainty about what will happen: that remains as empirical as ever. (*b*) The transcendence which is disclosed in faith is not the completion of a series, or of any imaginable number of series: on this point Kant was indubitably right. It is completion *beyond* the series, beckoning to every member at every point of the series, cheering, cleansing and transforming, but leaving to every member its own options, and therewith its own ineradicable right to folly. Such a transcendence in no way precludes the empirical approach to the understanding of the world, but is in fact its complement; and precisely because it is a transcendence. From that point of view, a transcendence which overtops the whole world is a better complement than one which resides in the depths of the human *psyche*; the former only elicits, the latter determines. Unless the depths are connected with other depths by underground passages: in which case it does not greatly matter. It is merely a question of choosing images. Personally I distrust depths; they are too far removed from rationality and self-control, and too closely associated with the evils uncovered by psycho-analysis. There is no divinity in their liberation unless it is also a reconstruction.

That, however, is not our main concern. We had to indicate where we stood in relation to transcendence. The answer is that our position cannot be stated without it. It also cannot be stated in terms of transcendence alone. There are too many empirically recognizable preliminary indications. What version of transcendence we look to is a relatively minor concern, so long as the result is not 'human, all too human'.

5. *Tension*

Between the anticipations of God disclosed in experience there is undoubtedly a tension. An orderly world cramps creation; a creative world disturbs order. But (cf. p. 71) though the ordering of creation limits it as creation, the creation of order establishes it as order. If we want to relieve the tension, it is from the side of creation that we must start.

Creation, we say, establishes order. Examples are imaginative social planning and musical composition.[21] But it undoubtedly displaces order. Original social thinking, and the movements which follow it, may in the end establish a new order, which may or may not be better than the old, but in the meantime they weaken the established order, and the immediate result may be the absence of any recognized order. As order is one of the anticipations of divinity, it is almost an article of faith to believe that it will return, but that is not to say that it is easily conciliable with the creative disturbance which displaced it. At this level the approaches to divinity are turned against each other. Similarly in a work of art, organization wars against inspired dispersion, and imaginative fertility against formal restrictions; and most artists either tilt to one side or are in a condition of unstable equilibrium. Our examples seem to show the tension perpetuated. Yet *some* degree of order proceeds from creation; creation is not dispersion of what is made but a making of what is not. And here we are close to the perennial problems.

The element of disturbance in creation arises from the fact that there is already an order in possession. But suppose there were not? In that case, not being driven into the role of a disturber by the presence of an existing order, might not creativity recover its natural role of producing order? If it were defective, it would doubtless not produce perfect order; but again, suppose it were not? In that case, the most perfect creativity would produce the most perfect order – on condition that the field was clear, i.e. if creation were out of nothing. So it might be argued: but the difficulty is that the 'most perfect order' would have to include creativity. If it did not, it would not be perfect; if it does, the tension re-opens. That does not weaken, for what it is worth, the argument for creation out of nothing; it does show that neither that nor anything else can remove the tension. There *is* something which, without removing it, can use it and fructify it. It is called, below, 'the divine concern'.

It will now be said: but what is in tension is only the shapes

---

[21] Musical composition, which in a sense creates the notes as well as the symphony, is the nearest human analogy to 'creation out of nothing'. When I consider how this patrimony is neglected in the search for noises purporting to 'imitate' nature, and even worse, for the incorporation of natural noises in the work of art, I feel I should like to be one of Plato's guardians.

or prolongations of God; God himself is free from tension, by
common agreement and by definition. But a prolongation is
not a weakening: if prolongations are in tension, that which is
prolonged is in tension also. What, then, about the simplicities
of faith? But these are directed to a God engaged in the work
of redemption, i.e. engaged in disturbing an inadequate order
to produce a better order. No freedom from tension here. What,
again, about the unity of the Godhead? But Christians at least
do not normally ascribe to it *absolute* unity. If God is in three
Persons, God covers a variety of functions, and unity depends
on the variety. The tension then reappears. In the *Age* news-
paper, Melbourne, December 24, 1968, there was a moving
front-page article by Arthur Koestler, imaginatively depicting
the human feelings of Christ on the Cross. It was denounced as
blasphemous by several sincerely Christian correspondents,
who forgot that it was only by being man that he could be God;
that he would not have gone through with the humanly speaking (and divinely speaking) ghastly business if he had not
had to be man to the last limit of suffering and humiliation.
Koestler did not mention the divine *incognito*, as Kierkegaard
did, but he did bring out forcefully the human foreground,
which is in constant danger of stained-glass-window stylization.
Those who prefer stained-glass windows to the actualities of
redemption would naturally be scandalized. But one-sidedly,
and with great dramatic power, Koestler drew out the human
actualities, and to those of us who find help in the divine
incognito he threw out a thought-provoking challenge. Whatever
else emerges, God in Christ, and God as Paraclete, are not
easefully at the controls, but wrestling with principalities and
powers and spiritual wickedness in high places.[22] Over a
major aspect of his being, God is actively in tension; and if, in
another aspect of his being, he is *au-dessus de la mêlée*, then there
is a tension between the untroubled and the agonizing within
his being. I only observe that if, in one aspect of his being,
God is, as the Latin phrase goes, 'impassive', there is not
merely a tension between the first and second persons, but a
radical opposition: and that he brought this out dramatically

[22] I believe this translation is inaccurate, but as a *précis* it is simply too
good to lose.

was for me at least the merit of Koestler's article. It puts 'impassivity' out for good and all. It is not much of a loss, if we consider that God as First Person is the God of the Old Testament, who is not at all 'impassive', and himself involved in a tension between justice and mercy.

The inevitable conclusion is that tension is inherent in the existence of God, and that in that respect his prolongations in the world are true witnesses. At the very best, for anything that can be said for 'impassivity' something else can be said for involvement, and 'impassivity' then becomes one arm of the tension. As we have seen, even that is doubtful, but it does not matter: that is all we need. If it is still asked: Why does the tradition have so much to say about 'impassivity', the answer lies in Pythagorean mathematics, the Platonic theory of Forms, and the Neo-Platonic vision of the One above Being. It was the tax paid by Christianity when it took over the inheritance of Greek *paideia*.

It remains to say that the notion of 'impassivity' in God is a philosophical misconstruction of something true and important, his permanence and his unceasing availability ('disponibilité' in Gabriel Marcel's happier French). Just as order has its place in the orbit of creation, so permanence in God is part of his initiative. In fact, the double prolongation has a double source. It is merely a matter of priorities. We have stated the view that creation comes first and order is derivative. But the tension remains, and if it did not, God would not be universally 'disponible'. To be accessible to all, he needs to have more shapes than one. There are times when an interval of quiet is needed before the next adventure. But I suspect that the 'peace which passeth all understanding' is peace in the midst of turmoil: that is why it 'passeth all understanding'. And to the over-burdened sheer quiescence is so attractive that in its name they have all but monopolized religion. That is why it is well to remember that God is a 'creator of creators'.

6. *Goodness*

In the light of the discussion of faith, reason and action in chapter VIII, we return to the subject of God's goodness – a central concept in every advanced theistic religion, and more than ordinarily ambiguous because of the failure of those who use it to clear up philosophical confusions.

As stated in chapter IV, 8, the position was that there are good reasons for believing in God, but also certain reservations, relating to suffering and evil. The goodness of a God in whose world such things happen is suspect. An attempt has been made to remove the reservations: first, by developing the doctrine of freedom; secondly, by extending the traditional panorama to include the experience of action; and thirdly, by exploring the implications of faith as a pre-religious phenomenon, and tracing its transition into intellectual assent. What remains to be done is to ask what changes, if any, these discussions enforce or facilitate in the ascription of goodness to God.

One change is clear: the Christian answer to the problem of suffering and evil, and the Christian re-interpretation of omnipotence, weaken the foundations of the commonest and most honourable objections. It remains to clinch the point by philosophical argument. For there are still confusions in ordinary religious diction, and they are not merely due to metaphor: they are due to incompatible philosophical assumptions.

1. Though this is not a popular deviation, it is a favourite among older-fashioned philosophers: God is represented, in the Greek mode, as 'that to which all things tend'. In that character, he coincides with 'good', which also describes, in the Greek mode, 'that to which all things tend'. This kind of 'goodness' is impersonal and unresponsive. Being unresponsive, it is also not responsible and cannot be blamed for anything that goes wrong with the world which seeks it, or for the failure of the world to seek it at all. The temptation to resort to it is that it lets us out of a standing difficulty. But it is wholly at variance with both the Old and the New Testaments, and implicitly replaces divine creativity by human aspiration. It is important not to resort to it for our very different purposes.

2. The goodness of God in the nineteenth century is that of a theological utilitarian: he brings about the best possible results estimated on the 'greatest happiness' principle, including rewards for service and punishment for disobedience. This is the popular deviation *par excellence*: God is the all-seeing eye

at the top of a Benthamite panopticon, untroubled, competent, and peculiarly concerned to sift the undeserving from the meritorious. The notion that redemption comes first is acknowledged in hymns and parables and gets a special mention on Good Friday, but it is interpreted externally, as if the object of the exercise were to placate a God obsessed by deserts, and not to bring human beings back to life and sanity. The result is that Christ is presented as *standing in* for mankind instead of *suffering with* mankind – he is not properly incarnate – the orthodox are steering dangerously close to Docetism. So we simply sit back and rest on the divine laurels. But the suffering of Christ is surely discomforting: it is a creative challenge to diminutive creators, in their lesser style, to do likewise.

This may seem to be a digression, but as a study in the theology of the utilitarian century it is, it would seem, damagingly on target. The whole point of it is that God's job is to make us happy, if we deserve it, and miserable, if we do not. This kind of goodness may pass muster in the courts, but they have a limited function. It is not the goodness of God, which reaches out after the undeserving and gives rise among men to the recommendation: 'Judge not, that ye be not judged.' It forgets that suffering is not only not the major evil but, when sacrificially accepted, an instrument of redemption.

3. The goodness of God, as the centre of his being, is somehow to be related to the secular fringes which lead up to him, order and creativity. Each of these manifestations of his being is also a manifestation of his goodness. As we have seen, there is between them both a tension and an asymmetry, with the accent on creation as the engine and order as the stabilizer. But, exploring the implications of faith, we have found that the centre of goodness is at the point at which God comes to grips with the counter-evidence. The goodness of God here sustains and fulfils the goodness of man just at the point where its natural resources flag. That leads to the concept of *agape*, *caritas*, in English: charity, love, or concern (in the deep Quaker sense of the word), demonstrated to men in a unique and unrepeatable but exemplary instance at a specific epoch-making moment of history. This is properly the last word on the subject and will be left for the climax.

4. It may seem throughout that 'the goodness of God' is presented, not merely metaphorically, but literally, in terms of a perfected humanity. The metaphors it is impossible to avoid; though it is difficult in the extreme to get them right.[23] But the temptation to take them literally is above all things to be avoided. So much of the trouble in theology, and even with the professionally conducted philosophy of religion, is due to a failure to distinguish between the finite illustration and the designated infinite. It is in particular important to avoid ascribing to God the limiting traits of human personality. It is difficult enough when the paradigm is eternal being; it is even more difficult when being is translated as activity and eternal as everlasting. Indeed, for God made man, it might even seem improper. But we must remember that God is structure as well as activity, and as structure he confronts the world with unattainable comparisons. At this secular point of the religious dialectic, God *does* wear an impersonal aspect: there *are* guide-lines, even stone walls, and those who prefer to knock their heads against them are at liberty to do so. There is nothing personal about their discomfiture: their fate is not a punishment but a consequence. If he intervenes in a historic occasion to save them from that consequence, he is indeed revealed in personal form, but even so he carries, as no mere human person can do, the whole divine authority. Moreover, though he deactivates the implacabilities, he does not abolish them; the stone walls (and the head-bashing) are still there, the difference is that they are no longer final. But in any case, the First Person of the Trinity is not dialectically replaced by the Second, nor is the Third a dialectical synthesis. All that all of them convey is needed to build up the picture of God, and even so we cannot compass it. If we choose to convey our sense of the strains created by the personal metaphor by using the word 'super-person', it may salve our consciences, but we shall be little the wiser. It is still true that the personal metaphor for Godhead is the least misleading; but the goodness of God is also displayed in inexorabilities more akin to natural law.

This, then, is the background for our climax.

[23] Cf. pp. 45–47 for the importance of using a battery of them.

7. *The Divine Concern*

In chapter IV it was noted that one empirical approach to God is from the side of personal existence, which defines itself in such a way that it is never fulfilled in experience, but owes to its unfulfilment all the fulfilment of which it is capable. This is indeed the classical model for fringes and prolongations. In speaking of order and creation we are still in the world of attributes and predicates; in speaking of persons we are in the world of activities in which the attributes or predicates are displayed. In the course of wrestling with the counter-evidence, we have seen how the emphasis falls on the exercise rather than the possession of qualities; what we believe and find confirmed is the supremacy of those qualities *in action*. We are driven to ask: how is it that they are supreme? What do they, and what does our faith, tell us about the subjugation of suffering and evil?

We have left this question to the last, because it is the climax, and without it all that has been written still hangs in the air, as an enchanting possibility. If there is no concern for the world, its regular structure, its creative potential, are instrumentalities waiting to be used. Such a concern is taken for granted in the simplest act of faith, as soon as it is confronted with the counter-evidence: and it is vindicated supremely in the full confession of faith in a Saviour and Redeemer. But, here as elsewhere, in the present ideological climate, it is better to stand from the other end and work upwards. If we find evidence of a more than human concern in ordinary secular contexts, it can no longer be said that we are appealing for evidence to a closed circle of the already convinced. On the contrary, we shall be making secularists testify against themselves; and in this kind of operation that is the only way of making progress.

To begin with, the divine concern is not restricted to its final focal point. It is felt all through the scheme of creation, including things commonly, and perhaps inappropriately, called inanimate. That things should be ordered with near-mathematical precision brings them right away into a scheme of excellence, on a more than human scale. If it is a fact, it is, in its own right, and not because human cupidity cashes in on it, a good thing. I do not know whether in this I show too much imagination, but I cannot but think it might so easily have been otherwise; the world might so easily have resembled the waste paper in a professor's basket. The fact remains that there is no logical reason why it should not have been. Equally, there would have been no 'world' if it had been. The atoms would have been lost and homeless, and if, as Whitehead suggests, part of their *esse* is *sentiri*,[24] they would have been themselves diminished by their lack of *rapport*. These musings are not merely fanciful; they express what the most careful empiricist knows, that the mathematical structures of the world are *found* rather than imputed. Let us say at this stage, *if* a benevolent creator had wished to produce a physical world as well as possible, he would have laid the mathematical foundations exactly as they are,[25] with the existing provisions for constitutional amendment.

This leads us again to creativity. We have already noted its traces in 'inanimate' nature; we have now to connect them with the divine concern. A divine concern for the world would be directed to getting as much as possible out of it; to activating at each stage unfulfilled capacities best to be developed. It could not rest content with the world as it is, unless it had no more to offer. But a human creator always leaves a margin for his successors to work in, and to suppose that God could produce only one world, like a one-book novelist, is not to pay him the highest honour. Concern would be shown by innovation as well as by stability, in the course of creative evolution, before even there was talk or thought of man. What *has* happened now reveals itself as what *would* happen if the world were an object of that concern. And, if we are tempted to be complacent about it, let us remember that the changes and adaptations in the structures of things bear witness to a total lack of complacence in God. It is in his unexpectedness as well as in his stability that our faith is founded.

In this context, if there is any concern at all, it must be a

[24] *Process and Reality*, p. 310.
[25] To that extent the eighteenth-century natural theologians were not wholly mistaken.

divine concern; there is no mutual concern amongst atoms. Or is there? Is that what is meant by gravitation? If so, the natural world is not in itself inanimate; the only really inanimate things are de-animated, like the philosopher's too familiar chairs and tables. Even so, it would be to ask too much of it that it should arrange itself for the best. The law-like togetherness which atoms 'enjoy' is exactly suited to their standing, and provides the proper foundation for the next leap forwards. As has already been suggested, as a spontaneous demonstration by elements not specially equipped for spontaneity, it is simply too good to be true (cf. p. 154). As a benefaction, as an expression of concern, it would be so well devised as to carry conviction with anyone not determined at all costs to disbelieve it.

There is a further forward-looking evidence of concern at this stage, and that is what is called 'the beauty of nature'. Again, there is a suggestion here that nature is beautiful because it is 'haunted', i.e. it is not fully discerned through its material aspect; and again I do not wish to deny it: I shall merely try to avoid the interpretations of it which are too obviously anthropomorphic or pantheistic. What must be insisted upon is that, e.g., the shape of a tree is not only pleasing to human inspection, but the exhibition of an inward perfection. But trees are living creatures: let us go back to seascapes and mountains and sunsets. There is undoubtedly a communion in these cases between the phenomena and the human. There is a 'balance of the picture' which the photographer or landscape artist seizes upon with delight, but it takes his discernment to pick the angles and the colours. But the shapes are *there*, the colours are *there*; we do not *invent* sunsets, we are susceptible or indifferent to them, but they are facts of the case. The physicist will explain what is happening, in much the same way that a trained critic will analyse a symphony, and we shall be grateful: one of the limitations of the poet, at least, in the presence of a sunset is his lack, if I may put it so, of inside information, and if his physics were better than is commonly the case he could speak with more authority. But physics is not a substitute for wholeness of vision: it is, in this age, a necessary contribution to it, but no more. If it were, physicists would be poets or artists, which, with the best will in the world, they are not. Sunsets are meeting points between artists and nature; and to serve as such, they have to have their own inalienable place in nature. They fire the imagination; they are not produced by it. They are part of the intrinsic furniture of the clouds and the sky: one might almost say, part of a benediction. If busy people miss the point, all one can say is that sunsets are far too good for them.

Here, then, as in the order of nature, without resorting to religion in what the secularist might regard as an offensive sense, we encounter factors which both belong and surpass, which both affirm themselves and bind together; which in their own right exhibit their doing (surely a benefaction!) and are *given* to us, given without our having earned them (again a benefaction), linking the two ends of creation in bonds that only the indifference of the rootless mechanical man can think of breaking. It can best be summarized by the invitation to consider the lilies of the field; they incite faith – from the very heart of nature.[26]

It is to this concern with nature that we are referred back from the human situation: 'He maketh his sun to shine upon the evil and the good.' No, we certainly should not turn our backs on God in nature, not even in aid of our highly moral enterprises; if they lose touch with nature, they are only too apt to call up an artificial sun constructed to shine only on the good: and then the counter-evidence has its field to itself. For it is precisely evil that prevents us from accepting the evidence as it stands. Anything that perpetuates it keeps us in doubt about God. Moral arrogance, the downgrading of people because of the evil in them, is a major part of the evil which it purports to downgrade. In our experience, love, concern, alone sees us as we are. Above all it does not pretend we are any better than we are. It says, no matter; even if we are *worse* than we think.

But, in our experience, that kind of concern operates un-evenly. It operates in exceptional cases almost to perfection on a

[26] It was this verse (Luke 12.27) that converted the great Japanese Christian Togohiko Kagawa, who also recorded that his countrymen found Peter and Paul 'over-importunate'. See his *Christ and Japan*, 1934, pp. 42, 99.

small scale. Good parents love their children for themselves, not for what they are. Friendship does not depend on merit. Promotion does, but that is another matter. In these narrower contexts, concern is both intimate and effective: that is why the family and private friendship freely entered into without backthoughts of policy are so favourable to the growth of agapaistic religion. But there is always the danger of arbitrary limitation, such as caused Mme de Staël to call marriage 'cet égoïsme à deux' and elicited that famous parody of Victorian family prayers: 'God bless me and my wife, my son John and his wife, us four, no more.' On the other hand, when extended to people in general, concern can only take the form of trying to serve the abstraction 'humanity', on which the proper comment is that expressed in the title (and the contents) of Gabriel Marcel's unsparing little work, *Les hommes contre l'humain*. Humanity is an alibi for pushing men about with a good conscience. So concern, among men, because of their finitude, is either personal and limited, or unlimited and impersonal. That is stating the matter kindly; it is frequently both limited and impersonal, as in the transfigured egoism of the nation state.

Yet it is there, and demands a fulfilment which it cannot achieve. That is a familiar fact of our finite condition, and it is only since we began to fancy ourselves as infinite that it has produced the kind of sulks which psychologists call 'frustration'. If we recognize a true infinite our own smallness will not matter. Very well, let us look for the fulfilment in an action of both personal and cosmic import. Such an action is, as we have seen, the terminal point of religious faith, and if it has actually occurred, if in a historic case the dilemma was broken and concern displayed both individually and, by extension, to all men (not of course to that well-dressed scarecrow, humanity), then we are entitled to talk about divine interposition. We are returning from an excursus into faith to attempt a conceptual account of the God disclosed to us, and we are now inclined to say: here we have it. The only question remaining is the empirical question, whether *in fact* there *is* a concern extending individually to all men.

On this issue, it will be necessary to consider again the

problem of the counter-evidence. Some men have every appearance of not being objects of *anyone*'s concern. I am not for the moment discussing the effect of believing a divine concern to be impossible: such a belief will certainly cause even beneficiaries not to recognize it when they see it. I am concerned with the ordinary run of mischance and suffering among unproblematical people who just can't cope. Here (it may be repetitious but the context is new) there are two things to be said.

1. What has been provided is an opportunity. No one can be forced to take it. God would not be showing concern in attempting it. Even on the human plane concern is weakened by compulsion. In God it would be in conflict with his nature as a 'creator of creators'. But the opportunity is there: it is provided in the continuous operation of divine concern through the Holy Spirit. If those whom it should possess, whether individuals or church organizations, fail to make themselves 'disponibles', the black mark is indeed against them – them, not God: God is not responsible for other people's failures, not even the failures of those who profess him. But in the meantime, there is a dangerous gap between need and availability, and unless we close it, it will be closed arbitrarily and impersonally by the social machine – to the permanent human impoverishment even of those whose interests are served.

Let us here ventilate all the doubts that we have about the gap. On the one hand, concern is diminished when it becomes a concern not for others, but for one's own righteousness. It is a treacherous region to move in, for what we begin by being righteous about is a concern for others; that is what righteousness consists of: and yet in the twitching of an eyelid concern for concern erodes concern itself. Think of what happened to the flaming concern of the seventeenth-century Puritans when they were pinned down in the next generation and went on the defensive. The result was that they were upright and dependable but, except for the few saints who turn up in almost any context, singularly unavailable. Think again of the virtuous and scrupulous modernists who are so busy clearing up doubts that they also are unavailable. Only the pressure of the concern itself can open up these closed channels; it has to become simple – and for those of us who are trussed up by intellectual scruple this is the hardest lesson of all.

Or consider a more difficult gap which in Western theological culture is often ignored. If I were a blowfly, I should picture the devil in skirts, and armed with a poison-spray. If I were a tiger, I should picture him in jodhpurs, and armed with a long-distance rifle. Who are these murderous intruders, disturbing a traditional pattern, without even the excuse of hunger? Where is the divine concern here? There are compensations, e.g. the fertility of the blowfly; and even a rough sort of justice, because, as the huntsman is to the tiger, so is the tiger to the antelope; but concern? Of all the gaps, animals worry me most; not only because they do not understand and can do little about it, but because they do not worry theologians enough. There is no Christian parallel to Yudhishthira, at the end of the *Mahabharata*, who refused to enter Heaven without his dog, and was told later that if he had not refused, he would never have been admitted at all. The most one can say in a baffling and troublesome case is this: that animals accept life; that they are roughly suited to and by their environment; that they take what is coming to them far better than we do; that the changes so fatal to their welfare are part of a creative disturbance; and that it is still not too late to pull them into the orbit of charity.[27] But they disturb me; and if I were an atheist, I should make the most of them.[28]

2. But, having ventilated these misgivings, we still hold to the central theme. There is no creature wholly out of reach of the divine concern. Extending backwards into nature, where it fulfils itself in accordance with the possibilities of nature, it mounts to its climax in the work of human redemption, which is founded in nature, clinched by historical revelation, and awaits only our co-operation with the one and the other.[29]

---

[27] St Francis saw the point, when he preached to the birds; so did Paley, when, alluding to the serpents in the African deserts, he wrote: 'Let them enjoy their existence: let them have their country. Surface enough will be left for man' (*Natural Theology*, 1804, p. 513).

[28] That Richard Martin, who first moved in the House of Commons against cruelty to animals (1822), should have been nicknamed 'Humanity Martin' is to the credit of humanity.

[29] 'Rise up, O men of God.' I have heard Barthians revile this hymn. But God having done everything for us, are we to do nothing?

Henceforth it is no excuse to say: we don't know. This is the way the scene appears when nature and revelation have been made to throw light on each other. There are anticipations of it in nature which incline us to accept it; after the great sacred events – the crucifixion, the ascension, and the for-all-time bequest of the Holy Spirit – the weight of the counter-evidence is lifted; but these events have to be read in their natural context to achieve their full impact. For example, it is little use to say that Christ died for us, unless we appropriate the heritage and live differently: and the difference is that if it had not been done, no one would believe that we could do it. It is as instigating faith, not merely as an object of faith, that redemption achieves its end. Unless we are redeemed into redeeming, we are not redeemed at all. And once the incomparable example is before us, it can be verified in lesser degree through the whole gamut of creation. Philosophy prepares the way: quite independently, it removes obstacles and elaborates the problems; but those problems are primarily practical, and the answers have to be lived through.

The divine concern, then, is 'the end of all our striving'. It establishes what is otherwise only promising. It is thus philosophically important that we should come to be aware of it. But it does not establish any position in philosophy. Rather it commands the philosophical enterprise as part of human excellence. If God has a concern for us, he has a concern for our activities; he will not frustrate or thwart them; he will build us up as we will let him. Some inkling of how this mystery can operate can be found in J. R. Jones's moving sermon to the University of Swansea.[30] As will be seen, I am in flat disagreement with Professor Jones when he says:[31] 'Nothing can constitute evidence for the existence of God.' But when he says, on the same page, 'love can give perceptive understanding of the meaning of the world', I find myself desperately wanting to agree with him. 'The understanding it gives,' he adds later, 'is perceptive, not problematic . . . meaning, although not comprehended, is somehow experienced . . . it is a perception, not a leap.' The suggestion that the love of God gives rise to

[30] In D. Z. Phillips: *Religion and Understanding*, 1967, pp. 141–53.
[31] *Op. cit.*, p. 147.

the *meaning* of the world (*whatever* it is) goes further than we are able to travel with him, because, as I see it, the meaning cannot be separated from the evidence; but the evidence being conducive rather than conclusive, it is still the love of God that assures us of the *meaning*, while helping to further certain secular speculations rather than others. His concern will be shown both in the building up of the philosophical preliminaries, and in the perceptive assurance of a meaning which still remains to be spelt out in detail.

That, then, is the picture of God built up empirically and completed in faith. It is, in many ways, traditional. It does not yield an inch to 'Christian atheism': there *is* a God, a God who is not merely an unusual way of looking at the world, but the condition of there being a world. It does not yield either to the subtler ploy of ploughing God back into the depths of our own being and continuing to speak of him as before. Yet, because it is empirically founded in observable facts, it is not 'wholly other', and because it is completed in faith, it remains intellectually in the realm of the probable, and exposed to the various assaults of doubt. The only way to get rid of doubt is to get rid of its causes. That is one reason why we are taught to pray: 'Thy will be done on earth as it is in Heaven.' Till that time, doubt and faith play upon and even sustain each other. 'The wheat and the tares shall grow together until the harvest.'

One consequence of this treatment is that intellectual honesty and religious faith are in no sense incompatible. They are frequently supposed to be, and not without reason. If faith is the acceptance of propositions which are not to be questioned, if philosophy is the closing of issues in a formed system, then they are entirely incompatible.[32] Even if faith is not the acceptance of propositions but philosophy continues to make totalitarian claims on our allegiance, there is, if not logical incompatibility, at least a permanent conflict of attitude. It is only the empirical conduct of the metaphysical enterprise together with the practical orientation of faith which keeps

---

[32] At least, unless the propositions accepted on faith are volatilized into philosophy. But this, as Kierkegaard stubbornly pointed out to a generation only too ready to yield to the temptation, is an offence against religion.

them in harmony without constraint. And this is a conclusion greatly to be welcomed.

8. *Miracles and Immortality*

As was noted at the outset (p. 38) the usual empirical elements in religion have been miracles and immortality. These, if accepted, have great persuasive value; they have happened, and cannot be dismissed as mere interpretations. It is no exaggeration to say that for most people they were the best part of the case for God. We postponed the issue and looked for standing characters of the world which a less believing (a less credulous) generation would have to admit; and we hinted that we might return to the subject in an already established theistic context. This is the time to redeem the promise.

On the matter of miracles, from the first days to the nineteenth century, they were part of the mental climate, factual and not in the least problematical. There were a few people who rejected them, but if they did they rejected God as a matter of course. Their tie-up with God was such that the mind moved easily from the one to the other. So it was natural for those who accepted them to proceed direct to God; the only question which had to be settled was whether particular miracles were authenticated.[33] When, following Spinoza, philosophers began to say 'God or nature' indifferently, any departure from the ordinary ways of return became ungodlike, and miracles a superfluity. God was expressed in the order of the world *and not* in the exceptional. When, following Hume, they interpreted nature herself empirically, a miracle, by the mere fact of being unusual, became unnatural. 'There must be a uniform experience against any miraculous event, otherwise the event would not merit that appellation.'[34] 'Nature' being defined in terms of 'uniform experience', anything uncongenial to that experience is self-contradictory. So miracles, instead of being a recommendation, become a liability to be accounted for – if possible.

[33] The devil could simulate them and we had to be reasonably careful.
[34] 'Of Miracles', in *Hume on Religion*, ed. R. Wollheim, p. 211.

Hume took it for granted that a miracle is 'a violation of the laws of nature'. The assumption has often been criticized: here we merely, and mildly, protest that if, as Hume supposes, laws of nature are founded on experience, there is no question of violation, because laws are only progress reports. Anything may happen later – improbably, but that judicious adverb does not justify talk of 'violation'. What is, however, more important is that miracles cannot be evidence for God, because only God could be evidence for miracles. That certain things happened or did not happen is not the point; they could have happened, though most unusual, in the course of nature. Here Hume was at fault: his epistemology makes it certain that anything that happens for the first time is to be discredited. But it may happen, or be observed, for the first time, and profoundly disturb the traditional body of observations, and *look* like a violation of the laws of nature, but in fact merely expand our conceptions of nature. Climates of opinion are here important. The healing miracles in the Gospels, fifty years ago, were miracles to believers and frauds to unbelievers, because of a limited set of assumptions about nature; now we are much more inclined to accept them as part of nature. Extraordinary mastery of mind over body is accepted in India; to that extent, it is less of a miracle, and more likely to be good history, at the same time.

No one of these considerations outlaws the traditional miracle: it merely builds a bridge between miracle and natural event, and gets rid of the absolute discontinuities which are the bane of philosophy, and of philosophy of religion in particular. But it does emerge that a miracle, if it occurs, is a special intervention of God, perhaps, as St Thomas observed, not *contra naturam* but *praeter naturam*, but not such as could be included in a revised scheme of nature. If this is so, then God comes first, and a miracle can be recognized as such only as a consequence. It figures in the total conspectus, not as empirical evidence, but as a divine dependency. Presented to us as fact or history, it will be judged and perhaps appropriated as fact or history, or accepted as a miracle proper, according to the intensity of our conviction that with God all things are possible. It is empirical as being an event, but it is a miracle only in a divine context. The most that the event itself can do is to shake the belief in the predetermined boundaries of science and thus to open the mind to a greater receptiveness: a condition in which God may more easily be envisaged as a possibility. Not that we wish to depict a gap between the event and its divine employment; but without a sense of the divine the event will not show itself as more than an event, and will either be rejected or rationalized. So it was perhaps wise not to use miracle as empirical evidence: until God is in the picture, the question will arise: Evidence for what? – and it will not easily be answered.

The other empirical element in Christian belief is immortality, and here the above considerations apply with even greater force. In so far as the interest in immortality expresses itself through the methods of natural science, it has nothing to do with any kind of theology, revealed or natural. It happens that there is currently a body of knowledge, cumbrously known as parapsychology, in which one possible explanation of certain intractable but undeniable phenomena is communication with departed spirits. As far as one inexpert in these affairs can judge, it is not to be dismissed offhand, but neither is it the only or even the best hypothesis for organizing the phenomena in question. Leaving the empirical issue open, we still note that if the survival hypothesis is the most adequate, it still tells us nothing about God. In fact, it suggests the diminished manikin of *Odyssey* XI rather than the Christian hope of immortality; but even if the prospects were brighter than they seem to be (after all, among a random sample of earth-walkers, we should not expect to find a Socrates or a St Francis) they still tell us nothing about the connexion between survival and quality of life. *This* kind of empiricism does not link up with deity, one way or the other.

Historically, among most practising Christians, the link lies in the conception of divine judgment, assigning survivors to heaven and hell (or, in a less drastic version of the doctrine, possibly to purgatory). Immortality is vitally important here and now because on our use of here-and-now depends an indefinitely extended future. On that it may be said in passing that any sense it may make depends on its being a consequence rather than a punishment. But in this version of immortality God is the presupposition. He is also the presupposition in the more radical Christian suggestion – here needing only to be cited and not argued – that the condition of overcoming death is having eternal life already, through participation in Christ. If, then, it is suggested that the approach to God is through immortality, the reply is that the approach to immortality, as commonly understood, is through God. Once again, wisdom was right to warn us that the traditional empirical approaches are no longer available: not, however, because what they assert is not true, but because it is now clear that they either assume what they are said to prove, or else do not prove it. So it is to be hoped that the method used in chapter III, that of starting from premises not dependent on religion, and tracing them back to their religious context, will be found both more effective, and more empirical.

9. *Conclusion*

Surveying here the work of many years, I am conscious of discrepancies and rival emphases. I cannot hope to clear them all up. There is one point, however, at which there is more stress today than when the venture started: it is illustrated in the argument of the last paragraph. It was argued that immortality can get along without religion, and is of religious interest only in the context of God. Why, then, can it not be argued that order and creation and personality can get along without religion, and find a place in religion only because God is postulated for other reasons? We have presumed, it will be said, to advance from order and/or creation to God because they are imperfectly exhibited in man and nature. But the sense of their imperfection already assumes God, and indeed inquiry among atheists of my acquaintance suggests that they do not feel it: their reaction is: nothing is perfect, so what? Many modern philosophers of religion, spirited racers by Wittgenstein out of Kierkegaard, accept this conclusion and insist that no philosophy of religion is possible which does not start from the assumption of God. They do not sketch the boundaries of the secular till God emerges from them (which is what we have tried to do): they elucidate the situation in which God is acknowledged from the beginning. In the recent collection, *Religion and Understanding*, edited by D. Z. Phillips, several contributors advance this point of view so cogently that if I were more concerned for consistency than for truth, I could wish I had not read it before writing *Finis* to the present venture. May I therefore conclude by trying to square accounts with them, in such a way as to acknowledge my admiration as well as my disagreement?

There is one point on which we agree completely. God *is* there from the beginning, and it does not take a philosopher to find him. But:

1. As mediaeval thinkers frequently pointed out, the order of approach is not the order of reality. Supposing you don't know about God, or have lost him: is there nothing you can do by the light of reason to improve your acquaintance, or revive your memories? The contributors to the collection must, I think, answer No: only God can break the deadlock. We, on the other hand, have urged that without him we can go half-way to meet him. In this we are more modest than the devisers of proofs: we have admitted that the counter-evidence can only be countered by divine action: but we do at least advance evidence which, if the counter-evidence *can* be countered, we regard as overwhelmingly persuasive.

2. This innocent and natural proceeding transgresses against the rule under which modern philosophers are licensed to consider religion; it is, in a modest way, metaphysical; it advances to at least provisional conclusions concerning the *being* of things; it is *not* merely the analysis or explication of an already given realm of discourse. Modern philosophers, on the contrary, if they are themselves religious, strike up an alliance with Kierkegaard, who denied the role of the intellect in the matter from the side of religion. Religion is from the one end admitted, and from the other extolled, on condition that it is not supported by reason. It is important to understand that this *is* the basis of what otherwise looks like a fine religious stance, and is in fact illuminated by many flashes of insight. It is important also to distinguish the statement that there is no purely intellectual knowledge of God (which is true) from the

statement that the intellect has no part whatever to play in the
approach to God (which I fear is misleading). It is to be suspected that those who are properly concerned to affirm the
first have allowed themselves to proceed to the second, without
adequate consideration.

3. There remains the analogy of talk about immortality. It
was objected that if survival can get along without God, so
can all the other so-called 'pointers', 'fringes' and 'prolongations'. So they can. And there is this resemblance between the
cases, that in both there is a sense of something missing. But
notice the difference. Survival without God is complete though
it may be trivial; order and creation without God would be
incomplete. If the secular argument from parapsychology were
to stand, survival would not lack anything of what it takes to
make it survival. But on our showing order and creation taken
by themselves would lack something of what it takes to be
order and creation. In fact – and this is probably the heart of
the matter – order and creation, and still more so 'person', are
descriptive concepts which are also 'value-concepts', the nature
of which it is to point beyond themselves to a transcendence
in which they are both expressed and surpassed. Both are
transformed by the presence of God; the former unexpectedly,
the latter by achieving their own perfection. So it was perhaps
wise to leave immortality (together with miracles, which are
divine by definition) to the crowning phase of the argument;
they suggest God only in so far as, or because, God is manifest
in them already. We have tried to work towards God from data
in which he is strictly 'incognito', and to show that the carefully secularized structures depend on the presence which they
do not by themselves reveal.

If we have succeeded, we have also vindicated the efforts
of natural reason to proceed towards God; that is to say, we
bring back metaphysics into the philosophy of religion. Not
in the grand old way; it is admirable, but when all is said we
work in the shadow of the 'empirical complex', and we cannot
expect to appropriate the universe single-handed. Moreover,
it would be death to intellectual adventure if we could. But
we can put together all the bits and pieces about God that
come our way, and experience the joy of seeing them con-

solidate in the course of a lifetime into a mobile and still developing pattern. That much philosophy can do, and must do. From that point on, faith takes over; faith, which underpins the necessities of action, and finds in action its vindication; supporting and completing and circulating within the more tentative constructions of the human intellect, which it dare not, for its own sake, ignore or defy. For thinking is part of the human endeavour which begins and is completed in faith, and is far too important to be left outside, when we go in to worship, on the cathedral steps. We shall always go on discovering, in the faith that there is always more to discover, and discern the presence of God throughout the unending journey.

INDEX OF NAMES

INDEX OF SUBJECTS

DATE DUE

MAY 5 198			
NOV 0 9 1995			
GAYLORD			PRINTED IN U.S.A.